Predictable
Surprises

LEADERSHIP FOR THE COMMON GOOD

HARVARD BUSINESS SCHOOL PRESS

CENTER FOR PUBLIC LEADERSHIP
JOHN F. KENNEDY SCHOOL OF GOVERNMENT
HARVARD UNIVERSITY

The Leadership for the Common Good series represents a
partnership between Harvard Business School Press and
the Center for Public Leadership at Harvard University's
John F. Kennedy School of Government. Books in the series aim
to provoke conversations about the role of leaders in business,
government, and society, to enrich leadership theory and
enhance leadership practice, and to set the agenda for
defining effective leadership in the future.

OTHER BOOKS IN THE SERIES

Changing Minds
by Howard Gardner

Bad Leadership
by Barbara Kellerman

Predictable Surprises

THE DISASTERS YOU SHOULD HAVE SEEN COMING, AND HOW TO PREVENT THEM

Max H. Bazerman
Michael D. Watkins

HARVARD BUSINESS SCHOOL PRESS

Boston, Massachusetts

08 07 06 05 04   5 4 3 2 1

Library of Congress Cataloging-in-Publication Data

Bazerman, Max H.
    Predictable surprises: the disasters you should have seen coming, and how
  to prevent them / Max H. Bazerman and Michael D. Watkins.
       p.   cm.
    Includes bibliographical references.
    ISBN 1-59139-178-4 (alk. paper)
    1. Disasters—Prevention. I. Watkins, Michael, 1956– II. Title.
  HV551.2.B39 2004
  363.34'7—dc22

                                                                    2004017441

The paper used in this publication meets the minimum requirements of the
American National Standard for Information Sciences—Permanence of Paper
for Printed Library Materials, ANSI Z39.48-1992.

To those who have suffered from
the failure of leaders to anticipate
and avoid predictable surprises.

Contents

Preface

Does your organization have serious problems that you know won't solve themselves? Are these problems likely to get worse over time? Could they eventually flash into a damaging crisis that will take most people in your organization by surprise? When we ask executives in private, public, and non-profit organizations these three questions, their answers almost invariably are yes, yes, and yes. Yes, serious problems exist. Yes, they are likely to get worse. Yes, they could flash into major crises for their organizations. The surprises, when they eventually occur, were entirely predictable.

In researching and writing this book, we sought to unravel a puzzle. Why does recognition of a looming problem so often fail to trigger an effective institutional response? Why do leaders, even those with the vision to recognize the approaching precipice, too often seem unable or unwilling to respond effectively? Why must a problem escalate into a full-blown crisis before costly corrective action is finally taken?

Our interest in predictable surprises was sparked several years ago, but crystallized in the aftermath of the events of September 11. The images of hijacked airlines smashing at full speed into the World Trade Center, and the Twin Towers falling in a mass of twisted debris, were indelibly imprinted on our minds. Like many, we sought to make sense of these horrific events. Why did it happen? What might be done to help prevent similar tragedies from occurring in the future?

The latter question catalyzed our early discussions about predictable surprises. The more we thought about it, the less we believed that the events of 9/11 were a true surprise. As the media uncovered more and more information about security and intelligence failures, it became increasingly clear that the attacks on New

York and Washington were, to a significant extent, predictable, based on information available to the U.S. government about the aims, organization, and methods of Al Qaeda. Severe deficiencies in the security of commercial airplanes, for example, were recognized not only by the terrorists, but by many in our own government.

As we probed deeper, we came to view predictable surprises as a common form of leadership failure, and 9/11 as a particularly devastating example. Both of us could point to numerous situations we had studied or observed that had the character of predictable surprises. Max's research on the destruction of the world's fisheries and the dangers of auditor conflict of interest (so dramatically borne out in the case of Enron) led him to believe that similar forces were at work on 9/11. Michael's observation of the failures of business leaders to prevent seemingly avoidable crises in their organizations likewise pointed to the existence of a more general phenomenon. Ultimately, we concluded that predictable surprise is an affliction to which many organizations—large and small; public, private, and nonprofit—fall prey.

Our first purpose in writing this book is to illustrate, analyze, and illuminate the phenomenon of predictable surprise. On a fundamental level, what renders leaders and organizations vulnerable to being predictably surprised? What crucial advice and tools would help leaders who have the requisite courage and vision to dodge the bullet? From real-world disasters at the highest level, such as the events of September 11 and the breakdown of auditor independence at Enron, to everyday challenges confronting managers of organizations large and small, we will document the failure of leaders to respond effectively to well-recognized challenges and, as a result, to be predictably surprised.

Our ultimate goal, however, is to help you prevent predictable surprises in your own organization. After looking deeply into the events and decisions leading up to September 11 and the fall of Enron in the first section of the book, we will then examine the reasons that leaders so often fail to prevent predictable surprises. Finally, we will develop a prescriptive framework that you can use to identify and prevent predictable surprises in the world around you.

In recent decades, historical events have prompted major contributions to the social sciences. President Kennedy's disastrous decision to authorize the Bay of Pigs invasion sparked Irving Janus's development of "groupthink," now a central concept in the study of group decision making. Likewise, Graham Allison's work on the Cuban missile crisis culminated in *The Essence of Decision*, arguably the most influential book ever written on international relations. The U.S. government's failed Vietnam strategy prompted many researchers to reach a deeper understanding of the tendency of humans to escalate their commitment to a previous course of action without rational justification. If this book has even a fraction of the impact of these classic works, the effort will have been worthwhile.

Acknowledgments

Our interest in the topic of predictable surprises grew from a conversation over "Ten o'clock coffee" in the Negotiations, Organizations, and Markets group at the Harvard Business School. Without this informal departmental institution, our collaboration might never have begun. The business school's "negotiations group" was inspired by the work of Howard Raiffa, a doctoral adviser to Michael Watkins, and Max Bazerman's most important informal adviser. Our analysis is rooted in Raiffa's visionary application of decision theory to ongoing global dilemmas.

Max's contributions to the book were heavily grounded in his research on auditor independence, conducted with George Loewenstein, Don Moore, Kimberly Morgan, and Lloyd Tanlu (see chapter 3), and by his writings on special-interest group politics, a topic covered in his 2001 book *You Can't Enlarge the Pie*, cowritten with Jon Baron and Katie Shonk.

Michael's contributions were influenced by his conversations about crisis prevention and response with professionals in the U.S. security community, especially the National Security Fellows at the Kennedy School of Government at Harvard University. His writings on "corporate diplomacy" and coalition building, the topics of his HBS elective course, and his 2000 book *Winning the Influence Game*, cowritten with Mickey Edwards and Usha Thakrar, also enhanced our understanding of predictable surprises.

Part III of the book grew out of an article we published in the *Harvard Business Review* in 2003, "Predictable Surprises." Our talented editors at HBR, Nick Carr and Gardiner Morse, influenced our understanding of predictable surprises. Jim Sebenius organized a session of the Negotiation Roundtable (of the Program on Negotiation at the Harvard Law School) that centered on our work, and the resulting discussion helped clarify our ideas. We have presented this work at the Harvard Business School, Columbia University, New York University, the University of Pittsburgh, Massachusetts Institute of Technology, Carnegie-Mellon University, the University of Chicago, Northwestern University, Stanford University, Tulane University, Duke University, and at a number of professional associations. The comments and discussions that followed these talks were critical to our thinking and our writing.

Jeff Kehoe, our editor at Harvard Business School Press, inspired us to sharpen our concepts and to make them useful and accessible to leaders across many sectors. Our most important debt goes our editor, Katie Shonk. An accomplished storywriter in her own right, Katie researched and refined many of the stories in this book, and we have benefited immensely from her skills.

—Max H. Bazerman
  Michael D. Watkins
  March 2004

1

What is a
Predictable Surprise?

A Preview

Were the earth-shattering events of September 11, 2001, predictable, or were they a surprise? What about the collapse of Enron into bankruptcy and scandal? We argue that they were both predictable and a surprise—they were predictable surprises.

We define a predictable surprise as an event or set of events that take an individual or group by surprise, despite prior awareness of all of the information necessary to anticipate the events and their consequences. Predictable surprises occur regularly in organizations, both public and private—the September 11 tragedy and the fall of Enron are simply dramatic recent examples.

Since the stakes are so much higher, and the risks potentially so much greater, for large groups—whether teams or organizations, local or national governments—we believe one of the main responsibilities of leadership must be to identify and avoid predictable surprises. Most leaders recognize growing systemic weaknesses in their organizations that have the potential to flash into major crises over time. Visionary and courageous leaders avoid tragedies by both anticipating and taking steps to mitigate the damage of such threats. But far too many leaders are predictably surprised. The United States' lack of preparedness for a terrorist attack using airliners rendered the nation terribly, and avoidably, vulnerable. Likewise, unwillingness on the part of U.S. leaders to deal with well-recognized weaknesses in the financial oversight of companies set the stage for Enron's collapse.

Consider the weaknesses in the U.S. aviation security system that led the terrorists to decide to use airplanes as weapons. The federal government knew that militant Islamic terrorists were willing to become martyrs for their cause and that their hatred and aggression toward the United States had increased throughout the 1990s. Terrorists bombed the World Trade Center in 1993. In 1994, terrorists hijacked an Air France airplane and made an aborted attempt to turn the airplane into a missile aimed at the Eiffel Tower. In 1995, the U.S. government learned of a failed Islamic terrorist plot to simultaneously hijack eleven U.S. commercial airplanes over the Pacific Ocean, then crash a light plane filled with explosives into CIA headquarters. Meanwhile, dozens of federal reports and Vice President Al Gore's special commission on aviation security provided comprehensive evidence that the U.S. aviation system was full of holes. Any frequent flyer knew how simple it was to board an airplane with items, such as small knives, that could be used as weapons.

When you put the pieces together, the threat of a predictable surprise emerges. Did the U.S. government know that four airplanes would be used to attack New York and Washington? No. Did the government know that both World Trade Center towers would fall? No. But U.S. government agencies and officials had all of the data they needed to know that dangerous deficiencies in airline security existed—ones that could be exploited in a variety of ways by anyone with ill intentions and a sufficient amount of planning and organization. The use of commercial airplanes as weapons on September 11 was therefore a predictable surprise. While advance knowledge of the terrorists' plans could have headed off the attacks, the U.S. intelligence community is only partially responsible for failing to "connect the dots." More broadly, it is the responsibility of the federal government to ensure that our skies are safe and secure. As was made clear on 9/11, our leaders failed miserably in this regard.

What about the collapse of Enron? Was it foreseeable and preventable? Immediately following the energy giant's bankruptcy, the firm's auditor, Arthur Andersen, faced intense scrutiny. How could Andersen have vouched for the financial health of a company that had been concealing billions of dollars in debt from its shareholders? Facing investigation for its role in the scandal, Andersen threw what some observers described as a "shredding party" of documents from its Enron audit. Ultimately, the firm was found guilty of obstruction of justice and ceased its audits of public companies.

At the heart of the Enron debacle is a conflict of interest that experts, including one of the authors of this book, have been warning about for years. In 2000, a number of researchers testified before the Securities and Exchange Commission (SEC) that the rapid growth of consulting divisions within the Big Five accounting firms (Arthur Andersen, Deloitte & Touche, Ernst & Young, KPMG, and Pricewaterhouse-Coopers) throughout the 1990s had made impartial financial audits impossible. With the firms relying on consulting work for much of their income, they found themselves in the compromised position of seeking the approval of the very companies whose books they were expected to judge without bias. The marked rise in fraud cases investigated by the SEC—up 41 percent from 1998 to 2001—was one sign of the potential for a dramatic predictable surprise. Separation of the Big Five firms' auditing and consulting functions, many advised, was needed to head off disaster. But, faced with vociferous opposition from Congress and from the auditing industry, including Arthur Andersen CEO Joseph Berardino, the SEC backed down. The predictable result: the collapse of Enron and Arthur Andersen, the loss of thousands of employees' jobs and retirement savings, and a stain on U.S. financial markets.

PREDICTABLE VERSUS
UNPREDICTABLE SURPRISES

In the aftermath of any significant crisis, legions of Monday morning quarterbacks inevitably assert that the people in charge should have predicted the disaster. Over the last thirty years, psychologists have documented this "hindsight effect," offering systematic evidence that people tend to believe in retrospect that an event was far more predictable than reality dictates.[1] Research finds that the hindsight effect describes the behavior of executives, and for our purposes, academics, analysts, and writers. Thus, we anticipate this response to our work and encourage our readers to consider whether we are guilty of the hindsight effect. We hope to clarify that the data needed to prevent the events of September 11 and the fall of Enron was available in advance, and that it was so overwhelming that responsible leaders should have acted upon it. Rather than splitting hairs about whether events at the margin were predictable surprises or not, we will examine cases in which the evidence was clear and overwhelming, was known to leaders, and yet was not acted upon. Further, we argue that in many organizations, there are predictable surprises clearly visible on the horizon that make an unambiguous case for action.

Of course, true surprises really do happen, surprises for which no one should be blamed. Forest fires occur naturally, even in areas where such fires are remarkably rare. Hundred-year floods occur, sometimes more than once in a hundred years. Other surprises occur that responsible leaders envisioned, yet deemed too unlikely and too costly to prepare for. When leaders have recognized potential threats, carried out thorough cost-benefit analyses, and decided that action is unwarranted, we are far less inclined to criticize them on the basis of hindsight. But based on our research and the many cases we have carefully studied, we make the normative argument that often, given the information that was potentially available, a responsible leader should have anticipated a surprise and worked to prevent it. Thus, we distinguish *unpredictable* surprises from *predictable* ones. Unlike an unpredictable surprise, a predictable surprise arises when leaders unquestionably had all the data and insight they needed to recognize the potential for, even the inevitability of, a crisis, but failed to respond with effective preventative action.

The predictable/unpredictable distinction is critical, separating predictable surprises from bad events that could not have been anticipated. However, as Professor Phil Tetlock of the University of California at Berkeley has wisely noted, events are not simply predictable or unpredictable; rather, they lie on a continuum of predictability. For this reason, we have chosen to avoid the impossibly difficult task of separating "somewhat predictable" events from the "moderately predictable." Instead, we focus on the argument that many catastrophes are extremely predictable, and that leaders should first confront the extremely predictable surprises that face their organizations. We argue that 9/11 and the collapse of Enron fall into this extremely predictable category, and we offer tools to prevent similar extremely predictable surprises from erupting.

CHARACTERISTICS OF PREDICTABLE SURPRISES

What are the distinguishing traits of a predictable surprise? We offer six general characteristics of predictable surprises, each of which can be found in the September 11 tragedy, the Enron scandal, and most predictable surprises that await us.

First, a shared trait of predictable surprises is that leaders knew a problem existed and that the problem would not solve itself. In many cases, such festering problems have been talked about in board meetings, executive sessions, Congress, and the Oval Office, and have been written about in the press. While leaders may have had differences of opinion about the urgency of the problem, the weight of evidence supported the need for action. As we will document, the administrations of George H. W. Bush, Bill Clinton, and George W. Bush all knew that aviation security and financial oversight of companies were deficient. These leaders were aware of a growing threat, yet failed to mobilize and respond accordingly.

Second, predictable surprises can be expected when organizational members recognize that a problem is getting worse over time. Some problems solve themselves; for example, the human body and the natural environment are robust and have the ability to cure themselves in many cases. But when scientific evidence (economic, biological, or other) suggests that a problem will not solve itself and will probably continue to escalate, a predictable surprise is likely. Although report after report told U.S. leaders that the nation's aviation security system was worsening by the day, while our enemies' power to take advantage of such weaknesses mounted, little was done. Similarly, the weight of evidence presented to the SEC in 2000 made it clear that auditors' lack of independence was a growing problem that could lead to disaster, yet the commission failed to enact real reform. Predictable surprises are not "bolts from the blue" that come without warning. Unlike unavoidable surprises, they are not failures of recognition, but failures of response.

A third feature of predictable surprises is that fixing the problem would incur significant costs in the present, while the benefits of action would be delayed. As we will argue in chapter 4, individuals, organizations, and governments have a strong tendency to discount the future. It is counterintuitive to spend scarce real resources now to prevent an ambiguous and merely potential harm from occurring in the future. New security and oversight systems aimed at fixing the aviation security and financial oversight systems in the 1990s would have required expensive direct costs from the federal government and from corporations. The benefits of preventative action would have simply been a reduction in the likelihood and magnitude of events such as the September 11 attack and the bankruptcy of Enron. Leaders and citizens alike would have observed no tangible return from their investment of time and money.

A fourth characteristic is related to the previous one: Addressing predictable surprises typically requires incurring a certain cost, while the reward is avoiding a cost that is uncertain but likely to be much larger. Thus, leaders know that they can expect little credit for preventing them. Measures aimed at avoiding predictable surprises require costs that constituencies will notice, yet politicians will not be recognized and rewarded for the disasters they help to avert. For this reason, they have little motivation to work to prevent predictable surprises and may choose instead to cross their fingers and hope for the best. Consider the electrical power system. We don't end each day thanking the power company for keeping our lights on. But if there is a protracted outage, even if it's due to necessary repairs, there will be hell to pay. Fixing aviation security before September 11 would have slightly increased travel delays and the cost of flying. But because the U.S. public could not envision the predictable surprise of failing to fix the problem, aviation security remained a low priority for politicians—including those who had been warned for years by reliable sources about the potential for a catastrophe on the scale of September 11. Nor did many U.S. citizens pay attention to the issue of auditor independence prior to the collapse of Enron. The most pressing social and economic problems are often also the most onerous and thankless tasks, because most citizens have not yet even recognized them. Wise leaders will recognize this odiousness as a feature of predictable surprises and work to educate their constituencies about the need for significant and immediate action.

A fifth characteristic is that decision-makers, organizations, and nations often fail to prepare for predictable surprises because of the natural human tendency to maintain the status quo. Above and beyond concerns about the cost and time requirements of change, when a system still functions and there is no crisis to catalyze action, we will keep doing things the way we have always done them. Acting to avoid a predictable surprise requires a decision to act against this bias and to change the status quo. By contrast, most organizations change incrementally, preferring short-term fixes to long-term solutions. To avoid predictable surprises, leaders must make the case for change and eliminate the status quo as an option. Thus, while some token efforts to improve airport security and to address auditor conflicts of interest were made in the 1990s, reforms fell woefully short of meeting these challenges. We accepted too many features of outdated, ineffective systems.

An unfortunate sixth characteristic of predictable surprises is that a small vocal minority benefits from inaction and is motivated to subvert the actions of leaders for their own private benefit. That is, while society is often desperate for its leaders to take decisive action on an issue, special-interest groups that benefit from the status quo will fight hard to block reform. As we will document in chapter 2, to prevent well-specified and much-needed improvements in security from being implemented, the airlines manipulated governmental decision-making via lobbying and campaign donations. The airlines' political action suggested that they were far more concerned with reducing their short-term expenses than with ensuring the safety of their passengers. Notably, they were the first in line for government assistance in the aftermath of September 11. Similarly, in 2000, as we describe in chapter 3, auditing firms had little trouble persuading Congress and the SEC that they were capable of providing unbiased audits of the same corporations they depended on for consulting profits. The collapse of Enron a year later made the disproportionate power of the Big Five firms, including Arthur Andersen, to distort government policy all the more painful in retrospect. Politicians and government regulators have been too easily swayed by the arguments of these special-interest groups.

Our goal here in drawing out these characteristics is to go beyond mere descriptive or analytical accuracy. Indeed, collectively, these six distinguishing traits of predictable surprises provide a useful set of signals that danger is present. If ignored, these characteristics can lead to tragedy. However, with sound leadership, and with the proper diagnostics and tools—which we will provide in this book—disaster can be avoided.

PROTOTYPES OF PREDICTABLE SURPRISES

We expect that our introduction of 9/11 and Enron made you curious about the predictability of these events, but may also have you wondering if the data is really there to make this accusation.

Chapters 2 and 3 (part I of the book) offer an overview of events relevant to the predictable surprises of the September 11 attacks and the Enron collapse. We believe that the data will eliminate any doubt about their predictability. But our goal is not to provide a comprehensive history of either set of events; rather, we aim to illustrate a pervasive leadership oversight—the failure to avoid predictable surprises. The notion of predictable surprises is a diagnostic concept, not just a post-hoc explanation of recent tragedies. Predictable surprises can and should be anticipated, rather than merely identified in hindsight, as the costs of prevention are far lower than the costs incurred in the aftermath of disaster. The U.S. government could not have predicted the specifics of these events, but should have better anticipated *and prepared for* a broad variety of catastrophes. Interestingly, organizations will achieve the greatest success if they adopt blanket

measures to prepare for a spectrum of disasters, rather than addressing potential surprises one at a time. The accounting reforms that
emerged after the downfall of Arthur Andersen were extremely narrow, focusing on specific flaws of Andersen's audit of Enron rather
than treating these flaws as symptoms of a major systemic problem.
These tentative reforms are unlikely to prevent future crises.

While we personally did not advocate for greater airline security
before September 11, the first draft of the Gore Commission on airline security report, written in 1996, contains all of the details that
U.S. leaders needed to identify and prepare for this predictable surprise (see chapter 2). In the case of auditor independence, Max H.
Bazerman, one of the authors of this book, was part of the effort to
persuade the U.S. government to take action before a predictable
surprise erupted. Bazerman co-wrote and published a 1997 paper entitled "The Impossibility of Auditor Independence" and testified before the SEC in 2000 that true auditor independence cannot occur
within the current U.S. financial system (see chapter 3).[2]

WHY DON'T WE ACT ON WHAT WE KNOW?

By now, we trust that you are thinking about the predictable surprises
in your own organization. Why do executives so commonly fail to act
on predictable surprises?

In part II of the book, we provide a multidisciplinary look at why
predictable surprises are so common within organizations. We will consider the cognitive, organizational, and political causes of predictable
surprises in a manner that can be generalized to most organizations.

Chapter 4 will focus on the cognitive reasons why we ignore the
threat of predictable surprises. We will argue that people tend to hold
positive illusions that lead us to interpret events in an egocentric
manner and to undervalue risks. In addition, our natural tendency to
discount the future reduces our willingness to invest now in order to
prevent a disaster that may be quite distant and vague. People also
tend to try to maintain the status quo, creating a barrier to the concrete
and often large-scale changes that are needed to head off predictable

opp
cost issue not
addressed.

surprises. Finally, most of us are more willing to run the risk of incurring a large but low-probability loss in the future rather than accepting a smaller, sure loss now. We don't want to invest in preventing a problem that we have not experienced and cannot imagine with great specificity. Thus, far too often, we only address problems after we have experienced significant harm.

Moving to the level of the organization, chapter 5 argues that for an organization to avoid predictable surprises, it must efficiently and effectively take a number of steps: Scan the environment for information regarding threats, integrate that information from multiple sources, respond in a timely manner, observe the results of the response, and incorporate lessons learned into the "institutional memory" of the organization. Organizations often err by failing to follow these critical processes. This may be because organizational "silos" impede the integration of information, or because individual incentives encourage people to behave in ways that damage the collective. Regardless, organizations are rendered vulnerable to being predictably surprised.

Finally, at the political level, chapter 6 shows that there are often a small number of individuals and organizations that are highly skilled at corrupting the political system for their own benefit. The failure of the United States to enact meaningful campaign finance reform for so many years, for example, created an election environment of legal corruption; even with the recent ban on soft-money donations created by the 2002 passage of the McCain-Feingold campaign finance reform, it remains far too easy for special interests to influence the political process and to help predictable surprises come to pass. Meanwhile, a politician's larger constituency will remain focused on the costs of action to prevent predictable surprises, while ignoring future benefits—which will often follow the leader's term of office. As a result, small groups that are intensely activated around an issue hold sway over a much larger polity that does not have strong feelings on the issue. When a predictable surprise occurs, politicians and journalists tend to focus on a small number of evildoers, rather than exploring systemic flaws that create incentives for abuse. Too often the tyranny of the minority, fortified by conviction, clout, and cash, keeps us from preventing predictable surprises.

DIAGNOSING AND PREVENTING
PREDICTABLE SURPRISES

Hindsight may be 20/20, but in part III, we show that leaders can prescriptively employ the concept of the predictable surprise to avoid future disasters. The key lies in establishing robust systems for recognizing, prioritizing, and mobilizing to prevent predictable surprises. Our primary goal is not to explain the past, but to highlight the future in a way that allows leaders to take action. We present systematic processes that leaders can implement, and we use these processes to identify predictable surprises that confront our broader society.

Chapter 7 focuses on how leaders can enhance their ability to recognize emerging threats. Drawing on stories such as the mistakes of the U.S. intelligence community prior to the 9/11 terrorist attacks, the failed merger of General Electric and Honeywell, and the crippling difficulties faced by Monsanto in its attempt to sell genetically modified food in Europe, the chapter explores the factors that contribute to recognition failures. We provide leaders with specific tools, including measurement system redesign, intelligence network building, scenario planning, and disciplined post-problem learning, to enhance their abilities to recognize looming trouble.

Chapter 8 explores how leaders can more effectively prioritize actions to prevent predictable surprises. To help leaders overcome barriers to effective prioritization, including "noise," competing priorities, diverse cognitive biases, and perverse incentives in organizations, we supply a powerful set of tools to strengthen prioritization. These include structured dialogue processes, rigorous decision analysis, and incentive-systems redesign.

Finally, chapter 9 examines how leaders can better mobilize support for tackling predictable surprises. Even if they recognize and prioritize action to address looming problems, leaders may be stymied by organizational inertia and active opposition from special-interest groups. While the courage to tackle tough problems is a prerequisite for success in mobilizing to prevent predictable surprises, it is not sufficient. Leaders can use techniques such as persuasive communication, strategic coalition building, structured problem-solving, and crisis-response techniques to accelerate mobilization.

SOME SPECIFIC PREDICTABLE SURPRISES
THAT DEMAND ATTENTION

In our concluding chapter, we identify some of the most important predictable surprises currently looming on the horizon. We will argue that predictable surprises can be expected due to the failure of our leaders to effectively address industry reliance on government subsidies; global warming; campaign finance reform; auditor conflict of interest; and future financial obligations associated with our aging populations and their impact on economies. At an industry-specific level, we face potential disasters from airlines' frequent-flyer programs and from the vague contracts that are so often written between firms. This treatment will allow readers to consider predictable surprises that can be effectively mitigated.

While the vision to identify predictable surprises may be rare, the courage do something about them is rarer still. We define courage as a willingness to act against one's own and others' short-term interests to avoid heavy long-term costs, as well as the capacity to persuade other influential parties of the need for action. The Clinton/Gore administration had the vision to recognize the need for radical improvement in airline security in the late 1990s. Unfortunately, it lacked the courage to act. Similarly, Arthur Levitt, the head of the SEC in 2000, had the vision to focus on the lack of auditor independence in the accounting world, but lacked the courage, as well as the clout, to stand up to special-interest groups to the extent necessary to avoid the Enron collapse. We will provide leaders with tested approaches to persuading influential constituencies to abandon the status quo. In doing so, we will hone leaders' ability to prevent predictable surprises from damaging their organizations.

If our efforts are somewhat successful, we will convince you that September 11 and Enron were predictable surprises. If we reach a greater level of success, you will finish the book believing that a conceptual structure exists for identifying predictable surprises. If we achieve the highest level of success to which we aspire, when you finish this book you will have identified predictable surprises in your organization and will begin to implement strategies to effectively respond to these threats.

PROTOTYPES OF PREDICTABLE SURPRISES

The core argument of this book is that leaders need to confront predictable surprises in their organizations. Yet while many leaders can identify the predictable surprises in their organizations, they are likely to overlook the potential magnitude of such problems. In part I, we seek to convince leaders that the events of September 11, 2001, and the collapse of Enron and Arthur Andersen were predictable. Rather than providing the most comprehensive history of these events, we overview these stories, integrating details to provides evidence for our argument: that each event was, in fact, predictable and avoidable.

In part II, we will describe the reasons that leaders fail to prevent predictable surprises. In part III, we offer a framework for identifying predictable surprises worthy of attention in your organization. The conceptual structure of part II and the prescriptive structure of part III could have been used by leaders to prevent the catastrophes covered in part I—September 11 and the corporate scandals of the start of the millennium. Of course, hindsight is easier than foresight. We conclude the book with a chapter that highlights likely future predictable surprises.

2

September 11

The Costs of Ignoring a Predictable Surprise

For all of those in the know about security, what happened on 9/11 was not unexpected.

—Gerald Dillingham, Aviation Security Director,
General Accounting Office

In the months that followed the September 11, 2001, terrorist attacks on New York and Washington, homeland defense leapt to the top of the government's agenda and the forefront of citizens' consciousness. Commercial jetliners had crashed into the World Trade Center, the Pentagon, and a Pennsylvania field, revealing that the security infrastructure of the United States was paper-thin. Suddenly, everyone was an expert on the flimsiness of cockpit doors, the knife loophole, and high turnover rate of airport security personnel—though prior to September 11, most of us had never given aviation security a second thought.

Consider the following declarations, similar to the headlines that appeared on the editorial pages of newspapers across the country soon after the attacks:

"FAA Needs Preboard Passenger Screening Performance Standards"

"Development of New Security Technology Has Not Met Expectations"

"Aviation Security: Urgent Issues Need to Be Addressed"

"Vulnerabilities Still Exist in the Aviation Security System"

In fact, these declarations are not newspaper headlines. Nor were they reactions to September 11; they were written before the tragedies. Each is the title of a U.S. General Accounting Office (GAO) report: The first was issued in 1987, the next two during the 1990s, and the last in 2000.[1] For more than a decade prior to September 11, the GAO, the investigative arm of Congress, had been warning the highest levels of government about the sorry state of security at U.S. airports and air-traffic control headquarters. September 11 was not only a predictable surprise, it was a predicted event. In dozens of thick reports, many labeled "Urgent" and "Critical," the GAO documented ongoing vulnerabilities in an air-transport system that were ripe for exploitation (see appendix A at the end of the book for a list of reports). Terrorism was one of the GAO's top concerns. Fifteen months before September 11, it warned: "The trend in terrorism against U.S. targets is toward large-scale incidents designed for maximum destruction, terror, and media impact."[2]

In the 1990s, two presidential commissions issued recommendations that led to the passage of two new aviation security laws. From 1996 to 2000, Congress provided the Federal Aviation Administration (FAA) with approximately $1 billion to fund its civil aviation security program, including more than $340 million for the purchase and deployment of security equipment in U.S. airports.[3] Yet by September 11, 2001, the FAA, Congress, the airlines, and two administrations had extremely little to show for their time and money.

Testifying before Congress nine days after the attacks, Gerald L. Dillingham, the GAO's director of physical infrastructure issues, repeated his plea for aviation security reform, commenting:

[P]revious tragedies have resulted in congressional hearings, recommendations, and debates, but little long-term resolve to correct flaws in the system as the memory of the crisis recedes. The future of aviation security hinges in large part on overcoming this cycle of limited action that has too often characterized the response to aviation security concerns.[4]

In this chapter, we consider the extent to which American leaders, through their "cycle of limited action," enabled the September 11 terrorists to believe that they could carry out their plan with deadly precision. In doing so, we will show that the failures of airline security on September 11 were a predictable surprise. Throughout the 1990s, U.S. leaders were aware that hatred toward the United States was growing among Islamic extremists. They also were aware of the ease of taking knives on board airplanes, the concept of turning an airplane into a missile, and the strategy of simultaneous hijackings. Why did they ignore the clear threats to the United States? Why did they do so little to prevent the surprise? This chapter will explore the cognitive, organizational, and political determinants of inaction prior to September 11. In doing so, we will develop the argument that the U.S. government and the airline industry should have acted on aviation security long before September 11, 2001, and that the events of that day were a predictable surprise.

We begin with a brief history of air disasters and the typical government response—thick reports, weak laws, and little action. We focus on the Gore Commission, a case study in denying the likelihood of a predictable surprise. Formed after the 1996 explosion of TWA Flight 800, the White House Commission on Aviation Safety and Security, headed by Vice President Al Gore, moved in a few months from a tough draft report that held the airlines and the FAA responsible for repairing the broken system to a final report condoning business as usual.

The government's inability to enact simple, measurable aviation security improvements, we will demonstrate, can be directly linked to faulty decisions by key individuals, a lack of courage on the part of our leadership, the organizational structure of our government, and the lobbying and campaign donations of private industry. Entrusted with the safety of the flying public, the airlines denied the very real possibility of a predictable surprise and did everything within their considerable power to block meaningful reform. The "cycle of limited action" is closely linked to the death of thousands on September 11.

On November 19, 2001, President Bush signed an aviation security bill that federalized airport baggage screeners and require screening of all checked luggage—important reforms that experts have been urging for years. It is possible that the death of 3,200 people in a single morning in America may have broken government gridlock in a way that the previous 2,000 deaths worldwide in terrorist-related aviation incidents since the late 1960s had not. But will new reforms be enforced, or will they be allowed to fade away until the next predictable surprise?

AVIATION SECURITY:
A HISTORY OF FAILURE

In the early days of commercial aviation, airplanes were as unprotected as city buses and subway trains are today. The FAA was established in 1958 with the dual—and conflicting—mandate of promoting air commerce and the safety of air travel. It wasn't until 1973, following a spate of hijackings to Cuba, that the FAA required airlines to screen passengers and their carry-on baggage for weapons. In 1978, Congress deregulated the airline industry by striking down government fare and route controls. The FAA continued to regulate the airlines' security efforts; airlines typically have hired private security firms to fulfill these duties.

The increased intensity of competition brought on by deregulation is supposed to benefit consumers through greater choice, lower prices, and better service and security. A *Consumer Reports* study concluded that this has not been the case for the airline industry. While it is true that airfares dropped 37 percent in the twenty-two years since the 1978 deregulation, airfares had declined at the same rate in the twenty-two years *preceding* deregulation. In fact, "deregulated full-coach fares in 2000 were 65 percent higher than their regulated equivalents in 1978, on average, even after adjusting for inflation."[5] Meanwhile, service and safety deteriorated as the airlines crammed more seats onto smaller planes and passed on security duties to the lowest bidder. For the airlines, security has both direct and indirect costs. Careful screening of passengers and their bags would mean flight delays, precious minutes and hours lost on the airlines' most expensive fixed-cost asset, the airplanes.

In light of the airlines' strong incentives to reduce the monetary costs of airport security, it was up to the FAA to police the industry and keep standards high. But in the decades that followed deregulation, the FAA proved itself incapable of ensuring even minimal levels of aviation security. The FAA did not establish standards for weapon detection rates, a shortcoming that the GAO, in one of its early reports on aviation security, blamed for poor screener performance. Tests in 1978 of X-ray screening operations showed an average weapon detection rate of 87 percent. The fact that 13 percent of test weapons went undetected, the FAA and the airline industry agreed, was "significant and alarming."[6] By 1986, detection had fallen to 79 percent for X-ray tests and 82 percent for metal detector tests, and stood at 87 percent for physical search tests—despite the fact that, as the GAO noted, flaws in FAA test procedures may have artificially inflated the screeners' success rate.

Why did the screeners have so much trouble carrying out their duties? The GAO reported in 1987, "the program continues to experience many of the personnel-related problems—high turnover, low wages, inadequate training—identified in a 1979 FAA/industry study."[7] Because screeners were being paid at or near minimum wage, turnover stood at about 100 percent annually. Training was often limited to watching a film; at one site, no one ever graded the tests that screeners took on procedures. The FAA found that some screeners let mock pipe-bombs pass through because they did not recognize them as weapons.

Why did the FAA accept the airlines' dismal security standards? Former Department of Transportation Inspector General Mary Schiavo noted in her 1997 FAA exposé *Flying Blind, Flying Safe,* "when [FAA officials] consider safety, they do so through a forty-year-old prism that skews their vision back to a time when the government heavily regulated airline prices and routes, when only a few brand-name carriers plied the skies and when all the airlines operated with the same procedures and rules."[8]

Only in 1996, after the crashes of ValuJet 592 and TWA 800, did Congress address the FAA's outdated dual mandate by reducing the agency's promotional duties and charging it instead with "assigning, maintaining, and enhancing safety and security as the highest priorities in air commerce."[9] Schiavo was unable to take comfort in this reform. In her 1997 book, she asserted, "The fact that the 104th Congress eliminated the FAA's mandate to promote aviation has not changed the long-standing tradition of loyalty to the aviation industry that prevails at the agency. I fear that the elimination of the mandate will make the public, the press and safety advocates complacent about the FAA's priorities."[10]

On December 21, 1988, Pan Am 103 blew up over Lockerbie, Scotland, killing 259 passengers and crew members and 11 people on the ground. A small amount of Semtex, a powerful plastic explosive, had been hidden in a cassette recorder packed in a suitcase. The attention of security officials turned from guns to bombs, and President Bush created the President's Commission on Aviation Security and Terrorism, which issued a series of recommendations aimed primarily at improving bomb-detection technology. As Congress drafted a new aviation-security bill based on the commission's report, the Air Transport Association (ATA), the airlines' trade group, balked at an FAA proposal requiring fingerprinting and criminal background checks of airport workers. Lobbyists for the ATA, which brags on its Web site that it has "played a major role in all the major government decisions regarding aviation since its founding," persuaded Congress that background checks would be an unnecessary drain on scarce resources.[11] The Aviation Security Improvement Act of 1990 required the FAA to step up research and development on an effective explosive-detection system. Background checks of airport workers were required only when a job applicant's record showed a gap of a year or more.[12]

Four years later, the GAO revealed that the FAA had made little progress in deploying new technology to detect explosives. The agency was stuck with a quagmire of forty-two different research projects with names such as "Pulsed Fast Neutron Activation," "Nuclear Quadrupole Resonance," and "Olfaction (Use of Dogs)." Many projects had been called off due to lack of success; others were hobbling forward despite "unsuccessful" or "inconclusive" early results.

According to the GAO, FAA researchers paid scant attention to human factors—the way technology would be used in the field—and seemed oblivious to the budgeting concerns of Congress and the airlines. The FAA estimated that approval of new detection devices was still five years away.[13] Congress finally mandated screener background-checks in 1996, but they were of little value; current employees were exempt, while many of the new screeners hired were recent immigrants with backgrounds that were almost impossible to verify.[14]

No surprise, then, that gaping holes remained in airport security. "In 1993," wrote Schiavo, "plainclothes agents from my office sneaked into some of the nineteen busiest airports in the U.S. They wandered around in off-limits areas, seldom challenged by airport or airline employees. . . . They got onto planes and into cargo holds. They wore no identification, dressed casually and didn't even pretend to belong there. They also carried guns, knives, fake bombs and a deactivated hand grenade through security screening points and X-ray machines." Two years later, "in 1995, my agents, together with FAA inspectors, carried fake bombs strapped to their bodies or in briefcases, marzipan candy or other substances arrayed on boards to look like plastic explosives, and guns and knives through metal detectors. They got into secure areas at the big international airports around the country. They were not stopped 40 percent of the time."[15] Hoping to alert President Clinton, Congress, and the flying public to these lapses, Schiavo prepared a report on her findings for the FAA. She was unnerved by the message she received at a meeting with FAA and Transportation Secretary Frederico Pena's staff in the summer of 1996: "they wanted me to bury the report. The Olympic Games were opening in Atlanta that same month. . . . The FAA, with the backing of the Secretary of Transportation, remained convinced it was best to withhold the report from the public indefinitely."[16]

Meanwhile, throughout the 1990s, evidence grew that Islamic terrorists intended to use commercial airliners as weapons against the Western world. In 1995, an Algerian terrorist group linked to Al Qaeda hijacked an Air France jet and threatened to crash it into the Eiffel Tower; the plot was foiled when commandos killed the hijackers during refueling.[17] The 1994 bombing of a Philippine Airlines flight to Tokyo was determined in 1995 to have been a test run for a plot to blow up eleven U.S. jetliners over the Pacific Ocean. As part of the plot, a Pakistani who had trained at U.S. flight schools would crash a light plane into CIA headquarters.[18] "It is likely that thousands of passengers would have been killed if the plot had been successfully carried out," the FAA stated in 1999.[19] Palestinian Ramzi Yousef and his co-conspirators were convicted for the Philippine Airlines bombing and for the U.S. airlines plot; Yousef was also indicted for his role in the 1993 attack on the World Trade Center, which killed six people and injured one thousand. In its September 11, 1996, report "Aviation Security: Urgent Issues Need to Be Addressed," the GAO cautioned, "Events such as the [1993] World Trade Center bombing have revealed that the terrorists' threat in the United States is more serious and extensive than previously believed."[20] The FBI Bomb Data Center reported that bombing attempts had climbed internationally from 803 in 1984 to 3,163 in 1994.[21]

THE GORE COMMISSION
AND ITS OMISSIONS

The explosion of TWA 800 in July 1996 put the spotlight back on aviation security. Two hundred thirty-nine people died in what was initially thought to have been a terrorist incident. Signaling a serious intent to improve the safety of the skies once and for all, President Clinton established the White House Commission on Aviation Safety and Security, put his vice president in charge, and filled it with security heavyweights, including former CIA Director John Deutsch and Department of Transportation Secretary Frederico Pena, as well as several relatives of air-disaster victims.

On September 9, 1996, the "Gore Commission," as it came to be known, submitted a promising preliminary report to the president. Gore called for twenty new safety and counterterrorism measures, including the establishment of safety and security consortia at all commercial airports and criminal background checks and fingerprinting of all screeners and employees with access to secure airport areas. The most notable recommendation: full matching of passengers and their checked bags prior to all domestic takeoffs and removal of unmatched baggage. Intended to prevent terrorists from planting bombs on flights they would not take, bag matching was already required on all international flights departing the United States. Pan Am's failure to follow international bag-match regulations resulted in the explosion of Flight 103. Insiders say commission member Victoria Cummock, who lost her husband John on that flight, convinced Gore that domestic bag-matching could prevent similar tragedies. In its draft report, the commission proposed that a test approach to domestic bag-matching be put into effect within sixty days.

To the airlines, bag matching didn't mean added safety, but delayed flights and enraged passengers. According to Victoria Cummock and former FAA security chief Billie H. Vincent, the airlines pressed Gore hard on the issue. DC lobbyists did not begin to disclose their profits publicly until 1997, following the passage of the 1995 Lobbyist Disclosure Act, so 1996 lobbying figures are not available. But in 1997, the ATA, the airlines' trade group, spent $2,570,000 to lobby the White House and Congress on aviation policy and legislation. In 1997, American Airlines spent a staggering $5,560,000 in lobbying fees; the same year, five other airlines—Delta, Northwest, Southwest, United, and US Airways—spent more than $7 million combined on lobbying.[22]

On September 19, ten days after the release of the draft report, Gore sent a letter of appeasement to Carol Hallett, president of the ATA. "I want to make it very clear," Gore wrote, "that it is not the intent of the administration or of the commission to create a hardship for the air transportation industry or to cause inconvenience to the traveling public."[23]

The day after Gore's letter was released, TWA—the airline whose crash had triggered the commission's work—gave $40,000 to the Democratic National Committee. In the next two months leading up to the 1996 presidential election, the other big airlines anted up big soft-money donations to the Democrats: $265,000 from American Airlines, $120,000 from Delta, $115,000 from United, and $87,000 from Northwest. In the election's closing weeks, the airlines gave the Democratic Party a total of $585,000—two-and-a-half times what they gave Republicans during the same period.[24] American's three checks, deposited October 18, 21, and 22, during the heat of the bag-matching battle, make up more than three-quarters of the company's soft-money donations to the Democrats in 1995 and 1996 combined.[25]

By all accounts, the negotiations leading up the release of the Gore Commission's final report in February 1997 were intense. Commission member and counterterrorism specialist Brian M. Jenkins pointed out that the commission had to juggle the agendas of many different constituencies: the airlines; cargo carriers; unions representing pilots, flight attendants, and air-traffic controllers; and civil libertarians concerned about terrorist profiling proposals; not to mention the 700 million passengers who fly U.S. planes each year. The airlines pushed hardest of all. "Our concerns continue to be bag match, bag match, bag match," one airline industry insider told *Newsday*. "We think that it will cause massive disruption in the system."[26] Facing pressure from all sides, the twenty-one members of the Gore Commission argued heatedly over bag matching and other issues the night before their report was due. They were unable to achieve unanimity. Disgusted with the watered-down stance on bag matching and a lack of concrete goals and deadlines, Victoria Cummock refused to sign the final draft.

The Gore Commission report, released February 12, trumpeted an overall goal of cutting aviation disasters by 80 percent over the next ten years. Given the predicted rapid growth in air traffic, success was crucial: "Boeing projects that unless the global accident rate is reduced," the report declared, "by the year 2015, an airliner will crash somewhere in the world almost weekly."[27] Although the explosion of TWA 800 had since been attributed to a fuel tank explosion, not a ground-to-air missile as first suspected, the commission continued to view terrorism as a key threat: "[I]t is becoming more common to find terrorists working alone or in ad-hoc groups, some of whom are not afraid to die in carrying out their design. . . . [T]errorists see airplanes as attractive targets. And, they know that airlines are often seen as national symbols."[28]

The report opened with tough talk, but the fifty-three recommendations that followed left serious doubt as to the feasibility of the commission's long-term goal. A mere shadow of its first draft, the report was written in vague language it lacked concrete goals and deadlines, and skirted the all-important issue of funding. The predictable surprises highlighted in the first draft were buried by the political actions that created the final report. The commission advised the government to purchase "significant numbers" of explosive detection machines for the airlines—but did not define "significant" or offer an installation deadline. Airlines should go forward with plans to equip cargo holds of all passenger aircraft with smoke detectors, the commission advised, but again deadlines were not mentioned. Securing aircraft and controlled areas of airports from unauthorized access was another ill-defined item on the commission's wish list: "Certify screening companies and improve screener performance" was another. How should the firms be certified? Should screener training be increased, or would on-the-job testing be adequate? When should the security firms have new hiring and training programs in place? The commission avoided these issues, but it did give the airlines two years to have their employees fingerprinted by the FBI. It refrained entirely from addressing the difficult task of updating the nation's outdated passenger-screening technology.

Regarding its most contentious issue, bag matching on domestic flights, the commission softened from a test program of full matches within sixty days to partial bag matching within ten months. Under the commission's "layered" approach to security, only the bags of passengers triggered by a profiling system would be matched to their owners. "We fully intend to move towards a full bag match when and as the ability to do that becomes clear," said Gore, but without incentives or deadlines, the promise rang hollow.[29] Aware that the FAA's rules take an average of three years to enact, the commission could have ordered the agency to issue an emergency directive on domestic bag-matching, but it did not.

"There's nothing in this report that's startling or new," commented ATA Vice President John Meehan.[30] This was doubtless a relief to the industry. With little accountability attached to the proposals, it would be impossible for the FAA or the commission to hold the airlines to the reforms.

"The final report contains no special call to action, no commitments to address aviation security system-wide by mandating the deployment of current technology and training with actionable timetables and budgets," commission member Victoria Cummock wrote in a scathing nineteen-page dissent attached as an appendix to the report.[31] Cummock found the commission's backpedaling on bag-matching especially galling. A system in which only the bags of profiled passengers are matched, she pointed out, would not have saved Pan Am 103: "[T]here never was a passenger ever associated with the bag containing the bomb. Since you can only profile passengers (not bags) the bag with the bomb would not have been detected."[32] Commented Toronto airport president and FAA security adviser Louis Turpen, "Pan Am 103 happened in 1988. It's now 1997. It took us less time to win World War II and to build the atomic bomb."[33] Commission member Kathleen Flynn, who lost a child on Pan Am 103, later told the *Boston Globe* that she believed the final report to have been influenced by political contributions. She noted, "the same thing happened under the Republicans."[34]

Soon after the Gore report was issued, journalists picked up on the spike in airline industry donations to the Democrats following the release of the commission's first draft. Security experts and safety advocates were struck by the timing. "It's a perplexing coincidence," said former FAA security chief Billie Vincent of American Airlines' generosity. "On its face, it would seem to be an outrageous exercise of influence with money."[35] Mary Schiavo concurred: "I think the timing is a little too coincidental for my taste."[36] American defended its $265,000 gift to the Democratic party by insisting that it was merely trying to "play catch-up" with competitors such as Northwest and United; besides, a spokesperson pointed out, the company had donated $100,000 to the Republicans around the same time.[37] "We are certainly no fan of the current fundraising system in Washington," said American public-relations director Chris Chiames, "but we have come to recognize that it's the way the city operates." The vice president's office denied a link between the donations and the commission's recommendations. Victoria Cummock felt otherwise: "We had one group of recommendations on September 9 that were tangible and forceful. I think the airlines basically bought a new set of recommendations after September 9."[38]

Congress folded many of the Gore Commission's recommendations into the Airport Security Improvement Act of 2000. Early drafts of the act addressed deadline and funding issues that the commission itself had not; baggage-screener training was to have tripled from a mandatory twelve hours to forty hours. But after being worked over by airline industry lobbyists, the act passed with watered-down language that allowed airlines to bypass the forty-hour requirement with their own training plans.[39]

The months leading up to the release of the Gore Commission's final report were remarkable not only for the airlines' support of Al Gore, but for Al Gore's support of the industry, as the *St. Petersburg Times* documented in 1999. Gore, looking ahead to his own presidential bid following Bill Clinton's reelection in November, became a "mouthpiece" for the airlines, charged Victoria Cummock.[40] In December 1996, in the midst of industry uproar over the commission's full bag-matching plan, Gore and President Clinton hosted a White House news conference for fifteen airline CEOs to reveal their plan to install smoke detectors in small jets. Motivated by the May 1996 crash of ValuJet 592, in which 110 passengers and crew died after a fire broke out in the cargo hold, the plan was intended to leapfrog over the FAA's rule-making process. "[The airlines are] jumping over the regulatory and the financial hurdles," Gore said in his speech. "And the winners will be the millions of Americans who fly on these planes."[41] Ten months after the press conference, the National Transportation Safety Board (NTSB) wrote to the FAA to say it was "disappointed" that the agency was taking so long to have the detectors installed. According to the NTSB, only *one* plane had been retrofitted since Gore's announcement.

Gore's willingness to lend a helping hand to the airlines was viewed by many as a preemptive attempt to win over powerful industries that might otherwise line up behind the Republicans in the 2000 presidential race. Gore succeeded in boosting airline contributions from 1996 levels, especially during the drafting of the commission's report, but overall, the industry put its money on the Republicans during the 1999–2000 election cycle (see table 2-1). Some observers recognized the danger implicit in Gore's coddling of the airlines: He would be vulnerable if a new air disaster exposed laxity in the Clinton administration's approach to aviation security. The risk was that "you might take credit for something that will later come back and bite you," University of Kansas political science professor Burdett Loomis said in 1999.[42]

TABLE 2-1

Airline Contributions to Federal Candidates and Political Parties: 1992, 1996, and 2000 Elections

Election Cycle	Total Contributions	Donations to Democrats	Donations to Republicans	Percent to Democrats	Percent to Republicans
1992	$1,625,117	$890,113	$727,104	55%	45%
1996	$4,069,317	$2,107,659	$1,946,098	52%	48%
2000	$6,794,539	$2,650,176	$4,107,890	39%	60%

Adapted from "Airlines: Long-Term Contribution Trends," Center for Responsive Politics, 2004, <http://www.opensecrets.org/industries/indus.asp?Ind=T1100> (accessed 14 March 2004). "Methodology: The numbers . . . are based on contributions of $200 or more from PACs and individuals to federal candidates and from individual and soft money donors to political parties, as reported to the Federal Election Commission." While election cycles are shown in charts as 1996, 2000, etc., "they actually represent two-year periods." For example, the 2000 election cycle runs from January 1, 1999 to December 31, 2000.

PREDICTABLE NEGLECT
AND SEPTEMBER 11

"Later attempts to track [the Gore Commission's] recommendations will result in problems with differing agency interpretations, misunderstandings, and outright opposition to implementation by individuals and/or organizations who oppose the specific recommendations," said Victoria Cummock in her dissenting letter. Her prediction proved chillingly accurate. In the days and weeks following September 11, as the nation's attention zeroed in on aviation security, it quickly became clear that the terrorists had counted on, and successfully exploited, a number of long-standing and predictable weaknesses in the system. Reporting to the White House immediately after the tragedy on the status of Gore Commission recommendations, the FAA admitted that very few had been implemented during the past four-and-a-half years. The *Los Angeles Times* revealed that, as of September 11, most of the recommendations "had been watered down by industry lobbying or were bogged down in bureaucracy."[43]

In the years prior to September 11, 2001, awareness grew within the federal government of the U.S. aviation system's lack of preparedness for a terrorist attack involving airplanes, and of the mounting likelihood of such an attack. In 1998, Stephen Gale, a terrorism specialist at the University of Pennsylvania, and two other experts analyzed the threat from airborne attacks for the FAA, based in part on analysis of the Eiffel Tower threat and the crash of a small plane on the grounds of the White House in 1994. The researchers presented the agency with two scenarios: (1) terrorists crashing planes into nuclear power plants on the East Coast, and (2) terrorists commandeering Federal Express cargo planes and crashing them into the World Trade Center, the Pentagon, the White House, the Capitol, the Sears Tower, and the Golden Gate Bridge.[44] "You can't protect yourself from meteorites," said Gale, paraphrasing an FAA official. "He was saying it was too hard."[45]

In December 1999, Al Qaeda terrorists armed with knives hijacked an Indian airliner to Kandahar, Afghanistan. To maintain control during the hijacking, the terrorists cut the throat of a young passenger and let him bleed to death—a tactic that the September 11 terrorists are suspected of using on flight attendants.[46] In July 2001, the Italian government closed airspace over Genoa and mounted antiaircraft batteries based on tips that Islamic extremists were planning to use an airplane to kill President Bush during a Group of Eight summit.[47]

Still the FAA and the airlines did little to improve aviation security. In the years following the Gore Report, most of the airlines balked at implementing even a partial bag-matching system for domestic flights. Some relied on profiling software called CAPPS (Computer Assisted Passenger Prescreening System) and searched the luggage of passengers "selected" by the system. CAPPS judges passengers on criteria that arouse a suspicion of terrorism, such as paying in cash or buying a one-way ticket, but it does not include input from law enforcement agencies. Security experts have derided the profiling system, which singles out 2 to 5 percent of passengers, as "myopic."[48] While suspicious passengers might have been interviewed by law enforcement on the same airlines' flights to Europe, they were not taken aside prior to domestic flights. This limited profiling was rendered almost irrelevant by the fact that the airlines refused to conduct bag checks on the second or third leg of a domestic flight. The system was wide open: A passenger selected as suspicious could simply get off the plane he intended to bomb at an intermediate stop. Profiling is doomed to fail in the United States for another reason, argued Mary Schiavo in *Flying Blind, Flying Safe*. "In other countries race, nationality, color of skin, sex, religious affiliation or even the possession of facial hair may peg a person as suspect," she wrote. Such stereotyping is outlawed by the Constitution and the courts, and rightly so. But because "the success of profiling with limited parameters is unproven," Schiavo argued in 1997, "profiling will never be the answer in this country."[49]

Our national concern for civil liberties necessitates thorough and color-blind security systems, including full bag-matching and use of state-of-the-art explosive detection machines. Yet the techniques used to uncover weapons and bombs prior to 9/11 were decidedly low-tech. The Gore Commission advocated the use of explosive detection machines to improve the accuracy, speed, and quantity of baggage searches. From 1996 to 2000, the FAA deployed 550 trace detection devices at eighty-one airports. Each of the $1 million machines was designed to scan 225 bags per hour, but the Department of Transportation revealed in 2000 that many machines were sitting idle, while others were used at a mere fraction of their capacity.[50] Reluctant to pay for the upkeep of their taxpayer-funded machines, some airlines continued to prefer hand searches. Under the airlines' "layered" approach to security, more than 90 percent of luggage was going into cargo holds unscreened.[51] Hustling bags onto planes remained the airlines' top priority, and no one was holding them accountable for safety.

Under pressure from the ATA to abandon its push for partial bag-matching, the FAA conducted a cost-benefit analysis of the proposed measure in 1999.[52] The FAA estimated that ten years of partial bag-matching would cost the airlines $2 billion, primarily in delayed flights. Regulators compared this expense to the estimated cost to the airlines of the explosion of one plane. First, they assigned a value of $2.7 million to each passenger's life. Next, they factored in a typical passenger plane: a Boeing 737, two-thirds full with seventy-three passengers and five crew members. After an explosion, the airlines would face $210 million in liability losses plus $16 million for the plane itself. Property damage and investigative and legal costs would bring the total to $271 million. A hard-nosed accountant might argue that even this huge loss of life and property might not justify the $2 billion ten-year cost of partial bag checks, or that the money might be better spent on other public security measures. But the FAA cited a study showing that air travel routinely slumps after a major air disaster. This loss of business would cost the industry $1.7 billion. Thus, the cost of enhanced security was roughly equal to the financial cost of losing one airplane.[53] Yet for the next two years, the FAA's partial bag-matching rule shuffled through the agency's bureaucracy. Meanwhile, plans for 100 percent screening of checked bags had been shunted off into the distant future—at some U.S. airports by 2009, at all of them by 2017.[54] No bag-matching regulation, neither partial nor full, was on the rulebooks on September 11, 2001.

Two of the terrorists aboard American Airlines Flight 77, which crashed into the Pentagon, were apparently singled out by the CAPPS profiling system. Nawak Alhazmi and Khalid Almihdhar's reservations were made on the Internet in late August with Visa cards, but they paid cash for the tickets ten days later at a travel agency, thereby triggering suspicion. Both of their bags were allegedly searched before being loaded into the cargo hold, but neither terrorist was questioned.[55]

"In our hearts," said ATA President Carol Hallett in a speech to the Travel Industries Association in Atlanta soon after the tragedies, "everyone must realize that the failure to use the techniques that are available today may be directly responsible for the events of September 11."[56] Unfortunately, the industry's change of heart came too late.

All nineteen terrorists apparently breezed through airport security with the knives and box cutters that some of them may have used to kill or injure crew and passengers. Airport security firms had a long-standing policy of letting passengers through security with knives less than four inches long. In the mid-1990s, the FAA discovered during a series of tests that a hunting knife carefully positioned in a carry-on bag is virtually undetectable by X-ray.[57]

"We recognize that the process of setting standards [for preboard passenger screening] will require time as well as consultation with the airlines and other interested parties," the GAO wrote in its first report on screening in 1987.[58] Thirteen years later, the FAA finally had written a rule requiring certification of private screening companies, despite objections from the airlines about the potential economic burden of standards. But as of September 11, the FAA had not yet published the rule in the Federal Register, the necessary final step before enforcement could take place. Meanwhile, employee turnover had jumped in some airports to 200 percent or more; starting salaries remained at or near minimum wage, and were often lower than the hourly rate paid by airport fast-food restaurants.[59] In March 2001, the GAO reported that screeners at American airports were still only half as effective at detecting weapons as their counterparts in European airports—many of whom are federal employees or members of law enforcement.[60] The airlines and airports accepted the FAA's $10,000 fine for each undetected weapon as just another business expense. During a two-year period in the late 1990s, airport authority Massport and the airlines paid $178,000 in fines for security violations at Boston's Logan Airport—one of the airports breached by the September 11 terrorists.[61] In 2000, Congress mandated background checks for all security screeners. In October of that year, Argenbright Security, which employed twenty-five thousand people at American airports, was fined $1.5 million for hiring untrained screeners with criminal backgrounds.[62]

The terrorists also counted on the flimsiness of cockpit doors. Since 1998, at least fourteen drunk or disturbed passengers have attempted to force their way into cockpits during flights, six of them with success. In June 1999, a passenger broke into an All Nippon Airways cockpit and fatally stabbed the pilot with an eight-inch knife. It was such incidents that motivated Israeli airliner El Al to create a fortified double-door system. But in the United States, pilots and the FAA preferred flimsy doors to help the crew escape in a crash. The airlines had their own reason for opposing sturdy doors: The added weight to the aircraft would increase fuel costs. "There are intelligent ways of making sturdy, light doors," commented University of Michigan aerospace engineering professor William Kaufman. "If El Al does it, why don't we do it, too?"[63]

The FAA admitted that its "often conflicting and time-consuming" rule-making procedures had slowed the implementation of many of the Gore Commission's security recommendations.[64] According to the GAO, it can take the FAA five years or more to begin the rule-making process, and up to fifteen years to complete it.[65] The industry contributes to the slow pace by filing objections, requesting delays, and calling for public hearings—whatever it can think of to stall a new rule. "Anything that would cost them money they could fight, and delay rule making for years and years," commented Democratic Representative Peter DeFazio of Oregon.[66] The FAA did expand its use of bomb-sniffing dogs at airports, as directed by the commission. But, as of September 11, the agency had not yet launched a commission-inspired program to assess the vulnerability of the nation's 450 airports to terrorism. Likewise, it was still collecting data on how to prevent intruders from gaining access to restricted areas of airports. One 1999 GAO report revealed that government investigators were able to gain access to secure areas without proper identification 120 times in a five-month period.[67]

"The American people have been lied to and lulled into a very false sense of security," said Victoria Cummock after the attacks. "In other countries, airport security is done by professionals. In this country, it's given out to the lowest bidder."[68] David Stempler, president of the consumer group Air Travelers Association, concurred: "Until [September 11], we were in a state of complacency in this country. We created a façade of security. . . . We had a system that was set up for failure."[69]

THE REAL COSTS OF INACTION

Consider a preliminary and incomplete list of the losses incurred by the world at large on September 11. The sheer human costs are unfathomable. Thousands of people lost their lives; many more thousands lost spouses, parents, children, siblings, and friends. Using the FAA's 1999 formula, which assigned $2.7 million to each human life, the liability loss of 3,200 people was $8.64 billion. New York City Comptroller Alan Hevesi estimated the "lost human productive value" of the thousands who died in the World Trade Center, many of them young people with high-powered jobs, to be $11 billion.[70]

Congress designated $40 billion for disaster relief in the days after September 11. The attacks on the World Trade Center cost

New York City between $83 and $85 billion, according to the city comptroller.[71] The Pentagon suffered about $1 billion in damages. In terms of insured losses, the attacks were the costliest disaster in history, totaling $40.2 billion.[72] Post 9/11, insurance rates for commercial and public works projects in major U.S. cities soared by 50 to100 percent.

Immediately after the attacks, senior executives and board members from the airlines joined with teams of lobbyists from forty-two Washington, D.C. firms—including former members of the House and Senate and former secretaries of transportation—to present a united front on Capitol Hill. Their argument: that because the terrorists attacks were undertaken in reaction to U.S. policy, not direct attacks on the airlines themselves, the government was responsible for bailing out the industry.[73] Congress agreed to give the airlines a $15 billion emergency bailout package ($5 billion in cash and $10 billion in loan guarantees).

The blow to the nation's tourism and travel industry was enormous. Fear of flying became a global epidemic, causing tourism to atrophy worldwide. The nine largest airlines lost $2.3 billion in the third quarter of 2001 alone; one hundred thousand airline employees quickly lost their jobs.[74] The six biggest airlines—American, United, Delta Air Lines, Northwest Airlines, Continental, and US Airways—lost a record $6.9 billion from October 2001 through June 2002.[75] US Airways filed for bankruptcy in 2002; by the end of the year, United Airlines, which was losing between $10 and $20 million each day, filed suit.

The war in Afghanistan cost $1 billion per month; new homeland security measures and agencies also cost billions. The U.S. Postal Service, which witnessed a decline of 6.5 percent in mail volume following September 11 and the anthrax scare, appealed to Congress for a $5 billion bailout.[76] A year after the attacks, forty-one American service people had lost their lives in "Operation Enduring Freedom" in Afghanistan, and 190 more were wounded. Many Afghani civilians lost their lives in the war; thousands were displaced from their homes.

When President Bush took office in January 2001, budget officials predicted a $313 billion surplus for fiscal year 2002. But an economic slump in great part attributable to the 9/11 attacks led to a $150 billion deficit for the year. With the nation entrenched in a global war on terrorism, the Office of Management and Budget projected the deficit to spiral to $455 billion in fiscal year 2003 and to $475 billion in fiscal 2004.[77] The government has been forced to borrow billions, putting the retirement incomes of Baby Boomers and younger generations in jeopardy.[78]

Add up the loss of thousands of human lives, the loss of trillions of dollars, and the loss of security that millions have experienced since September. Then consider this: The airlines and the politicians that backed them rejected the FAA's argument that they might someday face losses of $2 billion from a terrorist attack on a single airplane.

Hindsight is 20/20. None of us could have envisioned the *specific* horror of that Tuesday morning until we were watching it on television. But lack of intelligence regarding the details of the attacks is no excuse for lack of preparation. The holes in the aviation system that the terrorists exploited were thoroughly documented; many of our leaders had been reading about them for years. They were well aware that the system's weaknesses could one day prove irresistible to enemies of the United States. The failure of the airline security system has all of the ingredients of a predictable surprise.

In a 2000 report, the GAO noted that the absence of a "major security incident in the United States or involving a U.S. airliner in nearly a decade could breed an attitude of complacency in improving aviation security. Improving security in such an environment is more challenging and difficult."[79] Despite such reminders, politicians, FAA regulators, and airline officials chose to cross their fingers and hope for continued good luck rather than to protect the country against threats they had been warned were virtually inevitable.

THE CAUSES OF INACTION THAT CREATED A PREDICTABLE SURPRISE ON SEPTEMBER 11

Who was responsible for failing to stop the predictable surprise of September 11? The human mind intuitively searches for a single person or group to blame. But, like most complex failures, this one can be explained at multiple levels: cognitive, organizational, and political.

It is the role of leaders to have the vision and courage to understand these barriers and act to surmount them.

At an individual level, the decision-maker must surpass common judgment biases. The human tendency to discount the future and to accept the status quo helps to explain why many members of Congress accepted weak aviation-security laws. Most people will discount the need for fundamental change, at least until a tragedy occurs. In addition, people tend to ignore errors of omission. That is, we tend to ignore the harm that occurs from inaction and pay greater attention to harm that comes from action. When the benefits of action are vague, such as a long-term reduction in air disasters, individuals will be unwilling to accept sure losses, such as security fees and long lines at airports. Finally, we tend to have optimistic illusions about the future that prevent us from envisioning catastrophe. These innate cognitive barriers, which we will discuss in detail in chapter 4, prevent leaders from having the vision to avoid predictable surprises.

It would be comforting if cognitive biases were the end of the story. But the initial draft of the Gore Commission provides evidence that the vision for change existed in the Clinton/Gore administration. Ultimately, the failure to tighten airport security was a failure of courage. Facing formidable organizational and political barriers, the administration backed down, lacking the courage to act forcefully on its vision.

A number of government agencies stood in the way of Gore Commission proposals. Concerned about customer privacy and delivery delays, the U.S. Postal Service failed to cooperate with an agreement it signed with the FAA to screen parcels or hold them for twenty-four hours before putting them on planes. In addition, as of September 11, the FAA was negotiating with intelligence agencies to give airline officials access to confidential information about potential terrorists and plots.[80] The CIA alerted the INS about two of the 9/11 terrorists beforehand; the INS discovered that the men were already in the country. The FBI began searching for them, but no one bothered to tell the FAA to be on the lookout.[81] (We discuss the intelligence failures surrounding September 11 in chapter 7.)

The federal agency entrusted with the safety of U.S. civil aviation is the most obvious target of blame. Critics and supporters alike say the FAA has been paralyzed by its need to reach consensus among the myriad public and private interests it is supposed to regulate.[82] In a 1996 review, the GAO blamed organizational culture for "the agency's persistent acquisition problems, including substantial cost overruns, lengthy schedule delays, and shortfalls in the performance of its air traffic control modernization program." Lack of management continuity "fostered an organizational culture that has tended to avoid accountability, focus on the short term, and resist fundamental improvements in the acquisitions process." A 1996 Aviation Foundation and Institute of Public Policy report concluded, "FAA does not have the characteristics to learn and . . . its culture does not recognize or serve any client other than itself."[83] The agency's lethargy and inaction have led to accusations that it not only fails to prevent fatalities, but actually *contributes* to them. Noted Mary Schiavo in 1997, "the FAA itself was cited by NTSB as a cause or contributing factor in 214 accidents with 970 fatalities from 1983 to 1995."[84]

For some players in the tragedy, the FAA served as a convenient scapegoat. "It's a government failure," said Gore Commission staff director Gerald Kauvar of September 11. "We specifically said the FAA had to change, and they've proved resistant to change."[85] But FAA rulemaking procedures are a legacy of the Reagan administration's antiregulatory agenda. Forced to weigh the costs and benefits of each new security proposal via complex testing and approval processes, the agency grew increasingly sluggish and unfocused. "The FAA, despite its professionalism and accomplishments," said Stuart Matthews, president and CEO of the Flight Safety Foundation, "was simply never created to deal with the environment that has been produced by deregulation of the air transport industry."[86]

Thus, the predictable surprise of September 11 can also be seen as a market failure brought on by deregulation. Because the airlines survive from quarter to quarter, their reported earnings closely watched by Wall Street, they have a strong incentive to keep short-term costs low. The tendency to discount the future is overwhelming. Like rigorous audits of company's financial statements, maintenance of healthy fishing stocks, and a number of other cases we will discuss in other chapters, airline security is a "public good": Everyone benefits from it, but no single individual or company has a strong incentive to provide it. In fact, the incentive often is the opposite; the airlines, for example, will seek a free ride in the hope that groups such as the FAA will pick up the slack.

Economists generally agree that private markets are not the best mechanisms for providing public good. Thus, the airlines' penny-pinching on security may have been an inevitable consequence of an ill-conceived system. "Airlines should never have been delegated with responsibility of administering the security screening process," griped ATA spokesperson Michael Wascom. "It was delegated to us by the federal government. We are not a law enforcement agency." An NTSB official acknowledged, "They're in the business to fly from here to there. We're asking them to do something they don't want to do, they don't do very well, and they don't want to spend money to do."[87]

In addition to these major organizational problems, politics stand out as another glaring source of failure and neglect, especially in light of the $15 billion September 11 bailout package that Congress handed the airline industry. "We're going to lose good military personnel, because of the stupidity of the industry," said former FAA security chief Billie Vincent. "And now they're on the doorstep of the president with their hands out, saying, 'Help us, help us.' We wouldn't have been in this situation at all if they hadn't fought the things we were recommending in the first place."[88] Said security activist Bob Monetti, whose son died in Pan Am 103, "If it weren't for the fact that five thousand people are dead, it would be comical. Here these people have been fighting spending every penny on airport security and now they want a bailout?"[89]

By continually jumping to the airlines' aid in the years leading up to his 2000 presidential bid, Al Gore took a gamble that did not pay off. Not only did he lose the election, but after September 11, his work as leader of the aviation security commission paints a picture of a politician willing to swap public safety for soft money. Gore's decision to bet against a catastrophic predictable surprise may well have become an issue in the 2004 presidential race, had he chosen to run.

But Gore was hardly the first or last politician to be targeted by the airline industry. The 1990 Bush commission was no more successful in bringing about significant change. "The history of the [aviation] security issue and much of the debate," according to Senator Ron Wyden, "goes like this: Tragedy, Step 1. Outrage, Step 2. Barrage of proposals, Step 3. Reports, Step 4. Recommendations, Step 5. Step

6: lots of jawing about it. And Step 7, sort of incremental, long, drawn-out processes that don't get it done."[90]

The industry spent millions to ensure that politicians would not deviate from this script. In 1995 and 1996, airlines contributed to the reelection campaigns of ten out of twelve members of the House Appropriations subcommittee on transportation, the committee that funds the FAA.[91] President George W. Bush's 2000 campaign received more than $118,000 from the country's four top airlines (United, Delta, Northwest, and American), compared with Gore's $57,000 from all airline donors combined. Early in his term, Bush halted a potential strike at Northwest and pressured Delta pilots to accept a deal with management or face federal intervention. Under his watch, American's bid to acquire TWA sailed smoothly through the federal approval process.[92]

The pressures of Washington politics, as well as the magnitude of the event itself, may appear to qualify September 11 as a very particular type of predictable surprise. Indeed, it is an extreme case, both in its magnitude and its complexity. Whether through action or deliberate neglect, numerous organizations and individuals—politicians, government agencies, and corporations—contributed to the security vulnerabilities exploited by international terrorists. Yet the lessons of 9/11 apply even to the less extreme types of predictable surprises that occur within the business world every day. For instance, aviation security remained lax in the United States because no single politician or group was willing to take responsibility for fixing the broken system, while other groups remained intent on preserving the status quo. Such failures occur in offices and boardrooms every day, and we will return to many examples later in the book.

WHAT HAVE WE LEARNED?

On November 19, 2001, President Bush entrusted a new federal agency, the Transportation Security Agency (TSA), with the safety of Americans traveling by air, ground, and sea. The private security firms were handed their walking papers and the new agency was given a year to screen, hire, train, and oversee an army of federal baggage screeners and hundreds of airport security managers.[93] By the close of 2002, all checked luggage was to have been screened with explosives detection equipment.

Though generally a no-nonsense law, it does come with a clause that has industry fingerprints all over it. Republican congressmen attached a provision that allowed five airports (San Francisco International, Kansas City, Tupelo, Greater Rochester, and Jackson Hole) to retain their private screeners—a workforce funded by the TSA.[94] If the pilot program succeeds, in 2004, airlines will be allowed to replace their TSA workforce at all airports with employees from private companies.[95]

Within a year, forty-four thousand federal screeners were on the job, all of them U.S. citizens earning twice the average salary paid to private-sector screeners before September 11. The number of air marshals on flights rose, and cockpit doors were reinforced. But with only two U.S. companies manufacturing the $1 million bomb-detection machines, the agency was unable to get them up and running in all U.S. airports by December 31, 2002, the federally mandated deadline; many airports were resorting to stopgap measures, such as handheld "trace detectors" and sniffer dogs.[96]

Are Congress and the president prepared to hold the TSA and the airlines accountable for meeting expectations? In establishing the new agency, Congress removed oversight responsibility from the notoriously weak and inefficient FAA, yet did not go so far as to transfer aviation security from the Department of Transportation to the Department of Justice, as some experts had advocated. "[The airline industry] was very concerned about making sure [the new security agency] stayed at Transportation because they knew at the end of the day that they would have more luck influencing the way things go at DOT than at Justice," revealed one airline industry consultant.[97] The new agency is packed with FAA bureaucrats—as many as two thousand of them—and therefore risks succumbing to the same DOT culture that tolerated the FAA's lethargy.[98]

As in the past, it may be up to watchdog groups and activists, the press, and the GAO to monitor aviation security for the public. Then again, it could be that the predictable surprise of September 11 has finally persuaded government and industry of the folly of betting on the ineptitude of would-be terrorists. Gore Commission member Brian Jenkins expressed the uneasy mixture of guilt and rationalization that everyone linked to aviation security must have faced as that terrible day unfolded. "I don't think the airline industry delivered the security it should have," said Jenkins. "I don't think the government did enough or enforced the rules. And I don't think the public demanded the level of security it should have. But had we done better, would it have prevented the tragedy on September 11? Not necessarily. I just don't know."[99] We never will know if tighter laws and action would have presented the disaster. But we do know that preventing predictable surprises increases our chances of a safer society. By clarifying the nature and causes of predictable surprises, and developing diagnostic tools, we hope to play a small role in helping leaders develop the vision and courage to act on predictable surprises in the future.

3

The Collapse of Enron and the Failure of Auditor Independence

On October 16, 2001, energy-trading giant Enron reported $618 million in third-quarter 2001 losses and the largest earnings restatement in U.S. history—$1.2 billion of lost shareholder equity. For three years, Enron had overstated its profits by about 20 percent. Through a complex web of off-balance-sheet partnerships engineered by former Chief Financial Officer Andrew Fastow, Enron had schemed to hide its mounting debt and keep the company stock flying high. The shocking news caused Enron stock to plunge; investors soon faced collective losses of more than $6 billion. The Securities and Exchange Commission (SEC) launched an inquiry into Enron's unconventional accounting practices. "Where were the auditors?" became the refrain of op-ed pieces and radio call-in shows.

On October 23, a week after Enron went public with its bad news, David Duncan, the Andersen partner in charge of the company's audit, instructed his staff based at Enron's Houston headquarters to make sure the office was complying with Andersen's document retention policy. Andersen attorney Nancy Temple had forwarded the policy to Duncan as Enron's troubles emerged. For more than two weeks, like passengers bailing out a sinking ship, Duncan and his employees deleted Enron files from their computers and packed up Enron-related papers for destruction. They were still doing so on November 8, when the SEC issued a subpoena to Andersen on the Enron matter.

In December, Enron became what was then the largest corporate bankruptcy in U.S. history. Stockholders and former Enron employees whose pensions had evaporated filed civil lawsuits against Enron and Andersen for deceptive practices. In January 2002, Andersen alerted the federal government to the scope of its Houston office's destruction of Enron documents and fired David Duncan. Andersen clients defected from the firm by the dozen, as did the firm's foreign affiliates and satellite offices; the company's tax and consulting divisions courted buyers. On March 14, the Department of Justice announced that it was suing Andersen for obstruction of justice for shredding Enron documents in the face of SEC investigations. Andersen CEO Joseph Berardino resigned on March 26. Six thousand employees, most of them in the Chicago office, were laid off on a single day. In early April, David Duncan agreed to plead guilty to a felony, thereby becoming the star witness in the federal government's criminal trial against Andersen and reducing the likelihood that he would serve a jail sentence.

Did David Duncan act alone in ordering the shredding of Enron documents or was he just following orders? This question lay at the heart of the mid-2002 trial. Duncan and other Andersen partners testified that, following Enron's declaration of bankruptcy, they knew the Enron audit was riddled with errors and was likely to attract suspicion from the SEC. Duncan expressed his belief that his superiors in Chicago condoned the shredding in order to protect Andersen from future lawsuits. Other Andersen employees backed the defense team's claim that Andersen higher-ups were not involved, that the purging was routine, and that no significant files or paper were destroyed.

Duncan testified at Andersen's criminal trial that, while working on the audit, he did not find Enron's $1 billion in losses particularly worrisome. Duncan's was just the most recent in a string of poor professional judgments made by Andersen auditors. In June, the SEC had sued Andersen for issuing false and misleading audit reports on behalf of Waste Management, which had restated its 1992-to-1997 earnings by $1.7 billion, and for helping to cover up misdeeds by company executives. The auditor settled the suit for $7 million without admitting to or denying the accusations; nor did Andersen discipline any of the auditors involved in the case.[1] Andersen also faced scrutiny for faulty accounting of the Sunbeam Corporation and the Baptist Foundation of Arizona. Andersen seemed to have learned nothing from its role in these scandals—nor, apparently, had the accounting profession as a whole. As part of the accounting industry's peer review process, Big Five auditor Deloitte & Touche had looked over Arthur Andersen's audit work through August 31, 2001, including the Enron account, and passed the firm with flying colors.[2]

In the end, the jury surprised everyone by finding Andersen guilty in the Enron case, but not for document destruction. In mid-October 2001, Andersen attorney Nancy Temple had replaced the word "misleading" in a draft memo from Duncan referring to Enron's earnings misstatement with the more legalistically neutral phrasing "aggressive and unique." According to the jury, Temple was Andersen's "corrupt persuader," the source of justice obstruction. On June 15, hours after the verdict was delivered, Andersen announced the end of its auditing practice and stated that it would cease auditing public companies by August 31.[3]

The fall of Enron and Andersen has been widely portrayed as a case of massive corporate greed and arrogance. Certainly, these elements cannot be denied. The staggering levels of risk and secrecy upon which Enron was built, and upon which it foundered, cost the jobs and retirement incomes of thousands, contributed to a slump in the stock market, and may even have exacerbated California's 2000-to-2001 energy crisis. Similarly, the failure of Andersen auditors to challenge Enron on its elaborate accounting schemes reflects the lengths to which the firm was willing to go to maintain its most lucrative client. Despite a long-held reputation as the most straightlaced and objective of the major accounting firms, Andersen continually signed off on earnings statements that it knew to be "aggressive and unique" at best, "misleading" at worst. Managers at both firms were willing to sacrifice their own integrity for the sake of money and power.

But beneath the greed lies another facet of the Enron case that has been less closely examined, one that is particularly crucial to Andersen's lapses in judgment. No one could ever have predicted the dramatic downfall of Arthur Andersen, yet economists, psychologists, and other experts on human judgment and decision-making had warned the U.S. government and the private sector repeatedly about the potential for crisis in the accounting industry and financial markets. Specifically, many experts were concerned about the growing lack of independence of auditing firms and saw the failure of auditor independence as a predictable surprise just waiting to happen.[4] In this chapter, we consider the cognitive, organizational, and political forces that prevented U.S. leaders from working to stop the surprise.

THE ROOTS OF A PREDICTABLE SURPRISE

The future of the [accounting] profession is bright and will remain bright—as long as the Commission does not force us into an outdated role trapped in the old economy. Unfortunately, the proposed rule [on auditor independence] threatens to do exactly that. A broad scope of practice is critical to enable us to keep up with the new business environment, attract, motivate and keep top talent, and thereby provide high-quality audits in the future.

—Joseph Berardino, then-managing partner, Arthur Andersen, in testimony presented to the SEC's Hearing on Auditor Independence, July 26, 2000.

Ironically, given the link between accounting scandals and the plummeting stock market in 2002, the need for auditors was first recognized in the aftermath of the stock market crash of 1929. The Securities and Exchange Act of 1934 mandated independent audits of publicly traded companies and gave the SEC the authority to set financial reporting and accounting standards, a franchise the SEC delegated to the accounting industry. Under this system, accounting firms competed with each other for clients, typically on the basis of reputation, scope of services, and audit fees. This fatal flaw—giving companies the power to retain or fire their auditors—was a ticking time bomb placed at the heart of the system. From the very beginning, accounting firms found it necessary to curry favor with the very companies whose books they were supposed to examine without bias.

Since 1973, standards for audits of public companies have been set by the Financial Accounting Standards Board (FASB), a private-sector organization funded primarily by the accounting industry and its clients.[5] In 1977, the American Institute of Certified Public Accountants (AICPA), the accounting industry trade group, established an independent private-sector group called the Public Oversight Board (POB) to oversee and report on the public accounting of its member firms. Under the auspices of the POB, the biggest firms largely policed themselves via peer reviews conducted every three years. Objections and red flags were unheard of; no Big Five firm ever received a review alarming enough to trigger client flight. State boards and the SEC retained the authority to investigate and discipline cases of accounting improprieties and fraud. But the SEC's agenda has been subject to the winds of political change; for decades, the commission failed to dig deep into alleged wrongdoing.

Beginning in the 1980s, accounting firms began to supplement the low margins of their competitively priced audits with unregulated tax, management, and technology consulting contracts. As they tapped these seemingly unlimited new sources of income, the accountants insisted that the integrity and independence of their audits remained pristine. In the early 1990s, auditing work produced approximately 50 percent of the Big Five firms' revenue from publicly traded companies. A decade later, that figure was down to 30 percent.[6] The demand for information technology consulting services had exploded during the 1990s high-tech boom, enabling the Big Five firms to double their collective revenues to $26.1 billion.[7] By 2000, consulting profits (and margins) uniformly dwarfed auditing fees.

Table 3-1 illustrates the rapid growth of consulting work by the major accounting firms from 1993 to 1999. While U.S. audit revenues also increased from 1993 to 1999, consulting revenues grew much faster, eclipsing audit as a percentage of overall revenue.

In a 1996 report, the Government Accounting Office (GAO) commented on the risks posed to auditor independence by the expansion of consulting services:

> GAO . . . believes that questions of auditor independence will probably continue as long as the existing auditor/client relationship continues. This concern over auditor independence

TABLE 3-1

Estimated U.S. Revenues for Big 5/Big 6 Public Accounting Firms (in billions of U.S. dollars)

	1993	1994	1995	1996	1997	1998	1999
Estimated revenue by service line							
Auditing	$5,485	$5,823	$5,762	$6,195	$6,738	$7,812	$9,150
Non-audit services*	6,570	7,469	9,289	11,110	13,728	18,105	21,466
Total	$12,055	$13,292	$15,051	$17,305	$20,466	$25,917	$30,616
Estimated revenue mix by service line							
Auditing	45%	44%	38%	36%	33%	30%	30%
Non-audit services	54%	56%	62%	64%	67%	70%	70%

Compound growth rate of estimated U.S. revenues from 1993 to 1999

Auditing	9%
Non-audit services	19.5%

Source: Adapted from "Proposed Rule: Revision of the Commission's Auditor Independence Requirements," Securities and Exchange Commission, 17 July 2000, <http://www.sec.gov/rules/proposed/34-42994.htm> (accessed 14 March 2004).

Note: Management and information technology (IT) consulting increased at a rate of 26% per year.

*Non-audit services = tax services, management and IT consulting, and other non-audit services

may become larger as accounting firms move to provide new services that go beyond traditional services. The accounting profession needs to be attentive to the concerns over independence in considering the appropriateness of new services to ensure that independence is not impaired and the auditor's traditional values of being objective and skeptical are not diminished.[8]

In the late 1990s, Arthur Levitt, chairman of the SEC under President Clinton, began to take a close look at auditor independence. It had been nearly eighteen years since requirements on the issue had been amended—the same time period during which the Big Five's consulting divisions realized huge growth. In addition to the trends noted in table 3-1, Levitt found that, in 1999, 25 percent of all public companies—approximately 4,100—purchased nonaudit services from their auditors.[9]

Pressure on auditing partners to sell consulting services to their audit clients created an atmosphere in which the accountants were increasingly dependent on their clients for approval. Indeed, firms routinely factored "cross-selling"—the practice of selling nonaudit services to audit clients—into formulas that determined partner pay raises.[10] "Auditors weren't rich until they got into consulting," commented Michael Nemeroff, a Chicago attorney who helps senior executives hammer out compensation packages.[11] Former SEC chief accountant Lynn Turner said of his days as an auditor at Coopers & Lybrand in the 1990s, "Part of the [annual salary] evaluation was how well you generated new business. If someone brought in $25 million in consulting fees, they were a hero. Of course, bringing in that much audit work, you'd be a hero, too, but at the time audit was growing much more slowly than consulting."[12] A partner was likely to face a double blow from a client unhappy with a tough audit: responsibility for the end of both the auditing and consulting contracts and perhaps the end of his or her career. The stage was set for a predictable surprise. Levitt was particularly concerned about firms performing information-technology consulting for their audit clients. If one of the Big Five were to design and install a large computer system for a company, and if the system didn't work well, he theorized, the auditor might be afraid to criticize the work of its coworkers and jeopardize the consulting contract.[13]

The economic climate of the 1990s also increased the likelihood of a predictable surprise. As the stock market soared, companies felt compelled to keep Wall Street analysts and investors happy, thereby creating, according to Levitt, "an obsession with short-term earnings and short-term results." The bull market, Levitt later remarked in a PBS *Frontline* interview, "made every decision appear to be absolutely the right decision."[14] As ever more sophisticated instruments for investing became available, accounting increasingly became a tool for managing earnings to meet Wall Street expectations. In Levitt's words, accounting was transformed into a "numbers game," in which CFOs strong-armed their auditors to paint company earnings "in the most creative light possible."[15] Financial statements downplayed net income, or profits after all expenses, and instead drew attention to "pro forma income," "normalized income," and "income before non-recurring items"—formulas that, though perfectly legal, omitted or minimized significant expenses and liabilities.[16] Auditors became enablers, accepting aggressive accounting practices without complaint.

These systemic warning signs of a predictable surprise played out at Arthur Andersen in the years preceding the Enron scandal. In 2002 interviews with the *Chicago Tribune,* Andersen partners described an accounting practice that was caught up in internal bickering from 1997 to 2001, during and after its rancorous separation from Andersen Consulting. Hoping to quickly bounce back following the consulting wing's departure, Andersen became focused on rebuilding a lucrative consulting practice. Meanwhile, according to one partner, its audit work grew sloppy. The firm switched from "substantive auditing," a painstaking process requiring review of contracts and other specific documents, to less intensive procedures that focused instead on accounting processes and controls. In financial terms, the single-minded pursuit of new consulting dollars was initially a success. Andersen's revenue rose from $3 billion in 1992 to $9.3 billion in 2001.[17] By 2001, consulting work (tax, legal, corporate finance, and business consulting) made up 54.4 percent of Andersen's revenues ($5 billion); accounting made up 45.6 percent ($4.26 billion). During these years, Enron rose to become the firm's second largest client. In addition to auditing its books, Andersen was providing Enron with tax, business-consulting, and internal audit services.

As early as 1997, Andersen auditors uncovered inflated income in Enron's books, but they certified the numbers anyway. Andersen's most disastrous decisions surrounded the Raptors, the off-balance-sheet partnerships that Enron created as a hedge on its investments. In 2000, with two Raptors losing money and two making money, Enron sought to group the loans of all four partnerships together, thereby protecting its balance sheet. Andersen auditor Carl Bass, a member of the firm's Professional Standards Group, advised David Duncan that the only legal means of debt-sharing would be a cross-collateralization, under which the Raptors' obligations and assets would be merged for their lifetime. CFO Andrew Fastow rejected Bass's plan. Why? Because Fastow's personal earnings from the Raptors—

one of which, LJM, he personally headed—amounted to tens of millions of dollars, far more than his Enron salary. Bass's solution would decrease the value of the healthy Raptors, thereby helping Fastow's employer, but not Fastow himself. Fastow proposed instating a cross-collateralization that he personally could remove whenever he liked. "I did not see any way that this worked," Bass wrote in an e-mail to one of his superiors at Andersen. "In effect, it was heads I win, tails you lose."[18]

Bass was not only overruled, but removed from oversight of the Enron account. "Apparently," Bass wrote in an internal e-mail at the time, "part of the process issue stems from the client knowing all that goes on within our walls on our discussions with respect to their issues." Duncan signed off on Fastow's accounting sleight-of-hand, allowing Enron to cross-collateralize for only forty-five days—enough time for the company to report its earnings without revealing the Raptors' enormous losses.[19] When the forty-five-day window passed, further accounting gimmicks were used to hide the losses, at least one of which was in direct violation of accounting rules. The losses multiplied.

Arthur Levitt was unaware of the mounting disaster at Enron, but his uneasiness with auditor conflicts of interest was based on more than just a hunch. During the 1990s, as armies of consultants set forth into the workforce, the number of earnings restatements by U.S. public companies also multiplied by leaps and bounds. In 1981, just 3 companies issued earnings restatements. By 1998, that number had grown to 93; by 2000 it stood at 157. In total, more than 700 companies admitted to having issued seriously flawed financial reports during the 1990s.[20] In about 85 percent of these cases, Lynn Turner estimates, the companies themselves—not the SEC—went public with revised earnings announcements.[21] The SEC was uncovering only a fraction of accounting scandals on its own. Figure 3-1 shows the dramatic growth in restatements.

Restatements can be issued voluntarily, recommended by a company's auditor, or enforced by the SEC. Because they reveal seriously flawed or corrupt accounting, they are typically accompanied by a dramatic dip in a company's stock price. Turner estimates that investors lost more than $100 billion following restatements in the six years *preceding* Enron's restatement.[22] Some experts say that Levitt triggered the rise in restatements himself, by announcing in a 1998

FIGURE 3-1

Financial Reporting Restatements by U.S. Companies, 1990–2000

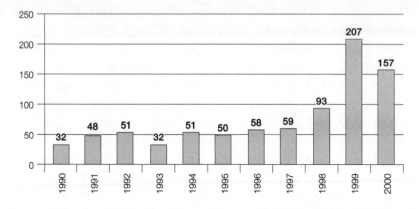

Source: Adapted from G. B. Moriarty and P. B. Livingston, "Quantitative Measures of the Quality of Financial Reporting," *Financial Executive,* July/August 2001: 53–56.

Note: In 1998 and 1999, the SEC aggressively prosecuted in-process research and development (IPR&D) write-offs in mergers and acquisitions. Nine IPR&D-based restatements are included in the 1998 total, fifty-seven in 1999, and one in 2000.

speech that he planned to take a more aggressive stance on earnings management.[23] But in the three years that followed the speech, 77 percent of the total market-value losses, or $50.2 billion, were linked to restatements by just eight companies: MicroStrategies, Cendant, McKesson, Lucent, Legato Systems, Raytheon, Texas Instruments, and Boston Scientific.[24] Levitt and Turner were particularly alarmed by the rise in fraud cases among big companies with household names.[25]

Other scandals convinced Levitt of the need to work toward greater auditor independence. In the summer of 1998, the SEC learned that executives in Coopers & Lybrand's Tampa office had been investing in companies that the firm was auditing, in direct violation of SEC rules. In total, more than eight thousand violations were uncovered within the firm. The SEC fined Pricewaterhouse-Coopers (Coopers & Lybrand and Price Waterhouse had merged during the course of the investigation) $2.5 million and asked the independent POB to investigate compliance with independence rules at the other major firms. But before the POB could finish its assigned task, its funding body, the accounting industry trade group AICPA, cut off funding for the inquiry. Displeased with the scrutiny, the accounting industry had shut down the investigation.[26] Meanwhile, the SEC was beginning to piece together evidence of accounting fraud at Waste Management. Arthur Andersen, SEC regulators believed, should have known that the financial statements it had audited for the company were misleading.

In sum, the SEC recognized numerous signs that corporate financial officers were succeeding in strong-arming auditors into accepting questionable accounting gimmickry. Levitt made auditor independence his top priority. Given the lack of accountability and the potential for huge disaster, the solution, Levitt believed, was a clean break between auditing and consulting duties. In fact, most of the Big Five firms were already taking steps toward spinning off their consulting divisions, whether by choice or by force. In January 1999, KPMG sold a fifth of its consulting unit to Cisco Systems and hoped to sell more. After years of infighting over profits and power, Andersen's consultants divorced the accounting firm in August 2000. Ernst & Young sold its consulting division to Cap Gemini for $11 billion in early 2000, around the same time that PricewaterhouseCoopers announced plans to spin off several of its consulting units. But Levitt was unimpressed by these spontaneous shows of independence. As soon as Andersen's consulting limb was hacked off from the parent firm, a new, even bigger one sprouted in its place. And while KPMG planned to sever links to its consulting division, auditors also intended to scoop up shares in the new company. Each firm had a different notion of "independence," each with its own ulterior motives and potential pitfalls.

Levitt decided to draft new rules that would greatly restrict the ability of the Big Five to sell consulting services to companies whose books they audit, but would leave them free to consult for nonaudit clients. With supply and demand remaining the same, Levitt envisioned a reshuffling of clients among the Big Five; there was no reason to expect that the auditors would suffer financially. Most important, the new rules might reduce the temptation of auditors to blindly accept their consulting clients' questionable accounting practices. This long-term benefit, Levitt believed, surely would be worth the short-term inconvenience.

Levitt presented his proposed reforms to the Big Five in the spring of 2000. The heads of Ernst & Young and PricewaterhouseCoopers appeared amenable to the changes, but Levitt was given quite a different reception in a joint meeting with KPMG, Deloitte & Touche, and Arthur Andersen executives. "'We're going to war with you,'" Levitt later paraphrased. "'This will kill our business. We're going to fight you tooth and nail. And we'll fight you in the Congress and we'll fight you in the courts.'"[27] Levitt and the Clinton administration clearly understood that the U.S. auditing system fell far short of its cornerstone of independence. They saw a predictable surprise developing, but didn't act forcefully enough to prevent it.

THE BIG FIVE VERSUS THE SEC

Levitt had already received early evidence of the accountants' wrath. In April, the heads of the House Commerce Committee, which oversees the SEC's funding and rule-making, sent the commission a letter that resembled a particularly tedious take-home economics exam, complete with a two-week deadline. Some of the sixteen multifaceted questions requested "empirical evidence, studies or economic analysis" to justify the SEC's proposed conflict-of-interest rules; others laid out convoluted hypothetical scenarios for regulators to assess. Many of the questions were quite pointed. "What are the investment restrictions to which employees of the SEC are subject?" read one. "How are they different from restrictions placed on accountants?. . . Estimate the number of violations that would exist if the stock restrictions applicable to the accounting profession were to be applied to the SEC and its staff on January 2, 2000."[28] The letter ended with what Levitt understood to be a threat from the committee's three leaders, Representatives Tom Bliley, Michael Oxley, and W. J. (Billy) Tauzin: "[Your] responses will help to determine if hearings on the SEC's oversight of the accounting profession are warranted."

Congressional hearings on SEC rule-making were unprecedented in Levitt's many years of experience. But he had underestimated the attachment of the Big Five to their "integrated" audits, as well as their influence on Congress. "They waged a war against us, a total war,"

Levitt later told *The New Yorker*.[29] The accountants hired seven lobbying firms to fight the independence proposal. Representative Tauzin "badgered me relentlessly," said Levitt, who received forty-five more letters on behalf of the accounting industry from congressmen.[30] The corporate world weighed in on the matter as well, inundating Levitt with letters in support of their auditors. In a September 20, 2000, letter to Levitt, Enron Chairman Kenneth Lay attested to the benefits his energy-trading company had received through one-stop-shopping with Arthur Andersen: ". . . Enron has found its 'integrated audit' arrangement to be more efficient and cost-effective than the more traditional roles of separate internal and external auditing functions."[31] In fact, Lay was only one of the letter's authors; it later emerged that David Duncan had cowritten it in consultation with Andersen's Washington lobbying firm.[32] In 2000, the year of Levitt's battle, the accountants donated more than $10 million to political campaigns and spent another $12.6 million on federal lobbying, according to the Center for Responsive Politics.[33]

In pursuit of his vision of auditor independence, Levitt held public hearings with investors across the country. In July 2000, he welcomed expert witnesses from government, corporations, accounting firms, and academia to testify before the SEC in Washington. The question at hand: whether firms that offered consulting services to their audit clients were putting the impartiality and reliability of financial statements in jeopardy.

Andersen Managing Partner Joseph Berardino, KPMG Vice President J. Terry Strange, and Deloitte & Touche Partner Robert Garland demanded that the SEC provide evidence of audit fraud arising from auditing firms' consulting business. "Given what is at stake," said Garland, "and the fact that there is no demonstrated problem, it would be irresponsible to take on the considerable risks surrounding the proposed rule."[34] Strange asserted that "nonaudit services improve audit effectiveness."[35] "[T]he proposal on the scope of services is not helpful," said Berardino. "In our opinion, we do think it will harm audit quality."[36] In his testimony, Berardino predicted that if Andersen were not able to offer its accountants plum consulting assignments, the firm would soon find itself with few quality job applicants. Berardino also argued:

[T]he more the auditors know about their client the better the audit is. If you or I were a CEO and wanted to perpetrate a fraud or cook the books, I think we'd want to keep the auditors in the dark. I don't think we'd be hiring them to help us implement our [IT] systems. I don't think we'd be helping them to look at our complex transactions.[37]

Max H. Bazerman, one of the authors of this book, and colleague George F. Loewenstein were among those who presented their opinions on auditor independence to the SEC. In a 1997 *Sloan Management Review* article with Kimberly P. Morgan entitled "The Impossibility of Auditor Independence," they argued that it is a mistake to focus solely on auditor neglect and corruption when evaluating the fallout from accounting scandals. Bias arises not only when judgments are reported, we wrote, but long beforehand—at the unconscious stage when decisions are made. For this reason, "audit failures are the natural product of the auditor-client relationship," they argue. "Under current institutional arrangements, it is psychologically impossible for auditors to maintain their objectivity; cases of audit failure are inevitable, even with the most honest auditors."[38]

They reached this conclusion from psychological research on "self-serving biases." Studies have shown that when people are asked to make impartial judgments, those judgments are likely to be unconsciously but heavily biased according to the individual's self interest. "Experts" in a given field, such as accountants or scientists, are no more successful at making impartial judgments than lay people.[39] The implication? When auditors have an incentive to keep a client happy, they are virtually certain to be biased.

As Bazerman, Morgan, and Loewenstein explained in the 1997 article, key features of the relationship between auditor and client leave the auditor terribly vulnerable to self-serving biases, some of which were introduced in the previous chapter of this book. First, they noted, the investors who will be harmed by an accounting misrepresentation are perceived as "statistical"; studies have shown that people are less concerned about harming unknown victims than known victims. An auditor is likely to be far more motivated to please his client, whom he knows and wishes to retain, than anonymous shareholders. Second, the negative consequences of being dropped by a client are far more immediate and vivid than the costs of an act of creative accounting, which may be delayed or never detected at all. In chapter 2, we saw how willing airline executives and politicians were to tolerate second-rate security in U.S. airports, in part because the immediate costs were so much more salient and predictable than the costs of a major terrorist incident. Third, because the auditor–client relationship often unfolds over years, deterioration in the audited company is likely to occur gradually; auditors start down a slippery slope by accommodating minor imperfections in the company's financial practices. Similarly, the aviation security system in the United States did not break down overnight; rather, a pattern of cost-cutting and tolerance for poor performance built up over time. Fourth, the fact that financial reporting standards are ambiguous and complex may enable auditors to rationalize self-serving judgments. Fifth, like all people, auditors have a remarkable capacity for denial, deluding themselves and others about the independence of their judgments. For all of these reasons, even if Solomon had been an auditor, he would have been hard pressed to avoid being biased in favor of the client. Increased competition for auditing clients, combined with the rapid growth of consulting, exacerbated the risk to auditor independence. "Much like the federal deficit," they wrote, "these problems are mounting and will get worse if not addressed.[40]

Three years later, in testimony presented to the SEC, Bazerman and Loewenstein backed the separation of auditing and consulting functions, but stressed that, as long as auditors are hired and fired by the companies they audit, unbiased audits are unlikely. "The current structure of auditing firms makes the creation of auditing independence impossible even among honest and well-intentioned auditors," they wrote.[41] Bazerman, Loewenstein, and Moore have since argued that, in order to create the appearance and fact of true independence:

1. Auditing firms should only provide auditing services.

2. Auditing contracts should be of a fixed duration, during which time the client cannot fire the auditor.

3. Companies should be prohibited from hiring accountants who have worked on their audit engagement.[42]

Arthur Levitt and his SEC team were convinced of the perils of auditor conflicts of interest; their task was to convince Congress to listen to them rather than to accounting industry lobbyists. In his quest for auditor independence, Levitt raced the clock. His eight-year term would expire with President Clinton's, a fact that did not slip by the accounting industry. The three firms opposing the SEC argued that more public hearings were needed before rules could be imposed. With the end of Levitt's term just months away, the SEC was called before the Senate to justify its proposal.

"In prosperous times, it can be easy to take investor confidence for granted," Levitt warned the senators. "But as those of us old enough to remember a bear market know, investor confidence can be lost in the blink of an eye."[43] PricewaterhouseCoopers chief James Schiro and Ernst & Young Chairman Phil Laskawy lent Levitt their support. "Although we did not believe independence was actually impaired by this service," Laskawy testified, "we could understand that, particularly with the large fees that sometimes were involved, an appearance problem could be present."[44] Laskawy also stated that Ernst & Young's accounting practice had not been hurt by the sell-off of the firm's consulting division.

But Jim Copeland, Deloitte & Touche's chief, complained that the SEC's proposed separation of consulting and audit work was unjustified given the lack of dramatic accounting failures in recent years. "Usually there is a train wreck or a stock-market crash prompting this sort of radical legislation," Copeland argued.[45] Essentially, Copeland urged the government to wait for a disaster, rather than acting to prevent a predictable surprise.

Siding with the auditing firms, key legislators failed to take the steps necessary to mobilize for a predictable surprise. According to Levitt, Representative Billy Tauzin "knew what the accountants were doing before I did. He was working very closely with them. I don't mean to sound cynical, but is it because he loves accountants?" Tauzin received more than $280,000 from the accounting industry in the 1990s, despite never having faced a serious challenger to his House seat. Levitt learned that House Appropriations Committee Member Henry Bonilla was prepared to cut the SEC's budget by attaching a rider to the commission's appropriations budget if Levitt didn't back down.[46] Leaders of the Senate Banking Committee, including Rod Grams, Evan Bayh, Phil Gramm, Charles Schumer, and Rick Santorum, scoffed at Levitt's suggestion that the mere appearance of impropriety necessitated change and joined the chorus of accountants and lobbyists crying for hard evidence. Levitt later revealed to *Frontline* that he did privately offer his critics in Congress the smoking gun they requested:

> We invited them to the commission, and they came. We went through a whole variety of financial fraud cases we were about to bring, including Waste Management. They left the hearing, and they didn't say that they were misled and heard nothing. But they didn't come away and say, "We've changed our minds." Clearly, we gave them the smoking gun. Nevertheless, they proceeded with letters, with calls, with veiled threats.[47]

As Levitt sought a deal that Andersen, KPMG, and Deloitte & Touche could live with, Ernst & Young and PricewaterhouseCoopers turned against him in the final hour. In what he later called his biggest mistake as SEC chief, Levitt gave up the fight. Certain that he would eventually be defeated by Congress, he agreed to let the firms continue to consult for their audit clients. The firms' only concession: to disclose the details of these relationships to investors. Disclosure, of course, only helps to expose intentional corruption; it cannot reduce an auditor's underlying bias. Levitt knew disclosure was inadequate, but it was the only measure felt he could pass. The very organizational structure that Levitt feared would lead to a disaster—the dependence on accounting firms for consulting dollars—prevented the Big Five from recognizing the need for change. According to Lynn Turner, when he and Levitt left the SEC in 2000, the commission had a backlog of 200 to 250 cases of accounting fraud under investigation.

Levitt blames his failure on the U.S. political system—specifically, the tremendous lobbying pressure and huge campaign contributions of the Big Five accounting firms. Between 1990 and 2002, accounting firms spent more than $53 million on political contributions.[48] During the 2000 presidential campaign, all of the Big Five firms were among George W. Bush's top twenty contributors (Ernst & Young, Andersen Worldwide, and PricewaterhouseCoopers each donated more than $100,000). While Al Gore did not fare as well industrywide, his largest contributor was an accounting firm; Ernst & Young donated $134,900 to his campaign. As of 2002, 94 of 100 senators and half of House members were recipients of the accountants' beneficence.[49] "It's almost impossible to compete with the effect that money has on these congressmen," Levitt said.[50] "If there was ever an example where money and lobbying damaged the public interest, this was clearly it."

THE TRAIN WRECK: THE PREDICTABLE SURPRISE OF CORPORATE FAILURE

Even the staunchest proponents of increasing auditor independence never dreamed of an accounting scandal as spectacularly destructive as the one that unfolded a year after the SEC hearings. The saga of the fall of Enron and Arthur Andersen offers a dramatic illustration of the dangers of allowing financial incentives to taint auditor independence. In the end, investors are estimated to have lost $93 billion dollars in the Enron crash.[51] In every sense, the Enron debacle was a predictable surprise. However, it was not a singular event. WorldCom, Adelphi, Global Crossing, Xerox, and Tyco all succumbed to financial scandal in the first half of 2002. Together, these troubled companies make up an entire arsenal of smoking guns. We have focused on Enron because it was the first and arguably most vivid disaster, and because it led to the demise of Arthur Andersen. As such, it offers other large auditing practices—as well as all types of organizations facing predictable surprises—the clearest cautionary tale one could imagine.

By accepting as much management, tax, and IT consulting work as Enron threw its way, Arthur Andersen left its auditors vulnerable to self-serving biases, and itself and Enron open to a predictable surprise. Details that emerged about Andersen's dependence on Enron reopened the debate about auditor conflicts of interest. During a February 2001 conference call regarding the Enron account, for instance,

Chicago- and Houston-based Andersen partners had discussed the firm's potential conflicts of interest as well as the fees they expected the account to generate in the future. Partners were concerned about Andrew Fastow's leadership of Raptor LJM and the income he received from the off-balance-sheet partnership. In addition, "We arbitrarily discussed that . . . [Enron] fees could reach a $100 million-per-year amount considering the multidisciplinary services being provided," Partner Michael Jones wrote the next day in an e-mail to David Duncan and another partner.[52] According to a statement filed with the SEC, Enron paid Arthur Andersen $25 million for audit work and $27 million for nonaudit services in 2000.[53]

At Andersen's criminal trial, David Duncan testified that he had huddled with his superiors in August 2001 after Enron VP Sherron Watkins revealed her worries about improprieties in the company's books to a friend at Andersen and predicted a potential Enron implosion. Watkins clearly envisioned a possible disaster. But Andersen accepted the opinion of Enron's outside law firm, Vinson & Elkins, that although the accounting practices were "creative and aggressive," Enron had not broken any rules or laws.[54]

At that point, Andersen was earning a million dollars a week from its various Enron accounts; more than half of that amount was paid for nonauditing work.[55] Further compromising independence, the ranks of Enron upper management were filled with former Andersen employees, including the company's president, vice president, and chief accounting officer.[56] "If you get too friendly and too relaxed, you can wind up nodding your head yes when you should be saying no," commented former GAO head Charles Bowsher, a former Andersen employee who stepped forward to advise the firm in its time of need. "There's a lot of art in addition to science in accounting."[57]

The Department of Justice's pursuit of Andersen was viewed as part of a larger Bush administration strategy to blame accounting scandals on the actions a small number of corrupt individuals and firms rather than on a broken regulatory system. "The Republicans have believed that . . . [i]f someone cheats, that's enough," said former SEC official Donald C. Langevoort. "Nail them. You don't need fancy rules about conflicts of interest, stock options, and those kinds of things."[58] The Justice Department team prosecuting Andersen focused heavily on the firm's past transgressions—its Waste Management and Sunbeam audits—as evidence of a pattern of crooked behavior. Eliminate Andersen, the logic went, and you fix the problem. But as the bankruptcies and arrests mounted, this argument grew harder to believe.

In the wake of the scandal, Deloitte & Touche and PricewaterhouseCoopers announced plans to follow KPMG and Ernst & Young in spinning off or selling their consulting units. But the "Final Four" accounting firms' actions suggested they were only paying lip service to the notion of deep reform. Between March and June 2002, before Andersen was even convicted, the Final Four swooped in to nab the well-fattened auditing and consulting contracts of at least 575 former Andersen clients. In the most recent fiscal year for which data was available, these companies reported paying Andersen nearly $1 billion in auditing and consulting fees combined; consulting and information technology fees made up 70 percent of the total, or about $700 million.[59] The four firms gobbled up not only Andersen clients and contracts, but thousands of former Andersen partners, managers, and staff. Meanwhile, their lobbyists worked overtime on Capitol Hill, trying to persuade Congress that they had no skeletons in their own file drawers.

LESSONS LEARNED?

"I don't personally believe that Andersen is any worse than any of the other firms," Arthur Levitt said in a *Frontline* interview soon after the firm was found guilty of obstruction of justice.[60] Following the Enron scandal, senators, CEOs, and even some accountants stepped forward to accept blame for opposing the SEC plan. "We were wrong. You were right," Senator Robert Torricelli told Arthur Levitt during his appearance before the Senate Governmental Affairs Committee.[61] With each passing week came a new congressional hearing into Andersen and Enron—eleven in all—along with promises for tough reforms designed to soothe investors and the troubled stock market. Representative Billy Tauzin, who had fought with the accountants tooth and nail against Levitt in 2000, called the case of Enron and

Andersen "an old-fashioned example of theft by insiders, and a failure of those responsible for them to prevent that theft."[62]

Perhaps the most striking change of heart on the issue of auditor independence was that of former Andersen CEO Joseph Berardino. Weighing in on the issue on June 4, 2002, three months after his resignation, Berardino announced his support for sweeping reform. Change was necessary, he said, to correct an accounting and auditing process that had become "a game of rules, loopholes, and legalisms."[63]

By mid-2002, earnings restatements had become an epidemic, each one met with massive stockholder sell-off. Lynn Turner estimates that through the 1990s and into 2002, investors lost almost $200 billion dollars as a result of earnings restatements by Enron, Global Crossing, Cendant, Waste Management, Sunbeam, Rite Aid, Lucent, Xerox, and other companies.[64] On June 25, 2002, telecommunications powerhouse WorldCom Inc. stunned investors by revealing that it had concealed $3.8 billion in losses during 2001 and the first quarter of 2002. The firm's auditor, Arthur Andersen, had failed to flag the rudimentary accounting trick—routine business expenses were listed as capital expenditures; the ruse was uncovered during an internal audit. On July 21, the company overtook Enron as the biggest bankruptcy in U.S. history.

As new scandals erupted at Adelphi Communications and Tyco, the House, the Senate, the White House, and the SEC each weighed in with a plan for reforming the accounting industry. The Senate's bill, proposed by Maryland Senator Paul S. Sarbanes and the strictest of the proposals, was fiercely opposed by the accounting industry. But the House and President Bush, reluctant to appear soft on reform, agreed to accept it largely unchanged.

The Sarbanes-Oxley Act signed by President Bush on July 31, 2001, reflects the view of the administration and Congress that deterrence of corrupt behavior through the threat of criminal prosecution of individual auditors and executives is the key to stopping the stream of corporate scandals. Speaking at the ceremonial signing of the corporate fraud bill, Bush declared, "The era of low standards and false profits is over. No boardroom in America is above or beyond the law."[65] The Act prohibits accounting firms from selling a broad range of consulting services to auditing clients and requires rotation of the partner in charge of audits of large corporations every five years. In addition, the Act establishes a "one-year cooling-off period" during which an accounting firm cannot audit a company if the company's CEO, CFO, or chief accounting officer was employed by the accounting firm and participated in the company's audit during the previous year. The Act lengthens prison terms for certain crimes, including document destruction, and makes it a crime to engage in a "scheme or artifice" to defraud investors.[66] Under the Act, chief executives and chief financial officers must certify their financial statements and face up to twenty years in jail if they "knowingly or willfully" permit misleading information to be issued in the reports. It requires swift disclosure of changes in companies' financial news and gives broad protections to corporate whistle-blowers.

A centerpiece of the Sarbanes-Oxley Act was the creation of a new, independent Public Accounting Oversight Board to monitor the accounting industry and discipline corrupt auditors. The SEC would oversee the new board and be required to review a greater number of financial statements. As we discuss in chapter 6, the board got off to a very shaky start. In late 2002, then-SEC Chairman Harvey Pitt, goaded by accounting industry lobbyists, machinated to keep reformer John Biggs from heading the board and instead championed William Webster, a former CIA and FBI chief with a limited but tainted record as a financial officer. The scandal forced both Pitt and Webster to resign, making a mockery of the Bush Administration's claimed intent of protecting American shareholders and workers from future corporate meltdowns. Speaking of the stalled oversight board to the *New York Times* in the final days of 2002, SEC historian Joel Seligman said, "They don't have a full board, they don't have a budget, don't have a staff, don't have an office, don't have a plan. It's as sad a beginning as one can imagine."[67]

Even if the Bush Administration changes course and demands accountability from the SEC and the oversight board, the Sarbanes-Oxley Act will only improve auditor independence and prevent predictable surprises to a limited degree. The overall shortcoming of this policy and other reforms is that they concentrate primarily on deterring corruption and pay scant attention to auditors' deep-rooted biases. Because auditor bias is unconscious, like many of the biases relevant to predictable surprises, efforts focused on deterrence are unlikely to improve auditor independence. While fear of prosecution may motivate auditors to decide to be honest, these conscious desires are unlikely to have much impact on unconscious bias. Another problem with deterrence is that the self-serving bias is much more sensitive to immediate incentives than it is to delayed, indirect disincentives. Therefore, auditors who believe they are honest, despite being biased, are likely to view criminal prosecution as a distant and unlikely possibility. The unconscious nature of the biases that lead to predictable surprises makes them particularly difficult to address and correct. In chapter 9, we discuss techniques aimed at reducing these biases from one's behavioral repertoire.

The prohibition on accounting firms providing consulting services to companies they audit is a step in the right direction. Accounting firms that advise their clients on how to become more profitable, while at the same time attempting to judge their clients' books impartially, face an impossible task. The new restrictions will ease pressure on auditors to moonlight as sales representatives for the other services their firms would like to provide. Unfortunately, the current proposals allow auditors to provide other advisory services such as tax planning, under certain conditions, with the preapproval of audit committees. Truly effective reform would prohibit auditors from providing any professional services at all.

Even full divestiture of consulting services from the auditing function is unlikely to solve the problem of auditor independence. A fundamental problem remains: Because auditors are hired and fired by the companies they audit, they are put in the awkward position of potentially casting negative judgments on those who hired them. The fundamental structure of the auditing system virtually ensures continuing independence violations. The Sarbanes-Oxley Act's requirement that accounting firms must rotate the lead partner on an audit every five years is an inadequate solution. Instead, the accounting firms themselves should have fixed, limited contract periods with their clients during which they cannot be fired. Contracts and fees should be specified up front and fixed for the duration of the audit term. At the end of the contract term, the auditor should not be rehired;

rather, the major accounting firms should rotate clients. As long as auditors are motivated to keep the client happy, it is unlikely that auditor bias will be reduced to any significant degree.

Another threat to independence touched on by the Sarbanes-Oxley Act concerns the career paths of accountants. As the Enron scandal unfolded, the common practice of Arthur Anderson employees taking positions with Enron, and vice versa, was revealed as a likely source of conflict of interest. Clearly, independence is compromised when an auditor hopes to develop job opportunities during the course of the audit. The one-year "cooling-off period" established by the Sarbanes-Oxley Act is insufficient. Auditors should be permanently barred from taking positions with the firms they audit.

Effective policies must completely eliminate incentives that create self-serving biases. For this to happen, policies must reduce the degree to which the auditor cares whether or not the client is pleased by the results of the audit. This is an extreme proposition, but without it, auditor independence will remain an illusion.

Aside from following new governmental restrictions, auditors must learn to recognize the effect of self-serving biases on their judgment. Professional schools have devoted significant attention to the issue of ethics in recent years, but schooling future accountants and executives on various ethical positions will not solve the independence issue. We see greater potential in the ability of social scientists to help professionals identify and understand the errors they make at an unconscious level. Once executives have been made aware of the self-serving bias, honest and visionary leaders of the accounting profession can bring about reforms in our accounting institutions that will eliminate bias, specifically by preventing the conflicts of interest that lead to bias. In addition, a greater awareness of the effects of bias would inspire audit leaders to stop citing "professionalism" as sufficient reason to trust an inherently biased system. These claims are inconsistent with all of the empirical evidence on human judgment.

We envision a system in which auditors serve not as "partners" or "advisers" to their clients, but in more impartial, distant roles, similar to that of tax collectors. Even if all of our proposals were implemented, however, it is still possible that auditors will remain biased due to social contact with their clients. We could go a step further and suggest that the auditing function be turned over to the federal government, but other problems are likely to result from such an overhaul. Our more realistic proposals could go a long way toward creating an independent auditing system.

"This is an important and useful step," said Arthur Levitt of the Sarbanes-Oxley Act. "But it's only one of many that must be taken to restore public confidence."[68] Separation of auditing and consulting functions is indeed a good first step, but it is not enough. The unsettling truth is that the fatal flaw remains. By failing to address the conflict of interest inherent in a system in which companies hire, fire, and therefore control their auditors, President Bush, former Commissioner Pitt, and Congress have ignored the root causes of the predictable surprise. Harvey Pitt's replacement, William Donaldson, has begun to enact improvements to the system. But they come too slowly, and the U.S. system of auditing is still far from independent. Perhaps the most surprising aspect of this predictable surprise is that even after the crisis occurred, we have failed to fix the system's obvious and fundamental flaws. Fresh disasters undoubtedly await us.

PART II

WHY DON'T WE ACT ON
WHAT WE KNOW?

To head off predictable surprises, we must understand the barriers that stand in the way of their prevention. Think about a predictable surprise in your organization, or consider 9/11 or the collapse of Enron. Why do such predictable surprises occur? When considering the source of difficult social problems, most people come up with a single explanation.[1] This is true of problems ranging from poverty to homelessness to teenage pregnancy. Researchers Chris Winship and Martin Rein argue that this focus on a single cause is one of the main barriers to creating effective social policy.[2] Ann McGill vividly illustrates this error by noting that partisans argue passionately over whether promiscuity or lack of birth control causes teenage pregnancy, when clearly both factors contribute to the problem.[3]

Seeking to avoid a single-cause explanation for predictable surprises, we argue that failures to prevent them occur at three levels—cognitive, organizational, and political.

Looking at chapter 2, partisan politics clearly obstructed improvements in U.S. airline security in the 1990s. Such political concerns cognitively blinded Al Gore and his commission to the magnitude of the danger they were imposing on the country. The organizational structure of the U.S. government, including the bureaucratic nature of the FAA, also played a role.

In chapter 3, we described how the major accounting firms lobbied heavily to keep a corrupt system in place for far too long. But organizational and cognitive factors also played a role in the fall of Arthur Andersen and Enron, and the close ties between Congress and the SEC were clearly relevant. By succumbing to intense lobbying from government and industry leaders, the commissioners at the SEC overlooked the magnitude of risk to which they exposed the country by failing to enact meaningful audit reform.

In chapters 4, 5, and 6, we dig deeper into each of these three categories—cognitive, organizational, and political—as we detail barriers to the prevention of predictable surprises. After describing these categories in detail, we present an action framework that will help leaders assess the changes they need to make in order to prevent predictable surprises in their organizations.

4

Cognitive Roots

The Role of Human Biases

T hink of the typical environmental activist, and you are unlikely to picture a chef in a busy kitchen, doling out hundreds of servings of meat and seafood a night. Yet many of the chefs who, throughout the 1980s and 90s, introduced their customers to such exotic dishes such as swordfish, Chilean sea bass, monkfish, sand dabs, Pacific snapper, and turbot now recognize that they fostered an unsustainable appetite for these species. They've since become leaders of a grassroots boycott of endangered fish, aiming to raise public awareness of the problem and give threatened species time to recover. The chefs became activists only after other groups, particularly national governments, failed to convince fishers of the need for changes in their harvesting behavior. By 2002, more than five hundred chefs nationwide had taken Chilean sea bass off of their menus. Since restaurants account for 70 percent of seafood sales, the chefs' boycott has had a real impact.[1]

But for many formerly plentiful and popular fish species, as well as entire fishing communities, the boycott came decades too late. In the 1960s, improved fishing technology subsidized by governments led to unsustainable fishing practices along the coast of New England.[2]

Trawlers from around the world descended upon the region, guided by Global Positioning System (GPS) satellites, and depleted one fishing area after another. Within years, a supply of healthy, tasty fish that had thrived for centuries suddenly fell into jeopardy.

Facing considerable political pressure from the fishers, the U.S. government slowly moved to expand its coastal waters and push back foreign boats. Before long, domestic fishers were fighting tenaciously for an increasingly small fraction of a scarce resource. In 1977, the New England Council enacted fishing quotas on cod, haddock, and yellowtail flounder, but under heavy lobbying from the fishers, revoked the limits in 1982.

Time and again, fishers shrugged off warnings from scientists that their livelihood would never recover if they did not harvest at sustainable levels. Positioning the mounting crisis as a choice between saving fish versus saving jobs, the fishers successfully lobbied the federal government to continue its financial support of fishing fleets. In doing so, the government not only failed to reverse the trend but actually contributed to an increase in the rate of extinction. Halibut, haddock, and cod disappeared from the Grand Banks, and fishers switched to less desirable dogfish, skate, and monkfish. Bluefin tuna fishers moved on to swordfish; when swordfish disappeared, the fishers pursued yellowfin tuna. Atlantic halibut, haddock, and cod have been replaced by smaller, less tasty, and more polluted fish.

In 2002, Ransom Myers and Boris Worm published the most extensive summary to date of the decline of the world's supply of the biggest and most important fish species, based on detailed global analyses.[3] They document the disappearance of 90 percent of each of the world's largest ocean species, including swordfish, marlin, cod, halibut, and tuna. They further show that it takes only about fifteen years for humans to destroy 80 percent of the population of any given species once that species has been targeted for exploitation. According to private analysts and the Food and Agriculture Organization of the United Nations, fishing subsidies amounted to about $15 billion per year as of 2003, or more than a quarter of the $55 billion annual global seafood trade.[4] "With modern satellite technology, fish finders and global positioning equipment, you can track and kill the last fish,"

Phil Kline, a former fishing-boat captain who advises the conservation group Oceana on policy, told the *Los Angeles Times*. "There is no place for fish to hide. It's like the era of the buffalo."[5]

The destruction of fisheries worldwide in modern times is one of the most clear-cut predictable surprises that the natural environment has ever faced. Species have diminished due to frenzied harvesting caused by too many fishers hunting down too many fish. Again and again, biologists warn governments of the threat of species depletion and even extinction; the government at first ignores but eventually accepts the data; fishers lobby against action; and the government backs off and continues its industry subsides. By the time the government finally takes action, the long-term value of the fisheries has been destroyed, and the fishers find themselves out of business anyway.

Time after the time, governments and fishers take far too long to act. Why?

The problem of overfishing is an example of a collective action problem known as "the tragedy of the commons." Collectively all the fishers would be better off if the common resource ("the commons") were conserved. But because each individual fisher has incentives to overconsume the resource, they can be expected to block cooperative agreements that would ensure the long-term health and sustainability of fish stocks. The predictable result of such irrational behavior is the depletion of fishing basins and species extinction. In chapter 5, we will show how incentives function within commons dilemmas. In this chapter, we will focus on the root cause of such incentives: the innate cognitive biases that predispose people to behave in a manner that, in the long term, harms them, the organizations they belong to, and society as a whole.

In the last few decades, researchers have shown that human judgment and decision-making deviates from rationality.[6] People rely on simplifying strategies, or cognitive heuristics, that lead them to make predictable errors. These errors, identified by behavioral decision researchers, have been applied to medicine, law, business, and public policy. In this chapter, we use this literature to describe and document the five cognitive biases most clearly responsible for predictable surprises:

1. We tend to have *positive illusions* that lead us to conclude that a problem doesn't exist or is not severe enough to merit action.

2. We tend to *interpret events in an egocentric manner*. That is, when considering the fairness of proposed solutions to a looming crisis, we allocate credit and blame in ways that are self-serving.

3. We *overly discount the future*, reducing our courage to act now to prevent some disaster that we believe to be quite distant.

4. We tend to *maintain the status quo*, and refuse to accept any harm that would bring about a greater good. In other words, we are reluctant to accept that some dramatic change will occur if we fail to address a mounting problem. Rather than confronting unpalatable choices, we avoid action altogether.

5. Most of us don't want to invest in preventing a problem that we have not personally experienced or witnessed through *vivid data*. Thus, far too often, we only fix problems after we ourselves experience significant harm or after we can clearly imagine ourselves, or those close to us, in peril.

In the remainder of the chapter, we explore these common biases and connect them to a number of other predictable surprises. We also show how biases can infect your own work decisions, and we provide advice for eliminating them from your behavioral repertoire. As you will see, these cognitive mistakes resonate with the stories presented in earlier chapters and permeate the common failure to respond to predictable surprises.

POSITIVE ILLUSIONS

Most people view themselves, the world, and the future in a considerably more positive light than is objectively justified or than reality can sustain.[7] Positive illusions have a number of benefits, such as enhancing and protecting self-esteem, increasing personal contentment, and helping us to persist at difficult tasks and cope with adverse and uncontrollable events.[8]

But this self-enhancement can also have destructive effects. It causes people to perceive themselves as being better than others with regard to a variety of desirable attributes.[9] It therefore leads them to have unrealistically positive self-evaluations across a wide range of social contexts. For example, in research studies, a majority of participants have been found to perceive themselves as being above average across a number of traits, including honesty, cooperativeness, rationality, driving skill, health, and intelligence.[10]

Unrealistic optimism is a bias in judgment that leads people to believe that their futures will be better and brighter than those of other people.[11] Most students expect that they are far more likely to graduate at the top of the class, get a good job, secure a high salary, enjoy their first job, get written up in the newspaper, and give birth to a gifted child than reality suggests. They also assume that they are less likely than their classmates to have a drinking problem, get fired or divorced, become depressed, or suffer physical problems. Similar patterns emerge for individuals in other age groups. We persist in believing that we can accomplish more in a day than is humanly possible, and we seem immune to the continued feedback that the world provides, pointing out our limitations.

People also falsely believe that they can control uncontrollable events.[12] Evidence suggests that experienced dice players believe that "soft" throws are more likely to result in lower numbers being rolled; these gamblers also believe that silence on the part of observers is relevant to their success. Ellen Langer found that people have a strong preference for choosing their own lottery card or numbers, despite the fact that this has no effect on the likelihood of winning.[13] Many superstitious behaviors result from a false illusion of control. Because such illusions encourage risky behavior, they can have significant adverse effects on gamblers and managerial decision-makers.

People are biased in how they explain the causes of events, taking a disproportionately large share of the credit for successes and accepting too little responsibility for collective failures.[14] Rod Kramer observes that this psychological pattern was well understood by President Kennedy, as quoted in Ted Sorenson's 1965 biography: "Victory has a thousand fathers, but defeat is an orphan."[15] Self-serving attributions can motivate leaders to reach the false conclusion that the efforts they have already made toward preventing a predictable surprise are sufficient and that no further action is necessary. Self-enhancement biases extend to the groups to which individuals belong.[16] People tend to believe that members of their group, such as the corporation they work for, are more honest, cooperative, trustworthy, diligent, and industrious than members of other groups.

Blaming others is a common pattern in politics. Kramer argues that the Watergate scandal occurred in part because President Nixon and others close to him denigrated the competence and motivation of his critics. The illusion of superiority was firmly behind the U.S. invasion of Cuba in 1962 that led to the Bay of Pigs fiasco. The Kennedy administration erroneously believed that a small number of U.S.-trained Cuban exiles could succeed in toppling the Castro regime. The result was a military failure and a significant threat to world peace, as the Soviet Union proceeded to arm Cuba with nuclear weapons.[17]

In recent decades, positive illusions have caused U.S. presidential administrations and their supporters to blame recent predictable surprises on the administration that immediately preceded or followed theirs. Supporters of George W. Bush, for instance, accept the view that Bush inherited the crises in airline security, corporate ethics, and the budget deficit from his predecessor, while Clinton/Gore supporters typically have denied blame and attributed these problems to failed Bush policies. In fact, there is plenty of blame to go around. Under both administrations, and under that of Bush's father, the FAA shrugged off repeated urgent warnings from the Inspector General and the General Accounting Office on the potential for air disaster, reverting again and again to the mantra, "Flying is safer than driving." Similarly, during the late 1990s, Congress ignored the warnings of SEC Chairman Arthur Levitt of the potential for financial disasters caused by auditor conflict-of-interest. Congress, the Big Five firms, and CEOs alike insisted on viewing proposed reforms of the auditing industry as evidence of overly zealous regulators, rather than a crucial call to action. Positive illusions reinforce politicians' convictions, while blinding them to the merits of alternate points of view. The result is often a predictable surprise. In chapter 6, we will discuss the role of political motivations in such debates.

The U.S. government has continued to avoid the mounting potential for global disaster created by the warming of the Earth's atmosphere. In 2002, the Bush administration's climate action report acknowledged that the United States would be substantially altered by global warming in coming decades, yet it failed to advocate solutions, such as controlling or reducing the country's heavy reliance on fossil fuels.[18] It is fascinating to note that those groups that would face the heaviest costs of measures aimed at addressing global climate change—auto manufacturers, oil and gas companies, elected officials closely tied to these industries, etc.—are those that most quickly develop the positive illusions necessary to ignore the challenge. Is it conceivable that scientists have overestimated the extent of future disaster? Yes. However, it is also possible that they have underestimated it, and that by the time we respond, it will be too late. We will consider the issue of global warming in greater detail in chapter 10.

Returning to the issue of fish overharvesting, it is amazing to note the vigor with which fishers deny that they have depleted a marine species almost beyond recovery. In each threatened basin, fishers claim that scientists and the government have raised unnecessary concerns. In the face of mounting evidence, fishers argue with great conviction that the depletion of a given fish population is only temporary, and that if the government would allow them to continue to fish without regulation, everything will work out. Often, these positive illusions forfeit the final chance to ward off the predictable surprise and save the fisheries from extinction.

EGOCENTRISM

Who is to blame for the predictable surprises of planetwide ecological disasters such as global warming, air pollution, and the depletion of fish stocks? The United States blames emerging nations for burning the rain forests and for overpopulation. Emerging nations blame the West for pollution caused by industrialization and excessive consumption caused by corporations overmarketing their goods. Within North America, consider the problem of acid rain. Tall smokestacks reduce local air pollution, but contribute to the regional problem of acid rain.[19] Citizens and politicians in northeastern Canada, the region most affected by acid rain, claim the pollution is caused by the industrialization of the Northeast and Midwest United States. To the Canadians, the causal connections are clear: The United States is to blame. Meanwhile, many interested parties in the United States (such as heavy industries and the politicians who support them) insist that there is no clear causal connection between U.S. smokestacks and the acid rain; they argue instead that acid rain is caused by the local burning of coal in Canada.

Of course, predictable surprises such as acid rain are complex, and they often have multiple causes. It is likely that both the United States and Canada are responsible for acid rain, but the blame game prevents either side from accepting responsibility and working to correct the problem. Even the most generous and future-thinking group will accept responsibility only for the damage that the group itself has caused. Unfortunately, we are rarely capable of making objective assessments of such matters.

Our views on environmental and societal issues such as acid rain and global warming are biased in a self-serving manner called "egocentrism."[20] While related to the positive illusions described above, egocentrism focuses on how one's viewpoint leads one to interpret information in self-serving ways. Going beyond assessments of oneself and others, egocentrism concerns the biased and preferential interpretation of events, and it highlights the difficulty of determining what is "fair."

Individuals can perceive a situation dramatically differently depending on the role they play. Psychologists David Messick and Keith Sentis argue that, when searching for a solution to a given problem, people first determine their preference for a certain outcome on the basis of self-interest, then justify this preference on the basis of fairness by changing the importance of attributes affecting what is fair.[21] Most people want a solution that all sides will view as fair, yet what we each consider to be fair is often biased by self-interest. Egocentrism leads all the parties in a given situation to believe that they deserve more than their fair share of a limited resource, as judged by an independent adviser. The problem lies not in our desire to be unfair but in our inability to interpret information in an unbiased manner.[22]

When two people write a book together, it can be expected that the sum of the percentage contribution that each author will attribute to himself or herself will add up to more than 100 percent.[23] This was also found to be true when husbands and wives were asked to estimate the percentage of the total household work that they performed.[24] Similarly, researchers Bob Sutton and Rod Kramer found that both sides of the Cold War attributed failure to reach agreement to the rigidity of the other side.[25] President Reagan told reporters, "We came to Iceland to advance the cause of peace . . . and although we put on the table the most far-reaching arms control proposal in history, the General Secretary rejected it." On the same day, General Secretary Gorbachev stated: "I proposed an urgent meeting here because we had something to propose . . . the Americans came to this meeting empty handed." More than just sound bites, these leaders' quotes reflect the egocentrism inherent in the diplomatic process.[26]

A theory of justice proposed by John Rawls suggests that fairness should be assessed under a "veil of ignorance."[27] Specifically, if individuals judge a situation without knowing what role they personally play, they will not be affected by their role. Thus, we can view egocentrism as the difference in our perceptions with and without the veil of ignorance. By deliberately assuming a veil of ignorance, individuals can learn to see beyond themselves and more effectively ward off a predictable surprise. This strategy is especially beneficial in the workplace, where considering the viewpoints of other parties (coworkers, competitors, regulators, and so on) is essential to gaining a well-rounded perspective on a looming crisis.

Returning to the failure of auditor independence in the United States, the egocentrism literature clarifies the impossibility of obtaining accurate audits from accountants who have a vested stake in their clients' success. When we closed chapter 3 with very strong recommendations regarding the need to eliminate conflicts of interest in the accounting profession, we were not expressing the belief that corruption is a general and unavoidable human trait. Rather, our opinion was based on the research conclusion that even well-trained, honest professionals view and interpret data in self-serving ways. As long as auditors are motivated to believe that their clients' financial data meets required standards, auditors will reach this conclusion more often than they logically should.

In late 2002 and early 2003, the U.S.-led search for intelligence data to support its desire to overthrow Iraqi dictator Saddam Hussein became a textbook case of self-serving interpretations of events. In the months leading up to the war, the Bush administration presented to the American people, the United Nations Security Council, and the world what it claimed to be reliable intelligence regarding the existence of weapons of mass destruction in Saddam Hussein's Iraq. "Facing clear evidence of peril, we cannot wait for the final proof—the smoking gun—that could come in the form of a mushroom cloud," Bush said in an October 7, 2002, speech.[28] And in his January 28, 2003, State of the Union address, Bush pressed the American people on the need for military intervention. "The British government has learned that Saddam Hussein recently sought significant quantities of uranium from Africa," he asserted.[29]

Hussein's progress toward building nuclear weapons became the primary justification for an immediate preemptive strike against the regime. Opinion polls showed that the American public accepted the president's claims, which translated into support for immediate war. And the administration likewise did little to discourage the widespread yet erroneous popular belief that the Hussein regime had strong ties to Al Qaeda and the events of September 11, 2001.

In the months after Hussein was overthrown, scant evidence emerged in Iraq of weapons of mass destruction. On July 7, 2003, with Iraq growing more chaotic and volatile by the day, the White House conceded that the information Bush cited in his State of the Union speech on uranium purchases had been based on forged documents. In a coordinated effort, Bush and his administration blamed CIA Director George Tenet for signing off on the intelligence data; Tenet himself accepted responsibility for the "mistake."[30] But months before the State of the Union speech, Tenet had personally intervened to remove from a prior presidential speech the claim that Iraq had attempted to purchase five hundred tons of uranium oxide from

Niger.[31] The CIA only signed off on the uranium line in the State of the Union address after references to Niger were removed and the charge was attributed to the British government rather than U.S. agencies.[32] It appears that high-ranking officials in the Bush administration, in their eagerness to prove that Iraq was an imminent threat to world peace, offered up for public consumption intelligence that was known to be dubious at best, fraudulent at worst.

The administration's desire to take on Iraq had its roots in the first Gulf War in 1991, but it picked up momentum in the aftermath of September 11, 2001, when Vice President Dick Cheney, Defense Secretary Donald Rumsfeld, and Deputy Defense Secretary Paul Wolfowitz began to lead the charge within the administration for a preemptive attack on Iraq. Wolfowitz and others in the "neoconservative" school had been advocating an attack on Iraq since the early nineties. As documented by journalist Seymour M. Hersh in the *New Yorker,* soon after 9/11, Wolfowitz created a self-described intelligence "cabal" within the Pentagon. The small group of policy advisers and analysts was founded on the belief that Saddam Hussein and Al Qaeda had close ties, and that Iraq had stockpiled chemical, biological, and possibly nuclear weapons that could threaten the United States.[33] Rumsfeld and his colleagues believed such an alternative intelligence group was necessary because the CIA, in their view, did not fully perceive the threat posed by Iraq. "[Rumsfeld's] byword . . . was that absence of evidence was not evidence of absence," said former CIA director James Woolsey, summing up the prevailing mindset within the Bush administration.[34]

Rather than objectively gathering facts and connecting dots, Wolfowitz's intelligence team "cherry picked"—they set out to find evidence that would support their preconceived beliefs and advance their agenda. Their intelligence sources included not only domestic and foreign agencies, but also parties with a political ax to grind, such as the Iraqi National Congress (INC), a group of Iraqi exiles eager to foment an American-led attack on the Hussein regime. Critics say that the Office of Special Plans simply went on a fishing expedition for any information that supported their cause, no matter how unreliable or self-interested the source.[35] "[T]he people in the Pentagon were susceptible to their own biases," commented journalist

Hersh. "Whatever intelligence they found that supported their pre-existing theories was the intelligence they believed."[36]

By fall 2002, finding itself increasingly marginalized by Wolfo-witz's intelligence team, the CIA asserted evidence of links between Iraq and Al Qaeda. Some analysts believed that CIA director Tenet felt obliged to tell Bush and the Pentagon what they wanted to hear or risk becoming irrelevant.[37] A former Bush administration intelligence official told Hersh, "One of the reasons I left [the administration] was my sense that they were using the intelligence from the CIA and other agencies only when it fit their agenda. They didn't like the intelligence they were getting, and so they brought in people to write the stuff. . . . If it doesn't fit their theory, they don't want to accept it."[38]

In retrospect, it appears that the administration formed its policies on Iraq upon an egocentric interpretation of information, a strategy that has threatened Bush's political clout as well as the global credibility of the United States.

Although in the lead-up to the war, some analysts raised serious doubts about whether Saddam Hussein posed an imminent threat to the United States, many U.S. citizens chose to take President Bush at his word. Why? In part, the trauma of 9/11 created a climate of fear that led the public to give the administration the benefit of the doubt. Also, confronted with the near-certainty of war, citizens could either decide that the country was going to war for a justifiable reason based on honest information provided by their leaders, or they could decide that the country was going to war for questionable reasons based on manipulated data. We argue that most people would be motivated to choose the former over the latter, and in the process, unconsciously, to allow an egocentric illusion to develop.

Who created the current corporate scandals—a few bad apples, the auditors, our capitalist system, investment bankers demanding quarterly results, or your favorite culprit? Who should pay the costs of fixing the system? Egocentrism creates a common obstacle to the prevention of a predictable surprise: the problem of gaining consensus on what is fair. When each party will only agree to solve the part of a problem for which they are responsible, the resolution of conflict becomes difficult. Environmental conflicts in particular tend to be highly complex, lacking conclusive scientific and technological information. Solutions typically require short-term economic sacrifices to attain comparatively uncertain long-term gains.

In a simulation of the New England fishery crisis described at the beginning of the chapter, researchers found evidence of egocentrism in the fairness interpretation of participants, who were M.B.A. and executive students.[39] In the study, four individuals assumed the roles of four fishing groups involved in harvesting the New England coastal waters. Like the real-world fishers, the student participants in the study harvested at a level that drove the fishing basin to collapse. The actual collapse had many causes, including a lack of incentive for fishers to reduce their catch, their refusal to believe scientists' warnings about species depletion, and government subsidies for the modernization of fishing fleets. This simulation added strong evidence that egocentrism was another leading cause of this overfishing. Specifically, each party tended to believe that it deserved a greater share of the resource than a neutral party would judge to be the case. In addition, the level of egocentrism observed was an excellent predictor of overharvesting.

Kimberly Wade-Benzoni and her colleagues documented the struggle of European nations to reduce pollution in the Rhine River, a problem that exemplifies the power asymmetry inherent in many international environmental disputes. As pollution and population rise worldwide, clean water has become an increasingly scarce resource and a growing source of conflict.[40] Two hundred and fourteen of the world's river basins are shared by at least two countries, and thirteen are shared by five or more.[41] Shared rivers like the Jordan, the Ganges, the Nile, and the Rio Grande have already been subjects of international dispute. Similarly, the Rhine River has become a point of contention. It flows through Switzerland, France, Germany, and the Netherlands, and its tributary the Moselle River flows through Luxembourg; these five countries share an interest in protecting the river.

In addition to its historical, political, and cultural significance, the Rhine provides drinking water, shipping, fishing, leisure and recreation activities, and ecological resources to each of the five nations. As the river passes through large cities and industrial regions, large quantities of toxic substances, including chloride, mercury, and cadmium, are discharged into it; more than one hundred such substances have been identified in the river. Hoping to reduce the levels of industrial pollution and wastewater discharged into the river, the nations have attempted to negotiate a solution.

Responsibility for polluting the river, as well as the level of benefit received from it, differs from nation to nation. Although all five countries contribute to the river's pollution, each one contributes a different amount. Downstream nations, especially the Netherlands, suffer the brunt of the pollution, and therefore are the most interested in finding a solution. Meanwhile, their upstream counterparts are far less motivated to acknowledge the existence of a problem, let alone to negotiate a settlement.

Because of these asymmetries in power and motivation, each actor ascribes a different degree of importance to the various issues. Focused on pollution-free water, the Netherlands, in the downstream territory, insists that effective measures aimed at reducing contamination be adopted by the upstream states. In contrast, France (an upstream country) advocates "a more pragmatic and gradual treatment of the issues" and encourages greater discussion of the economic aspects of the problem. Thus, as each country focuses on fairness arguments that serve its own best interest, egocentric interpretations of fairness are formed: The downstream countries concentrate on fair allocations of clean water, while the upstream countries focus on fair consideration of economic issues.

The connection of egocentrism to the degradation of the Rhine is quite consistent with other real-world environmental issues. In recent global climate-change negotiations, developing nations have blamed the existing problem on the excessive consumption patterns of developed nations. At the same time, the developed nations insist that the problem cannot be solved unless the developing world agrees to limit its expansion of a polluting power base and its destruction of the rainforest. While all parties agree that both behaviors contribute to the problem, they make fairness judgments in an egocentric manner.

DISCOUNTING THE FUTURE

Would you prefer to receive $10,000 today or $12,000 a year from now? Many people would choose the former, despite the fact that 20 percent would be a very good return on your investment in a year. Most homeowners do not adequately insulate their attics and walls, and fail to buy more expensive, energy-efficient appliances even when they would recoup the extra costs in less than a year. Large organizations also tend to discount the future in favor of immediate concerns. When one of the finest universities in the United States undertook a major renovation of its infrastructure, it failed in many cases to use the most long-term, cost-efficient building products. A very high implicit discount rate with regard to the future guided its construction decisions; present benefits (reduced up-front costs) were given greater weight than future costs (increased energy consumption). Paradoxically, the construction process was sacrificing returns on the university's endowment that the financial office would have been delighted to receive.

Research studies consistently turn up such myopic preferences, which seem to reflect an extremely high discounting of the future.[42] That is, rather than consciously evaluating options from a long-term perspective, people tend to focus on short-term considerations. At an individual level, we overly discount the future in ways that we are likely to regret later. At a societal level, the problems brought about by this tendency are more severe. Effective leaders have the necessary vision to convince society that it must act to maximize long-term welfare. But Herman Daly argues that many environmental decisions are made for the world "as if it were a business in liquidation."[43]

A critical aspect of most predictable surprises is that managing them requires the investment of resources now in return for some future, uncertain reduction of loss. The fishers discussed in the opening of this chapter needed to forgo current catch in exchange for benefits that might accrue only to future generations. Unfortunately, too often there are actors who resist making such sacrifices. In recent years, groups ranging from fishers to airline executives to the partners of the Big Five accounting firms have obtained substantial short-term benefit from resisting change or otherwise failing to act to avert predictable surprises. The benefit of action is often diffused to a broader population of citizens, who as a whole lack the knowledge or incentive to act on the issue.

Why do fishers consistently attempt to thwart coordinated efforts to reduce the total catch to sustainable levels? Because of the general tendency of decision-makers to deny the long-term effects of their behavior. When people focus on present gains, they are likely to discount the future, even if they personally would reap the benefits of taking future interests into account. A high discount rate may work against an individual's own self-interest, or it may cause harm on an intergenerational, global scale.[44] When the threat of a predictable surprise is imminent, both aspects may be present.

Members of the Financial Executives Institute consider overweighting of the present at the expense of the future by investors and managers as the greatest threat to global competition. Researchers Elizabeth Mannix and George Loewenstein blame high discount rates for the failure of businesses to devote significant resources to long-term investment, customer loyalty, and research and development.[45] According to this view, business decision-makers choose to maximize present gains at the expense of potential future benefits. One could argue that overweighting the present is not only foolish, but also immoral, robbing future generations of opportunities and resources. When making decisions that will affect others down the road, do we have a moral obligation to act in their best interest? If so, we should consider them as silent parties at the negotiation table.

Fishers have been strongly motivated to believe that the scientists are wrong, that the oceans are not being depleted, and that proposed regulations are too strict. "You base everything you tell us on what you really don't know," one fisher complained on the television show *Frontline*. "We're going to be told we've got to do all this stuff, but nobody knows anything. . . . You guys have got some jobs, but I don't think we're going to have any if you keep on. Save the fish, but what about the people?"[46] The fact is that decisions concerning the future will always contain some degree of uncertainty. Uncertainty allows for wishful thinking, but reality is too often deaf to our wishes.

Discounting the future interacts with the biases discussed earlier—positive illusions and egocentrism. Insisting that the scientists are flat-out wrong, the fishers cling to the positive illusion that the fish supply will improve with no adjustment to their behavior. They choose to ignore the fact that small to moderate changes in their fishing practices could eliminate the eventual need for massive change, such as the loss of their jobs. This wishful thinking often reflects an

crux of debate

egocentric desire to deny that one is contributing to a bigger problem. When a problem becomes so big that it can no longer be denied, wishful thinking leads us to blame others and let ourselves off the hook. After the U.S. fishers have fended off regulation of the domestic fishing basin, and the fish have disappeared, the fishers typically blame the government—for not instituting regulations earlier, for handing out subsidies, or for allowing foreign trawlers to fish off of U.S. coasts. All of these accusations, of course, are valid. But it is also true that the fishers themselves are to blame for discounting the future: for failing to take responsibility and supporting new, constructive government policy. By refusing to admit that changes in their collective behavior could help alleviate the problem, they have contributed to a predictable surprise.

Of course, discounting the future is not just about fish. Poverty in retirement is caused by the failure to save and invest earlier in life. As we will explore in chapter 10, federal deficits emerge from the desire to provide public services today, while avoiding the costs associated with those services. The easy solution is to discount the future and pass on the debt to future generations.

THE OMISSION BIAS AND THE STATUS QUO

Individuals, organizations, and nations tend to follow the often-heard maxim, "Do no harm." While this may often be a useful moral guideline, when followed too closely it can have adverse consequences. Sometimes, to avoid a situation that would cause great harm, society must accept trade-offs that require the infliction of a smaller harm. To avoid a predictable surprise, relatively minor inconveniences, such as long lines at airports or a security surcharge on plane tickets, are often necessary to prevent a much greater harm, such as airplanes flying into the World Trade Center and the Pentagon. The socially prescribed rule "do no harm" inhibits us from taking preventive actions that cause some degree of harm, even when the harms are relatively small or affect only a small part of the population. As a society, we are much more prone to make errors of omission (doing nothing) than errors of commission (causing harm).[47] Disabled from taking wise action to prevent predictable surprises, we accept the dysfunctional status quo. As we will explore in the next two chapters, organizational and political forces often conspire to maintain the status quo. But at its core, the "omission bias" is psychological: By nature, most people are reluctant to accept the need to inflict harm on themselves or others.

In a study of hypothetical vaccination decisions conducted by psychologists Jonathan Baron and Ilana Ritov, participants expressed an unwillingness to vaccinate children against a disease that was expected to kill 10 out of 10,000 children when the vaccine itself would kill 5 out of 10,000 through side effects.[48] People would not accept any deaths from the "commission" of vaccinating—even when their decision would cause five additional deaths. In other words, the error of commission that resulted in five deaths was seen as a greater harm than the error of omission that caused ten deaths. Clearly, this preference defies logic; we would argue further that a decision that leads to five unnecessary deaths is immoral.

Many people are similarly reluctant to commit themselves to programs that would help others at little or no personal cost, such as organ donation. Such programs cause minor harm (loss of organs after death) and create major benefits (saving lives). Yet consider that on average, fifteen thousand people die in the United States each year while waiting for an organ to be found. Only 4,500 of 11,000 eligible donors give up their organs; many eligible donors fail to authorize donation on their driver's licenses or their grieving families refuse to give consent.[49] Why do so many people fail to participate in organ donations programs? Obviously, lack of foresight and selfishness must be taken into account. But even when Baron and Ritov reminded participants that they or their loved ones might find themselves waiting in vain for an organ, they tended to give greater consideration to the potential loss of their organs after death. The omission bias allows people to believe that they are completely moral if they obey a list of prohibitions while otherwise pursuing their narrow self-interest. The predictable surprise? A national shortage of organs.

Related to the omission bias is the innate human tendency to maintain the status quo. People are often unwilling to give up what they already have—their "endowment"—for a better set of options. Why? Because, as psychologists Daniel Kahneman and Amos Tversky have noted, losses typically loom larger than gains.[50] Imagine that you are offered a job that is much better than your current job in some respects (such as pay, responsibility, and vacation time) and marginally worse in others (such as location and health insurance benefits). What would you do? An objective analysis would suggest that if the gains are greater than the losses, you should move to the new job. But because of the psychological tendency to pay more attention to losses than to gains, we tend to seek to preserve the status quo and, as a consequence, forego a net gain. When observing the snail's pace at which Congress enacts reforms, it is helpful to note that, because of the number of people affected by each decision, virtually all changes at a governmental level require certain losses in exchange for greater gain.

Bill Samuelson and Richard Zeckhauser found that people tend to be reluctant to make changes to their investment portfolio, even when changes make sense from a financial perspective, because any change can result in regret when the stock market moves in an unpredicted direction.[51] These researchers presented a thought exercise to a group of individuals who had a working knowledge of economics and finance. Participants were asked to imagine that they had inherited a large amount of money from a great-uncle. They were asked which of four possible investments they would pick: (1) a stock with moderate risk, (2) a risky stock, (3) U.S. Treasury bills, and (4) municipal bonds. The four investments were described in detail. Four other randomly selected groups (from the same subject population) also were told that they had inherited an investment from a great-uncle. Each group was told that the inheritance consisted of one of the four investments from the preceding list (one group was told that they inherited a stock with moderate risk, a second group was told that they inherited a risky stock, a third group was told that they inherited a U.S. Treasury bill, and a fourth group was told that they inherited a municipal bond). All participants were asked whether they would keep the investment that they inherited or trade it for one of the three other investments listed above. Participants overwhelmingly chose to keep the investment they received, rather than picking the investment best suited to their unbiased preferences; they showed a strong preference for maintaining the status quo. Paralleling this work, the median number of times that professors change the mix of investments in their retirement fund across the length of their career is zero.[52] We have an amazing tendency to accept the status quo.

When you fail to make prudent changes to your retirement fund, you are only hurting yourself and your family. When our leaders accept the status quo, we run the risk of disaster. In a wise essay about global warming, economist Thomas Schelling argues that, rather than making no adjustments to our behavior and hoping for the best, we should instead prepare for a predictable surprise that is even larger than that predicted by scientific models. "There isn't any scientific principle according to which all alarming possibilities prove to be benign upon further investigation," Schelling notes.[53] Thus, the best strategy may be to take a middle course but also to make sure we can adapt quickly if catastrophe strikes. However, even this middle course of action faces considerable inertia, as any alteration of the status quo would require painful changes on the part of individuals and industries.

Even as the scientific evidence of global warming has grown stronger in recent years, elected officials and the public have remained reluctant to take action. Along with other political and economic barriers, the desire to maintain the status quo hinders acceptance of effective solutions to prevent a predictable surprise. Paradoxically, the omission bias makes us reluctant to take actions to reduce global warming, even though we know that inaction will lead to harmful changes away from the status quo. Compounded with our tendency to discount the future, our tendency to preserve the status quo leads us to ignore changes that will be required of us later—even if these changes will come at a great personal cost.

The cognitive mistakes described in this chapter are insidious and pervasive, cutting across populations and contexts. The desire to maintain the status quo and to avoid errors of commission help to explain a number of the predictable surprises we have touched on: why fishers obstruct any change to their fishing habits, why the public did not demand effective airplane security prior to September 11, and why the Big Five accounting firms blocked reforms to their industry in 2000. The failure of society to respond to these predictable surprises has created massive costs to our society, including to those who were far removed from the specifics of these tragedies. The tendency to keep our heads in the sand is understandable, but not acceptable. Unfortunately, as we will see next, often it is only vivid disaster that motivates change.

VIVIDNESS: WE DON'T FIX IT IF
WE CAN'T TELL IT'S BROKEN

In his book *Judgment and Managerial Decision Making*, Max Bazerman asked readers:

> Which of the following lists caused more premature deaths in the United States in 1999?
>
> 1. Tobacco use, obesity/inactivity, and alcohol
>
> 2. Cancer, heart disease, and auto accidents

Highly influenced by the vividness of the causes listed in group B, most people choose this list. In fact, list A provides the three leading causes of premature death in the United States in 1999.[54] Auto accidents were eighth on the list of premature killers, and cancer and heart disease were even lower. Yet the vividness of these types of death in the media biases our perception of the frequency of events. Thus, we tend to underestimate the likelihood of premature death due to tobacco addiction, overeating, and alcoholism, and we miss opportunities to reduce these hazards through preventative measures such as school and workplace health programs.

Vividness of information affects many of our most important decisions about life. Although most people recognize the seriousness of AIDS, many individuals fail to take adequate measures to avoid contracting the disease. In the fall of 1991, however, sexual behavior in Dallas was dramatically affected by a vivid story concerning AIDS that may not even have been true. In a chilling interview, a Dallas woman who called herself C.J. claimed that she had AIDS and was trying to spread the disease out of revenge against the man who infected her. After this vivid interview aired, attendance at AIDS seminars in Dallas increased dramatically, AIDS became the main topic of Dallas talk shows, and HIV testing surged across the city. Although

C.J.'s possible actions were a legitimate reason for concern, it should have been clear that one woman could not have been responsible for any significant percentage of the total number of AIDS cases in Dallas. There were many more important risks to consider regarding AIDS transmission. Nonetheless, C.J.'s vivid report influenced many people's behavior far more than the mountains of data available.

Tversky and Kahneman assert that when an individual judges the frequency with which an event occurs by the availability of its instances, vividness matters: An event whose instances are more easily recalled will seem to be more frequent than an event of equal frequency whose instances are more difficult to recall.[55] The researchers cite evidence of this bias in a study in which two groups were read two different lists of names of well-known personalities of both genders. One of the groups was read a list in which the women included were relatively more famous than the men included, but the list included more men's names overall. The other group was read a list in which the men included were relatively more famous than the women included, but the list included more women's names overall. After being read their group's list, participants in both groups were asked whether the list was composed of more women or men. In both groups, participants incorrectly guessed that the gender that included the relatively more famous personalities occurred more often on the list. Participants apparently paid more attention to vivid names than to less well-known ones, leading them to inaccurate judgments.

While this example of vividness may seem fairly benign, it is not difficult to see how vividness—or its lack—might contribute to a predictable surprise. In many real-life situations, people fail to act until confronted with vivid data. In the case of predictable surprises, action is required to avoid the disaster, but until the disaster occurs, the need for change is not vivid. Without the vividness of an actual disaster, our leaders fail to take action. For this reason, fishers in overharvested areas typically fail to support fishing quotas until their own livelihood is threatened. For this reason, Congress failed to support the SEC's call for auditor independence reforms in 2000. And for this reason, Americans remained unconcerned about airport security until we watched the horror of 9/11 unfold on television. Our leaders can expect us to be numb to government warnings and data. It is their task to provide the vision for change, even when the need is not yet vivid.

The vividness bias is well understood by political leaders, who sometimes exploit it to rally public opinion in support of desired courses of action. By referencing nuclear weapons and painting images of mushroom clouds over U.S. cities, the Bush administration sought to make the threat posed by Saddam Hussein vivid to the public. To justify the resort to preemptive war, the threat needed to be perceived as immediate.

When the course of action for which leaders seek to rally support is the right one, it is essential that they paint pictures of the consequences of inaction as vividly as possible. But vividness can also be abused, as leaders seek to prevent needed change or rally support for questionable or illegitimate actions. As we will discuss in chapter 6, special-interest groups often will cite doomsday scenarios in seeking to protect their perquisites.

SUMMARY

The biases described in this chapter—positive illusions, egocentrism, discounting the future, the omission bias, the desire to maintain the status quo, and inattention to data that is not vivid—are the most fundamental, innate sources of predictable surprises. The errors work together, and they work in conjunction with the organizational and political factors we will explore in the next two chapters. We need to understand the multitude of causes and to attack each of them in order to reduce the risk of future predictable surprises.

If these biases are hard-wired in all of us, what hope do we have of eliminating them from our behavioral repertoire and confronting future predictable surprises head on? In fact, there is plenty of reason to believe that individuals, elected officials, and organizations are capable of developing a more rational approach to important judgments and decisions. At management and professional schools, students are routinely taught to audit their decision-making process for the biases described in this chapter. Identifying these biases is the first step toward changing one's views and behavior in a positive direction. By acknowledging their role in the cycle of overharvesting, and by opting out of the destructive system, the chefs who refuse to serve threatened fish species stand as an example to those who continue to deny the detrimental effects of their own biases. As consumers and voters, we can send a similarly strong message by educating ourselves on the fishing crisis, by refusing to buy overharvested species, and by lobbying our representatives in government for a tougher stance on fishing subsidies and quotas. In doing so, we may inspire others to take a closer look at the biases that can, in fact, do real harm. And in doing so, we may contribute to the prevention of the next predictable surprise.

While training to avoid biases is the most obvious implication of this chapter, in some cases, even training is likely to have limited effect. Linda Babcock and George Loewenstein have documented the amazing robustness of egocentrism, and the consistent failure of training efforts.[56] Thus, regarding auditor independence, we argued for eliminating the structural basis of the conflict of interest, rather than relying on moral persuasion or training. Understanding the limits of human cognition allows leaders to create structures in which these limits will do less harm. In the next two chapters, we develop conceptual ways to think about these structures.

5

Organizational Roots

The Role of Institutional Failures

On April 29, 1995, a small group of Greenpeace activists boarded and occupied the Brent Spar, an obsolete oil-storage platform in the North Sea owned by Royal Dutch Shell.[1] The boarding happened just weeks before Shell's British arm was planning to sink the platform in a deep trench in the North Atlantic. Joined by members of the European media, the Greenpeace activists announced their intention to block Shell's plans because they believed toxic residues in the Spar's storage tanks would damage the environment. Greenpeace timed the operation for maximum effect—a month before European Union (EU) environmental ministers were scheduled to meet and discuss North Sea pollution issues.

Shell rushed to court and successfully sued Greenpeace for trespassing. In the glare of media coverage, the activists were forcibly removed from the platform. For weeks afterward, as the cameras continued to roll, Shell blasted Greenpeace boats with water cannons to prevent the group from reoccupying the Spar. It was a public relations nightmare, and it only got worse. Opposition to Shell's plans— and to Shell itself—mounted throughout Europe. In Germany, Shell gas stations were boycotted and vandalized. Pilloried by the press and by governments, Shell finally retreated. It announced on June 20 that it was abandoning its plan to sink the Spar.

The attack on the Spar had clearly come as a surprise to Shell. But should it have? Other oil companies, fearing an industrywide backlash, had privately protested Shell's plans. Greenpeace had a history of occupying environmentally sensitive structures. And the Spar was nothing if not an obvious target: Weighing 14,500 tons, it was one of the largest offshore structures in the world and one of only a few North Sea platforms containing big storage tanks with toxic residues. But despite the warning signs, Shell did not see the calamity coming.

"We had perhaps done things too properly," reflected Chris Fay, the head of Shell UK, after the debacle. "We had covered all the scientific angles. We had covered all the technical angles. We had certainly very much covered all the legalistic angles. And you could say maybe that was a bit inward thinking. We hadn't taken into consideration hearts and emotions, which is where people are coming from."[2]

What renders organizations—from businesses like Shell to governments to nongovernmental organizations (NGOs)—vulnerable to being predictably surprised? Organizational surprise is likely to have complex roots. At the level of the organization, a predictable surprise may result from a host of factors, including:

- Failure to devote necessary resources to collecting information about emerging threats

- Reluctance to disseminate information that is deemed too sensitive to share

- Gaps in individual knowledge

- Failure to integrate knowledge that is available but dispersed across the organization

- Individual negligence and malfeasance

- Responsibility that is so ambiguously defined that no one has an incentive to act until it is too late

- Lapses in capturing lessons-learned

- Long-term erosion of the fabric of institutional memory due to personnel losses

Shell likely suffered from many of these weaknesses as it approached its decision regarding the Brent Spar. Such flaws are widespread in organizations of all kinds. When trouble areas emerge, wise managers will act to address them immediately, rather than turning away in the hope that these early warnings will not flare into a predictable surprise.

ORGANIZATIONAL FAILURE MODES

How can organizations avoid being predictably surprised? The answer is straightforward in conception but difficult in execution. For an organization to avoid predictable surprises, it must efficiently and effectively engage in four critical information-processing tasks:

1. Scan the environment and collect sufficient information regarding all significant threats.

2. Integrate and analyze information from multiple sources within the organization to produce insights that can be acted upon.

3. Respond in a timely manner and observe the results.

4. In the aftermath, reflect on what happened and incorporate lessons-learned into the "institutional memory" of the organization, in order to avoid repetition of past mistakes.[3]

Organizations become vulnerable to predictable surprises when one or more elements of this information-processing system break down. In particular, predictable surprises arise when organizations experience the following types of failures:

- *Scanning failures*—failures to engage in adequate scanning of the external and/or internal environment, either due to lack of resources or to organizational inattention regarding important classes of threats.

- *Integration failures*—failures to put together disparate pieces of information possessed by various parts of the organization, or to analyze available information into actionable insights.

- *Incentive failures*—failures of people in key positions to act on available insights because they lack the incentive to do so, or because their personal incentives clash with those of the organization.

- *Learning failures*—failures to distill key lessons from experience and to disseminate those lessons to all relevant parts the organization, or to preserve memory of past failures and approaches needed to avoid them.

In this chapter, we explore these four types of organizational failure and explain how they can lead to predictable surprises in organizations of all types, including those in the corporate world. We illustrate these failures with real-world examples—Shell Oil's efforts to sink the Brent Spar, the Japanese attack on Pearl Harbor, and the U.S. and UN intervention in Somalia—and explain how managers can work to avoid similar catastrophes (even if on a smaller scale) in their own organizations.

SCANNING FAILURES

Scanning failures occur when organizations fail to collect available information about emerging threats.

Selective Attention

Beliefs about what is "possible" or "impossible" can lead key members of the organization to focus their attention on certain problems, while allowing more serious ones to develop in plain sight.[4] The consequences of this selective attention are amply illustrated by Shell's battle with Greenpeace.

As it prepared to sink the Spar, senior leadership at Shell focused on a narrow "impact horizon" that neglected the predictable reactions of key constituencies and the effect of the decision on the organization as a whole. Specifically, Shell leadership concentrated on engineering and legal issues such as dealing with the British government, marshalling scientific evidence in support of the proposal, and developing elegant engineering solutions to the problem of safely disposing of the Spar. Eric Faulds, the head of construction for Shell UK, summed up the company's prevailing attitude: "We are trained as engineers to look at a problem, analyze possible solutions, and come up with a balanced answer . . . based on science and fact to the maximum possible extent. We can't base it on emotions."[5] This disregard for the emotional impact of its plans caused Shell to overlook a predictable public reaction. In the tradition of all good guerrilla organizations, Greenpeace exposed this point of vulnerability and shifted the battlefield.

Scanning failures also occur when decision-makers discount or ignore evidence that does not fit with their beliefs. When multiple, potentially competing sources of information and analysis exist within an organization, leaders may "cherry pick" among them, choosing to listen to assessments that fit what they want to hear and tuning out dissonant opinions. Describing the causes of major intelligence failures in their book *Strategic Intelligence for American National Security*, Bruce Berkowitz and Allan Goodman highlight this risk:

> [A] range of views usually exists in the intelligence community on most issues. So, if an official does not agree with the assessment one agency provides him, he is likely to be able to find one more supportive from some other agency. It is worth noting that in virtually every case that has been studied of an alleged intelligence failure between 1960 in 1980, the investigators have concluded that even if the intelligence community had possessed the right information or had reached the correct judgment, the policymakers would probably have ignored or rejected their findings.[6]

This dynamic can contribute to crippling self-censorship among those charged with identifying potential threats. To win internal bureaucratic wars and retain their influence with key decision-makers, they quickly learn to tell their masters what they want to hear. In the lead-up to the 2003 war in Iraq, this dynamic appears to have distorted U.S. and British intelligence assessments of the threat posed by Iraqi weapons of mass destruction as well as postwar plans to re-build Iraq. As we described in chapter 4, key leaders in the Bush ad-ministration sought out assessments that supported their preconceived convictions about Iraq and systematically ignored dissonant views. The result? False claims about Iraq seeking uranium from Niger and about connections between Iraq and Al Qaeda.

Noise

A second type of scanning failure occurs when signals associated with a threat are masked by a high level of background noise, which either emerges naturally from the environment or is intentionally cre-ated by an adversary aiming to confuse organizational leaders. By "sig-nals" we mean clues, indications, or other evidence of an impeding crisis. "Noise" refers to conflicting information that points to other critical problems or explanations for the threat. When the signal-to-noise ratio is low, it becomes very difficult for the best analysts to dis-cern genuine threats from false indications.

High levels of background noise played a role in allowing the Japanese to launch a surprise attack against U.S. bases at Pearl Harbor on December 7, 1941. On the "date which will live in infamy," Japanese aircraft carriers approached the Hawaiian Islands unde-tected and launched their fighters and bombers, raining wave after wave of bombs and torpedoes upon the American fleet in Pearl Har-bor.[7] Later the same day, Japanese attacks on U.S. bases on the Philippines, Guam, Midway, and Wake Island also achieved com-plete tactical surprise.

In her compelling analysis of the causes of the Pearl Harbor intel-ligence failure, *Pearl Harbor: Warning and Decision*, Roberta Wohl-stetter notes that U.S. analysts were flooded with information in the lead-up to the attack. Directly highlighting the problem of discerning signal from noise, she states, "It is only to be expected that the rele-vant signals, so clearly audible after an event, will be partially ob-scured before the event by surrounding noise."[8]

The signal-to-noise problem is further compounded by the orga-nizational consequences of repeated false alarms. When an organiza-tion's environment is hostile, it is natural for analysts to err on the side of caution. Better to be chastised for being too cautious than hung for being too optimistic, say Berkowitz and Goodman, summing up the "warning function" of the analyst, as contrasted with the "prediction function."[9] Analysts initially tend to be overreactive, which causes multiple false alarms. These false alarms create an immunization—fatigue on the part of other organizational members, and a desire among analysts not to raise another false alarm. When those responsible for scanning the environment move from being overreactive to being underreactive, the organization will fail to recognize a true threat when it ultimately arrives.

Overload

Those responsible for scanning the environment can also suffer from information overload, which keeps them from recognizing the full range of potential threats. As a result, their efforts either become too diffuse to be useful, or they are forced to ignore "lower priority" areas. In either case, the organization fails to see an emerging threat until it is too late. Note that overload can occur when (1) the resources devoted to intelligence gathering and analysis are insufficient for the volume of information to be processed, or (2) the range of potential threats increases, either slowly over time or very rapidly, without compensating adjustments in resource allocation, as was the case in the lead-up to Pearl Harbor.

When stressed by overload and forced to focus their resources, the mind-sets of key people in the organization can create serious vulnerabilities. Before the Pearl Harbor attack proved them terribly wrong, U.S. intelligence analysts had dismissed the possibility that the Japanese could launch a torpedo attack in the shallow and constrained confines of Pearl Harbor. Torpedoes dropped from airplanes, they knew, needed a significant depth of water to avoid premature explosion. As a result, antitorpedo netting had not been laid in the harbor. This reassuring assessment permitted analysts and decision-makers to focus their very limited resources on preparing for other threats that were deemed more likely to materialize. But unbeknownst to the Americans, the Japanese had been working feverishly to develop torpedoes that rapidly armed themselves in shallow water.[10]

Managers will recognize selective attention, noise, and overload as the common state of most organizations. If leaders fail to orchestrate a search for possible predictable surprises, the result is a high likelihood of scanning failures.

INTEGRATION FAILURES

Adequate scanning is just the first step toward preventing a predictable surprise. Next, leaders must make sure that the information gathered is effectively integrated and analyzed. Integration failures occur when various units or individuals in an organization possess all of the information necessary to perceive a predictable surprise, but fail to develop "actionable insights" about emerging threats.

Silos

Integration failure is typically caused by the existence of distinct "silos" of expertise and information flow within an organization— storehouses of valuable resources that others in the organization cannot access. Leaders must constantly make trade-offs between what researchers Lawrence and Lorsch termed "differentiation," the need to create and sustain deep pools of expertise, and "integration," the need to integrate and synthesize knowledge across these pools to achieve desired results.[11] As the overall complexity of any organizational "project" increases—be it an effort to sink an aging oil platform or to follow complex corporate governance systems—so too does the need for increased differentiation. The organization therefore develops multiple, deep wells of expertise, which in turn trigger a need for greater integration. The goal of full integration provides a real challenge for leaders.

The simplest type of integration failure occurs when various members of an organization have pieces of the puzzle, but no one has them all, and, critically, no one knows who knows what. On the basis of her exhaustive investigation of the lead-up to Pearl Harbor, Wohlstetter concluded that the U.S. government had all the information it needed to anticipate and prepare for the attack, but was unable to "connect the dots" in time to take action. She opens the book by saying, "Pearl Harbor provides a dramatic and well-documented example of an attack presaged by a mass and variety of signals, which nonetheless achieved complete and overwhelming surprise."[12] Her book ends, "If our intelligence system and all our other channels of information failed to produce an accurate image of Japanese intentions and capabilities, it was not for want of the relevant materials. Never before have we had so complete an intelligence picture of the enemy. And perhaps never again will we have such a magnificent collection of sources at our disposal."[13]

In short, an organization's knowledge never equals the sum of its members' knowledge. Various parts of the organization may have all of the information necessary to perceive and prevent a predictable surprise, but no person or unit is capable of putting it all together. In theory, senior management should play the role of synthesizer, compiling the fragmented information into "the big picture." But the barriers to this goal are great. Organizational members filter information as it rises through hierarchies. The temptation to withhold or gloss over sensitive, confusing, or embarrassing information is great. Those at the top inevitably receive incomplete and distorted data, and overload may prevent them from keeping up-to-date with incoming information.

Secrecy

A second type of integration failure is rooted in what might be called "the fundamental paradox of intelligence gathering": Sometimes information gathered through environmental scanning and analysis seems too sensitive to be shared broadly within an organization. This is true when information sharing might lead to leaks or changes in organizational behavior that would send signals to the "enemy." It's also the case when information sharing could compromise the sources and methods used to gather the intelligence. The problem may be compounded by a desire on the part of people "in the know" not to share information that is a source of power and influence, for fear of diminishing their own status. Regardless, the net result is that valuable information is not shared internally, and even top leaders can remain in the dark.

This problem played out in the Pearl Harbor attack. U.S. cryptographers were successful in breaking the highest-level Japanese PURPLE diplomatic code, as well as other less important codes.[14] Decoded intercepts painted a comprehensive portrait of Japanese strategic intentions and even yielded a directive to the Japanese Embassy in the United States to destroy key documents at a specific time just before the attack. But to avoid compromising sources and methods, the distribution list for PURPLE intercepts was kept very short, and some people decided on their own accord not to share critical information with higher-ups. As a result, key assessments about Japanese plans didn't flow to levels in the government that could have anticipated and prepared for the attack on Pearl Harbor. Wohlstetter notes that the "zealous guarding" of intercepted high-level Japanese messages by a small group of recipients led them to make a series of false assumptions that "erred on the side of optimism."[15] Here, organizational and cognitive factors—in this case, positive illusions—reinforced each other in contributing to a predictable surprise.

These mistakes offer a key lesson for managers. Even when you're embroiled in top-secret negotiations, it's important to do your homework and consult with top-level advisers. To ward off a predictable surprise, you need to temper optimistic assumptions about a deal's success with a thorough and open-minded examination of potential obstacles.

INCENTIVE FAILURES

An organization's leaders may have actionable insights about impending predictable surprises, but lack sufficient incentives to forestall them. Incentives are an excellent predictor of the behavior of individuals within organizations. Incentive failures occur when people in the organization have the requisite insight needed to prevent emerging problems, but fail to do so either because they lack an incentive to take action or, even more perniciously, because they have an incentive to cause the organization harm.

Collective Action Problems

Organizational members often confront situations in which their individual incentives encourage them to act in a manner that harms the organization as a whole, and thus contributes to predictable surprises. One major class of incentive failures is known as *collective action problems*. In such problems, people are collectively better off if they cooperate and contribute to solving (or avoid creating) a problem, but have individual incentives not to cooperate. Efforts to create or preserve social value fail in the face of individuals claiming value for themselves.

The classic illustration of a collective action problem is the *prisoner's dilemma* game.[16] In this stylized formulation, two felons jointly commit a crime and are arrested. After their arrest, they are separated and each is offered the same deal: "If you confess and your partner doesn't, you will get one year in prison and your partner will get seven. If you both confess, you will both get five years in prison." The police are confident that if both prisoners refuse to confess, they will be convicted on lesser charges and each end up with a three-year sentence, an outcome that both prisoners correctly surmise. Their combined jail time will be six years if neither confesses, ten if they both confess, and eight years if one confesses and the other doesn't. Thus, the best joint outcome is for neither to confess. But think about the incentives of the two individual "players." Each reasons, "If my partner confesses, then I'm better off confessing too. And if my partner doesn't confess, I'm still better off confessing." Each knows that the other will reason the same way, so both confess and both get five years—a lose-lose outcome.

Defection—choosing not to cooperate and looking out exclusively for one's own interest—occurs in organizations as well as individuals. Trust is one antidote to the problem, but it can be difficult to build and sustain. Another remedy is the ability to punish those who defect. When people play games such as the "prisoner's dilemma" repeatedly, rather than just once, the threat of defection in future "rounds" tends to promote cooperative outcomes.[17] Consider the OPEC oil cartel's relative success in preventing its members from overproducing oil and undermining the group's larger agenda. Cooperation becomes less likely when players belong to a relationship of limited duration. As the end approaches, they may begin to defect, a phenomenon known as the "end-game effect." Such self-interested behavior can be a primary contributor to a predictable surprise.

In chapter 4, we presented the global fishing crisis as a collective action problem, or commons dilemma: The short-term interests of individual fishers are at odds with the long-term interests of the fishing industry and society at large. Predictably, this clash resulted in the devastation of fishing stocks. In such cases, coercive regulation by a central authority, such as an international regulatory commission with the power to pursue and punish violators of fishing bans and quotas, may be necessary to sustain the commons.

The challenge to federal, state, and local governments of providing public goods, such as security, roads, education, or basic research, is another class of collective-action problems. Market forces typically do not provide sufficient incentives for individual citizens to make the necessary contributions or sacrifices for the common good. Instead, everyone has an incentive to act as a "free rider" and to let others make the necessary sacrifices. In the absence of adequate taxation and investment in public goods, the result is systematic underinvestment in resources that would increase social welfare.

Collective action problems arise in all types of organizations and can contribute to predictable surprises. A company's incentive systems, for example, may promote unhealthy internal competition among salespeople serving a shared pool of customers (the precious common resource). Predictably, such competition can lead to customer dissatisfaction. Customers who receive numerous, seemingly uncoordinated sales calls will become irritated, and they won't know whom to call if a problem arises.

Members of an organization may also take a free ride in the hope that others will assume responsibility for emerging problems. Organizational silos disperse responsibility as well as information. Sometimes everyone behaves as if someone else were in charge of heading off looming problems, and no one feels compelled to act. This situation becomes especially dangerous when organizational members perceive that taking preventative actions will yield them little reward if they are right and significant penalties if they are wrong.

Organizational decentralization also can play a role in exacerbating collective action problems. Leaders of decentralized units are often explicitly rewarded for pursuing parochial interests, but not for looking out for the good of the larger organization. Decentralization is not a problem when a crisis falls within the scope of defined units. Shell's decentralized matrix management structure, composed of autonomous national business units, did a good job of dealing with "normal" problems such as customizing marketing efforts to local customers. But when bigger issues spilled across unit boundaries, leaders could very easily find themselves working at cross-purposes.

Shell's organizational structure was ill suited to dealing with crises that crossed national lines. Because the Brent Spar was located in a British-controlled area of the North Sea, responsibility for the platform's disposal was naturally vested with Shell UK. Shell UK, in turn, sought the necessary permissions for disposal from the British government and consulted with British environmental groups. It was Greenpeace that broadened the incident's scope, focusing its public relations attack not in Britain but in Germany. Although Shell's German operating company had no part in the decision to dump the Spar, it became Greenpeace's central target. This pressure directly impacted the German unit's financial performance and executive compensation, resulting in the unfortunate spectacle of senior Shell managers in Germany publicly criticizing both the disposal plans and their British colleagues.[18]

Notably, predictable surprises often play out over time frames substantially longer than the typical tenure of organizational leaders. This creates a variation on the free-rider problem. "Why," a leader might ask, "should I be the one to grapple with this problem and take all the heat when nothing is likely to go wrong during my watch? Better to focus on my short-run goals and reap the rewards." In the business world, the more often managers are transferred between jobs, the higher the risk that significant problems will be left to fester. Why would a senior auditor for Arthur Andersen call Enron on some questionable accounting move, when the auditor would run the risk of losing Enron's business and his job? In such instances, the value of maintaining one's professional reputation for integrity can seem like a concern for the distant future.

Conflicts of Interest

Conflicts of interest, such as the auditor-independence issue described in chapter 3, are a second major class of incentive problems that contribute to predictable surprises. In conflicts of interest, people have incentives to take actions that can be expected to benefit them (at least in the short term) but harm people or groups whose interests they ostensibly represent.

The classic formulation of conflicts of interest is the *principal–agent problem*. In this situation, a principal—someone who controls valuable resources—allocates decision rights, or the right to make decisions on her behalf, to an agent.[19] Agents dominate a number of professions, including auditing, real estate, law, and investment banking. While agents can provide their clients with invaluable advice and service, a fundamental problem is built into the principal–agent relationship: An agent is likely to have his own distinct interests—oftentimes financial—which he may illegitimately seek to advance at the expense of the principal's interests. The agent's divergent interests and the principal's consequent distrust of the agent's motives give rise to a fundamental problem of information and control. Specifically, it is impossible for a principal to design an incentive system that perfectly aligns an agent's interests with her own. Nor is it possible for the principal to perfectly observe or control the actions of the agent; monitoring the agent would be costly, and the agent will always have access to information that is unavailable to the principal.

Conflicts of interest can render an organization vulnerable to predictable surprises. Take the case of Wall Street investment banks that seek highly profitable underwriting business from companies while publishing analyst reports that influence investors' perceptions, and consequently the stock prices, of those same companies. In 2002, Sanford Weill, the chairman of Citigroup, came under fire for apparently using corporate resources to provide personal assistance to Jack Grubman, a star analyst at Citigroup subsidiary Salomon Smith Barney. Weill allegedly helped Grubman's children gain admission to a prestigious day-care program in return for issuing a more favorable report on AT&T, an important client of Salomon's investment banking unit. Broader organizational politics also appears to have played a role in Weill's actions. As *The Economist* reported, "There is much speculation, and some e-mail evidence, that the recommendation helped to win support for Mr. Weill's successful ousting of [Citigroup's co-CEO, John] Reed, from Michael Armstrong, AT&T's chief executive, who also happened to sit on Citigroup's board."[20] The resulting damage to the reputations of Weill and his company was entirely predictable.

Not all principal–agent relationships are doomed to end with a predictable surprise. The potential for damaging conflicts of interest can be substantially diminished through a variety of means: (1) thoughtful design of incentive systems that align the interests of principals and agents to the greatest degree possible, (2) creation of monitoring systems that oversee agents' activities in a cost-effective manner, and (3) harsh penalties for self-serving behavior that damages the organization. Wise leaders will keep close tabs on their principal–agent relationships and implement systems and penalties aimed at preventing abuse.

Illusory Consensus

Organizations also can suffer from the illusion of consensus, an incentive problem rooted in the twin desires of most bureaucracies to avoid expending energy and incurring blame. It is all too easy to treat lack of active opposition to a course of action as positive support. Those who harbor doubts may keep quiet because they assume that decision-makers are armed with better information, or because they want to avoid being held accountable for mistakes. As soon as a predictable surprise occurs, however, those who were silent suddenly have an incentive to distance themselves from failure by going public with their concerns.

In the process of gaining approval to dispose of the Brent Spar, Shell consulted extensively with the British government. In turn, British officials informed other countries with North Sea interests about Shell's plan, but they did not actively attempt to secure buy-in from, for example, the German government. Once Greenpeace turned up the heat on Shell in Germany, the German government had every incentive to distance itself from the proposal. German officials quickly voiced "concerns" and then outright opposition to the Spar sinking, leaving the British government twisting in the wind.

The mirror image of the "illusion of consensus" problem is the problem of "suppressed dissent." Suppressed dissent can arise when one part of an organization is vested with *too much* responsibility for a particular issue and seeks to retain its primacy. If marketing personnel have traditionally held sway over key product-design decisions, for example, they may push for a product that the operations department knows will be very difficult to manufacture. Predictable results include late changes to the design, production delays, and a cost that is significantly higher than expected.

In such situations, other parts of the organization, including those with important information or perspectives to add, aren't consulted or may even be actively pushed out of the decision-making process. The result? Too narrow a perspective is brought to bear on the issue, and potential problems go unrecognized or are given too low a priority.

Illusory consensus is closely compatible with the concept of groupthink, which describes how members of an organization suppress their critical doubts and allow the false appearance of a consensus to emerge. Many leaders, such as John F. Kennedy in the Cuban Missile Crisis, have successfully managed illusory consensus by keeping their desired choices from the group, so as not to sway others' thinking; by asking group members to play the role of devil's advocate; and by asking them to consider information that runs counter to the prevailing view.

LEARNING FAILURES

Organizations suffer learning failures either when they fail to learn from experience or to disseminate lessons within the organization, or when hard-won knowledge is lost through erosion of institutional memory. The predictable result of failures in knowledge creation and preservation is the unnecessary reoccurrence of problems that the organization has previously confronted.

Organizational Learning Disabilities

In the aftermath of an organizational crisis, leaders have the opportunity to reflect on the experience and generate "lessons-learned," which can then be disseminated throughout the organization. Lessons can be taught to individuals in the form of cause-and-effects models and rules of thumb, or they may be codified into more formal guidelines, checklists, procedures, and processes.[21] Organizations suffer from "learning disabilities" when leaders miss out on opportunities to reflect and codify the lessons generated from past mistakes.

Even when leaders do capture lessons-learned, they may fail to disseminate these lessons appropriately within the organization. The flip side of the integration challenge discussed previously, organizational "learning disabilities" emerge when key lessons are not transmitted from the point of generation back to the front lines.

To understand why organizational learning may not occur, it's important to distinguish between the different types of knowledge. Knowledge can be explicit and tacit, as well as individual and relational.[22] The "explicit versus tacit" distinction is illustrated by the differences in how people are trained to be physicists versus artists. The prospective physicist reads about mathematics and science, attends lectures in her field, and solves problems that have right and wrong answers. Much of the knowledge she must acquire is *explicit*—it can be written down in books as rules, laws, and procedures, and it can be transmitted from a more experienced person to a less experienced person through papers, lectures, and seminars.

By contrast, the prospective artist learns largely by doing—by making art herself—and by being coached by experienced "masters." Much of the knowledge she must acquire is *tacit*—it cannot be written down as rules, laws, and procedures, and it can't easily be transferred from a more experienced person to a less experienced person in written or verbal form. In fact, master artists sometimes are not able to articulate their own recipes for success. They only know good work when they see it.

Of course, elements of science are present in art and vice versa. Similarly, knowledge possessed by organizations is part explicit and part tacit, part science and part art. Explicit knowledge, such as rules, procedures, and processes, can be transferred from one person to another verbally or in writing without a great deal of degradation. Tacit knowledge can only be acquired by doing, by being shown, or by working with others.

We can illustrate the second distinction between individual knowledge and relational knowledge in the context of organizational learning by looking at what it takes to build great baseball and basketball teams. One can put together an excellent baseball team by picking the best players in the major league for each position. Because baseball players operate relatively independently of one another, the resulting all-star baseball team can be expected to perform well. No matter whom they're playing with, good batters are good batters, and good fielders remain good fielders. In baseball, individual knowledge is much more important than relational knowledge.

But if you selected star players from the National Basketball Association for each position, would you end up with a great team? Possibly, but not likely. Basketball demands a high level of interdependence among team members; thus, relational knowledge is critical. Superior basketball teams play well because the players have learned to integrate their skills and develop shared "playbooks" through a great deal of practice. The stars might simply get in each other's way, making the whole much less than the sum of its parts.

In Table 5-1, we summarize the key types of knowledge that organizations accumulate as they learn.

The key implications of this summary for organizational learning are:

- Tacit knowledge gained by individuals who have confronted a problem is more difficult for an organization to capture than explicit knowledge. Think of the employees responsible for maintaining production equipment in a manufacturing plant. They come to know all of the idiosyncrasies of many, seemingly similar machines—a knowledge that is very difficult to codify and transmit.

- Relational knowledge gained by groups confronting a problem is more difficult to capture than individual expertise. When faced with a crisis, for example, experienced teams know

TABLE 5-1

Types of Organizational Knowledge

	Individual Knowledge (Expertise possessed by individuals)	Relational Knowledge (Knowledge of how to work effectively as a group)
Explicit knowledge (Transferable verbally or through writing)	• Rules • Laws • Procedures • The "science" of a profession	• Organizational charts • Formal decision-making processes • Plans for coordination • Written communication protocols
Tacit knowledge (Transferable by being shown or working with someone who has experience)	• Rules of thumb • Techniques • Approaches to group decision-making and problem-solving • The "art" of a profession	• Approaches to individual decision-making and problem-solving • Negotiated divisions of responsibility • Key sources of information and influence • Trust and credibility

which members are going to perform which tasks, and who is going to react in what ways. They don't have to consult procedures to mount a quick and effective response. Once again, this knowledge is difficult to capture.

- Tacit-relational knowledge—the knowledge that individuals have but cannot easily articulate to others—is the glue that holds the organization together, and it is the most difficult type of knowledge to preserve.

Organizations often fail to learn from past mistakes because they lack the mechanisms needed to share and codify, to the greatest extent possible, key lessons-learned. Such failures may occur because the organization is in a state of overload. Organizations in a reactive, "firefighting" mode can become trapped in a permanent state of crisis-response that impedes learning. When organizations are driven to the point where they have to repeatedly "patch" serious problems, because they lack the time to identify and correct underlying root causes, the stage is naturally set for predictable surprises. Organizational learning can also suffer from collective action problems, if no one has incentives to make the personal investments necessary to promote learning.

Organizations can identify and learn from their mistakes by conducting post-crisis reviews. In the aftermath of the Brent Spar debacle, Shell set up a process to capture key lessons-learned from the experience, which resulted in numerous changes to its organizational structure, processes, and procedures. Perhaps the pinnacle of organizational learning systems is the U.S. Army's mandated "after action review" process, and its central repository for those reviews, the Center for Army Lessons Learned (http://call.army.mil/). But no organization is too small to absorb its mistakes and work to ensure that they do not happen again.

Memory Loss

Even when an organization is diligent enough to capture and disseminate lessons-learned from past crises, these lessons can slip through the cracks when another problem area emerges. Predictable surprises can occur when an organization fails to remember key lessons-learned from the past. Absent ongoing investment in preserving organizational memory, erosion will occur. It may be rapid or creeping, but it is inevitable.

Organizations suffer memory loss every time an experienced employee leaves his or her job and is replaced by someone less experienced. Explicit knowledge can be transmitted in written or verbal form, but tacit individual knowledge can only be transmitted from person to person, and this transmission takes time. The loss of experienced personnel can therefore be devastating.

Valuable relational knowledge also is lost during personnel changes. Returning to our sports metaphor, consider the fact that replacing one individual on a baseball team is likely to have little impact on the team's overall performance. But replace a starter on a basketball team and critical knowledge is immediately "forgotten"; the finely honed balance of the team is thrown off. Of course, in any sport, replacing the entire team means that all of the group's accumulated relational knowledge will be lost. The new team must build its own base of relational knowledge from scratch. The same is true of all organizations. Those with high turnover—whether due to layoffs, strikes, or low morale—are likely doomed to repeat their past mistakes.

Fortunately, organizational memory typically contains significant redundancy. In a given organizational unit, it is rare for all experienced personnel to depart at the same time, and those who remain can help to educate new members. At the same time, the erosion of capabilities in critical areas can be subtle and all the more pernicious when it goes unnoticed.

The dangers of organizational memory loss are vividly illustrated in the tragic case of the intervention of the United States and the United Nations in Somalia in 1992–1993. In late 1992, the situation in Somalia had reached a crisis state: Armed clans were fighting viciously for control of the country, a drought had devastated agriculture, and hundreds of civilians were dying daily from disease and starvation. On December 9, 1992, the United States launched a large-scale military operation in Somalia to make possible the delivery of hundreds of thousands of tons of desperately needed food and other supplies.[23] Led by former U.S. ambassador to Somalia Robert Oakley, the UN-approved Unified Task Force (UNITAF) operation was designed to suppress the armed factions and to provide security for international aid agencies.

On May 4, 1993, the United States concluded the UNITAF operation, declaring the military-humanitarian effort a success. The $1.6 billion operation had saved an estimated 10,000 to 25,000 lives. In making the decision to withdraw, the U.S. asserted that it was time for the United Nations to step in with the UN Operation in Somalia (UNOSOM), the follow-on operation it had agreed to lead.[24] UNOSOM's far-reaching mandate, approved by the UN Security Council in late March, included disarming the still faction-ridden country, resettling thousands of refugees, and helping the Somalis rebuild their economy and achieve national reconciliation.

Interventions in crisis spots such as Somalia require a high level of interdependence among the political, military, and humanitarian players. To be effective, a team must work together to gain experience with each other's relative strengths and weaknesses and to develop shared "playbooks." Oakley finished his tour of duty in March and the United States pulled out of Somalia in early May, removing most of the military units, as well as psychological operations, newspaper and radio capabilities, and a strong intelligence force. In the process, they took with them all of their hard-won experience about how to navigate the dangerous currents of Somalia. There was essentially no overlap with the incoming leadership and no effort to document and share lessons-learned. As a result, UNOSOM never benefited from the institutional memory developed during UNITAF. All of the tacit knowledge acquired by individuals about, for example, how to operate in the streets of Mogadishu or how to negotiate with Somali warlords was forgotten. During the transition from UNITAF to UNOSOM, important relational knowledge also was irretrievably lost.

With UNITAF's departure, U.S. Admiral Jonathan Howe, the new UN special representative in charge of both the military and civilian components of UNOSOM, faced an alarming array of challenges. Resources contributed by UN member nations—including weapons, equipment, and people—fell far short of what was needed. UNOSOM had less than a quarter of its planned staff of 300 in place at the time of the U.S. withdrawal. Only 16,000 of an authorized 28,000 troops were in country, with Pakistan replacing the United States as the dominant force. The Australians and Canadians, among the most experienced and well equipped of the remaining forces, were drawing down troops in preparation for departure.

The United States appeared unwilling to play a major role after its own costly operation in Somalia. "Somewhere there was a gap," declared Robert Oakley. "The awareness of the weakness of the United Nations did not lead, after the change in administration in Washington, to the sort of concern and active involvement on the part of the United States government in making sure that UNOSOM was really up to the task."[25]

The result of this organizational memory loss was a predictable surprise. Regular contact between the Somali faction leaders and U.S. and UN representatives, carefully nurtured by Oakley during UNITAF, broke down. On June 5, Pakistani soldiers conducted a surprise inspection of a weapons site controlled by the followers of Mohamed Farah Aideed, the most powerful of the Somali warlords. The inspection went without incident, but as the soldiers headed back to base, they were attacked. Twenty-four Pakistanis were killed and more than fifty wounded before the fighting ended. In an emergency session, the UN Security Council unanimously passed a resolution blaming Aideed's organization for the attacks and affirming UNOSOM's authority to "take all necessary measures against all those responsible for the armed attacks."[26] To better protect UN personnel in Somalia, Howe pressed for a greater U.S. military presence. The Pentagon refused a request for Special Forces and heavy tanks, but did send some additional equipment.

On June 12, one week after the Pakistanis were killed, U.S. AC-130 gunships and helicopters systematically destroyed Aideed's radio station and five of his main weapons sites. On June 17, a combination of air and ground forces demolished his organization's command and control complex. On July 12, the U.S. Quick Reaction Force (a modest U.S. force left to assist the UNOSOM operation) attacked a meeting of Aideed's senior leadership, provoking a series of clashes and reprisal killings. Four American military police were killed on August 8 when their jeep was blown up by a remote-controlled mine.

In an attempt to capture Aideed, U.S. Delta Force commandos rounded up twenty-four of his associates in hostile territory. As the commandos prepared to leave, two helicopters assisting in the operation were shot down by rocket-propelled grenades. Army Rangers rushed to the scene without heavy armor protection. By the end of the fifteen-hour rescue mission, graphically portrayed in the film *Blackhawk Down*, eighteen American soldiers and one Malaysian had died, one American had been taken hostage, and seventy-seven Americans had been wounded.[27]

Congress reacted to the American deaths with outrage and called for the immediate and complete withdrawal of U.S. troops from Somalia. On October 6, President Clinton decided on a withdrawal date of March 31, 1994. U.S. troops pulled out at that time, leaving behind only a small contingent to protect the U.S. Liaison Office. Almost all European UNOSOM participants left as well, and complete withdrawal of the UN presence soon followed.

The operation was widely viewed as a severe setback for the United Nations. "For the first time in the history of the UN, we left an operation without taking it to free and fair elections, or political reconciliation," says Elizabeth Lindenmayer, principal officer for the UN's Department of Peacekeeping Operations. Six months after the UN pulled out of Somalia, many of the same forces that propelled the country into collapse in 1991 and 1992 were at work again. Crop yields were down, this time because of floods. Malnutrition and disease increased, looting was prevalent, and a new round of battles was underway in Mogadishu among the Somali warlords.

While an expanded mission and inadequate resources unquestionably contributed to the failure of UNOSOM, the loss of organizational memory stemming from the abrupt departure of U.S. forces most crippled the intervention in Somalia. Despite Aideed's hostile rhetoric at the end of May, for example, UNOSOM's handful of new counterintelligence agents—a major cutback from UNITAF's fifty—hadn't uncovered any evidence of a planned attack. And while Oakley had carefully nurtured dialogue with the warlords, Howe eschewed it. "The difference in UNOSOM," declared General Anthony Zinni, deputy to the military commander of UNITAF, "is they just brushed the Aideeds and Ali Mahdis and the faction leaders aside and decided to create this grassroots, democratic country with district and regional councils and little village elders out there under the acacia tree."[28] Sadly, this memory loss was entirely predictable and preventable.

Costly and unnecessary memory loss afflicts most organizations. Any time that a significant change in personnel occurs—in a project, a team, or a critical organizational unit—important knowledge can be irretrievably lost. Similarly, any time that responsibility for a critical activity, such as the launch of a new product, is transferred from one unit to another, critical insights can fall through the cracks.

Leaders must therefore make knowledge preservation a core activity. This means identifying when key transfers of personnel and responsibility occur in their organizations and intervening to make sure that thorough and accurate knowledge-transfer is high on the agenda. Often this means pushing units to delay personnel shifts or to provide employees who can serve as the "bridge" between the unit that is passing on responsibility and the one that is taking it on.

SUMMARY

The failure modes described in this chapter—failures in scanning, integration, incentives, and learning—are key contributors to predictable surprises in organizations. A weakness in any link in this chain of information-processing renders an organization vulnerable. The failure modes also often compound and reinforce each other. Learning failures, for example, can result from a lack of integration, or from a lack of incentives among the organization's leaders to invest in capturing lessons-learned.

While there are no easy solutions to these failures, there is much that organizations and their leaders can do to mitigate them. Systematic scanning of the environment, driven by clearly set priorities and explicit hypotheses, can increase the likelihood that emerging problems will be spotted. Leaders should pay careful attention to the design of organizational integration mechanisms, such as liaison roles and teams, to ensure that appropriate communication and integration occurs. In this manner, they can compensate for the barriers created by differentiation and silos. Leaders can work to overcome incentive problems by designing incentive and monitoring systems and by establishing and enforcing strict penalties for self-serving behavior. Finally, by devoting necessary attention and resources to the capture, dissemination, and preservation of lessons learned, leaders can help prevent history from repeating itself.

The organizational factors that contribute to predictable surprises are compounded by the biases described in the previous chapter. They also can be amplified by the political factors described in the next one.

6

Political Roots

The Role of Special-Interest Groups

In the aftermath of a predictable surprise, interested parties will go to extreme lengths to avoid meaningful reform, typically by arguing that the surprise is as unlikely as lightning to strike the same place twice. Perhaps nowhere is this strategy more common than Washington, D.C. Consider what happened in the accounting industry following the collapse of Enron and Arthur Andersen. Even as firms such as WorldCom and Global Crossing tumbled like dominoes in similar scandals, the major auditing firms continued their mantra: A few "bad apples" were ruining their reputation. At its core, the system was healthy, they claimed; the great majority of auditors were untainted by conflicts of interest. Taking this cue, the Bush administration continued to slap civil and criminal charges against a few of the most egregious violators while quietly taking steps to ensure that deeper reforms would fade along with the media spotlight.

Consider the actions of SEC Chief Harvey Pitt in the months following the July 2002 passage of the Sarbanes-Oxley corporate reform act. As we discussed in chapter 3, Pitt came to office as a lawyer whose former clients had included most of the largest auditing firms (as well as Enron, Tyco, and WorldCom), promising to end the threats to consulting fees that the industry faced under Arthur Levitt. But in the aftermath of Enron, WorldCom, and numerous other corporate failures, the public demanded action. The centerpiece of the Sarbanes-Oxley legislation was the creation of an independent accounting oversight board whose duties would include registering public accounting firms; establishing auditing, ethics, and independence standards; and investigating wrongdoing.[1] Five board members, vetted by the SEC, would steer the group's agenda. Through its appointees, the SEC would signal whether or not it was truly dedicated to reducing auditor conflict of interest and restoring integrity to a tainted profession.

Reform advocates were pleased by early rumors that Pitt intended to appoint John Biggs, the well-respected head of pension fund TIAA-CREF, to lead the new board. An outspoken proponent of serious auditing reform, Biggs supported auditor rotation on assignments as well as significant limits on consulting work.[2]

The threat of strong SEC leadership and enforcement led the accounting industry to launch a spirited, behind-the-scenes lobbying campaign against Biggs. Arthur Andersen had dissolved just months before, yet the industry remained desperate to avoid meaningful federal oversight. The firms and their lobbyists protested to members of Congress that the SEC planned to punish them for the actions of a few bad apples—the same argument they had made successfully during Arthur Levitt's crusade against auditor conflicts of interest in 2000. Again the accountants were able to sway legislators over to their side: A number of lawmakers, including the coauthor of the new reform law, Representative Michael Oxley (R-Ohio), reportedly contacted Pitt and urged him to consider dumping Biggs. "[Biggs] was the perfect choice to police the profession," the New York Times wrote, "which is why industry lobbyists and their allies in Congress worked so hard to derail him."[3]

Predictably, John Biggs fell from SEC favor. A familiar name in Washington politics emerged as the front-runner. William Webster, a former FBI and CIA chief with little experience in the financial world, was the SEC's new choice. With his law enforcement credentials, Webster was viewed as a likely practitioner of the "bad apples" approach to corporate scandal, through selected high-profile arrests and prosecutions.

At the height of the battle over the oversight board, a GAO report revealed that one in ten U.S. companies had restated its earnings at least once since 1997. According to the GAO, the pace of revisions, as well as the size of the companies forced to restate their earnings, was growing.[4] Clearly, the fact that 10 percent of U.S. companies had recently faced accounting irregularities suggested that conflicts of interest had infected more than even a few bushels of apples. Nonetheless, the SEC and the Bush administration continued to focus on high-profile prosecutions, presenting the illusion of corporate accountability to the public, while working to ensure that enacted reforms lacked teeth. The SEC's five commissioners, three Republicans and two Democrats, voted for oversight board chair nominees along party lines: Biggs was out, and Webster was in—at least for the moment.

Dissenting with the SEC majority, Commissioner Harvey J. Goldschmid, who voted for Biggs, characterized the process that had selected Webster as inept and flawed. Within a week, evidence emerged to support his claim. Webster revealed to the *New York Times* that, during the vetting process, he had informed Harvey Pitt that he had doubts about his own suitability for the board post. Webster told Pitt that he had sat on the auditing committee of U.S. Technologies, a company facing fraud accusations. "I said if this is a problem, maybe we shouldn't go forward," Webster recalled telling Pitt.[5] It later emerged that U.S. Technologies' three-person audit committee, headed by Webster, had voted to fire the company's auditor, BDO Seidman, after the firm raised concerns about U.S. Technologies' internal financial controls.[6] In dismissing BDO Seidman, Webster appeared to have exhibited the disregard for corporate responsibility and auditor independence that he would be expected to uncover, punish, and eliminate as head of the oversight board. Yet according to Webster, Pitt claimed that SEC staff had looked into the matter and dismissed its significance. Parties involved in the U.S. Technologies case insisted the commission never contacted them; in fact, Pitt failed to inform his fellow commissioners about the scandal. For Pitt, it was the last in a long string of political missteps, each rooted in his overly friendly relationship with the accounting industry. With the Bush administration facing deep embarrassment, Pitt ordered an investigation into his own actions, then quickly resigned, as did Webster.

We cannot know with certainty how Webster would have led the oversight board, had the Bush administration's wishes been fulfilled. But Webster's past does offer some indications. This was not the first time he had been summoned to the national stage to tone down reforms drafted in the aftermath of a predictable surprise, reforms intended as a last defense against similar, future surprises.

In chapter 2, we described the groundswell for aviation security reform that rose up in the aftermath of the 1988 bombing of Pan Am 103 over Lockerbie, Scotland, in which 270 people were killed. Congress prepared a new aviation-security bill based on the recommendations of President George H. W. Bush's blue-ribbon Commission on Aviation Security and Terrorism. Predictably, lobbyists for the Air Transport Association (ATA), the airlines' trade group, strenuously objected to the bill, complaining in particular about an FAA proposal requiring fingerprinting and criminal-background checks of airport workers. The ATA hired William Webster to testify to Congress against the precaution at a 1992 hearing. Webster, a trusted voice on matters of national security, told Congress that he did not feel the proposed security reforms were necessary.[7] Shocked by Webster's lax stance on security, Minnesota Representative James L. Oberstar recalled asking him point-blank: "Would you be taking this position if you were still director of the FBI?"[8] Webster's testimony was successful: In the final bill, background checks were required of airport workers only when a job applicant's record showed a year's gap in employment.[9]

After September 11, 2001, Webster was called upon to defend his 1992 stance against tighter aviation security. "I was trying to keep them from spending money in the wrong place," he claimed.[10] But the former CIA and FBI chief had no history of lobbying for other types of security measures. Rather, his postgovernment work was restricted to paid lobbying to help the airlines keep their security costs low. Given his history, Webster's excuse rang hollow. As head of the accounting oversight commission, would Webster once again have served as a tool of industry, fighting against the tide of reform, with little consideration of the next predictable surprise? We cannot know for sure, but luckily this danger was averted.

The previous two chapters have highlighted the cognitive and organizational causes of predictable surprises. This chapter complements these explanations by examining how political factors exacerbate the likelihood of a predictable surprise. We begin with an overview of the role of special-interest groups in the United States today. Next, we provide a short history of campaign financing and lobbying to clarify how special-interest groups grew into their current destructive form. We document the amazing role of politics in supporting what may well be the biggest killer in the realm of predictable surprises—cigarettes. We examine the exploitation of September 11 and the corruption of homeland security by politicians and corporations, and consider whether we are doomed to repeat the same surprises again and again. Finally, we conclude with concrete proposals aimed at repairing a broken political system.

AN OVERVIEW OF SPECIAL INTERESTS

In this book, we use the term "special interest" to refer to groups that seek gains for their members with little or no concern for the overall effect of their goals on society, even when the gains to their group are much smaller than the total social cost. It's important to note that some groups, such as activist and charitable organizations, have brought great gains to society at large. Thanks to these groups' political influence, Americans can now take numerous beneficial social reforms for granted. Even when groups backing a specific ideology disagree with each other, they are at least fighting for what they believe to be best for all. By contrast, special-interest groups work not to better the lives of the broader citizenry but to improve outcomes for their members. For the sake of a chosen few, special-interest groups impose an undue social burden on everyone—in the form of increased taxes, air pollution, lack of funding for education, and so on.

The term "welfare" tends to conjure up images of poor women accepting government handouts to keep their families fed. In fact, the most generously funded welfare recipients in the United States are not the poor, but America's corporations. Federal money spent on Aid to Families with Dependent Children, food stamps, and Medicaid comes to about $85 billion annually. The total annual cost of corporate tax breaks and subsidies is conservatively estimated at $87 billion per year and may exceed $167 billion.[11]

It is difficult to put a price tag on corporate welfare since its definition can be slippery, depending, for example, on whether tax breaks are included in the equation. Whatever the numbers, when Congress makes its annual budget cuts, it's corporations, not the nation's poor, who find their handouts protected time and time again. A prime example is the "economic stimulus" bill hammered out by Congress in the aftermath of September 11, 2001. Originally drafted to promote economic growth and help out those most hurt by the disaster, the final bill made a mockery of these good intentions. The 2002 Act handed out $114 billion in corporate tax cuts and $97 billion in corporate depreciation write-offs over a three-year period.[12] Just 7 percent of the total bill went toward helping the unemployed; for every dollar allocated to jobseekers, eight dollars went toward corporate tax cuts.[13]

Some economists and politicians justify corporate welfare as an important tool for creating jobs and stimulating the economy. However, neither side of the political spectrum has come up with convincing evidence to support these claims. Indeed, basic economic theory suggests that, overall, society would be better off without subsidies of any kind.[14] Subsidized goods such as cigarettes sell well in part because subsidies keep retail prices artificially low. This may be good for the cigarette makers, but it puts companies that produce nonsubsidized goods at a disadvantage, because consumers spending money on subsidized products have less money left over to buy unsubsidized ones. In addition to distorting the marketplace and violating basic tenets of economic competition, subsidies take funding away from government social programs and contribute to the national debt.

A comprehensive description of all of the U.S. government subsidies currently in effect would fill numerous books. In this chapter, we offer a quick overview of some of the most egregious examples.

Mining

Back in 1872, Congress enacted the General Mining Law to regulate the extraction of nonfuel minerals such as gold, copper, and silver. Intended to promote settlement of the West, the law offered up attractive incentives to prospectors, even by nineteenth-century standards.

One hundred twenty-five years later, the General Mining Law has never been amended. Incredibly, the following provisions remain on the books today:

- Anyone discovering a "valuable mineral deposit" on open public lands has a right to mine it, no matter what other non-mineral values exist.

- Anyone proving the existence of "valuable mineral deposits" may patent (purchase) the land and minerals at 1872 prices— $5 an acre.

- No royalty is required for the value of ores taken from public lands.

- No environmental standards exist.

- No reclamation provisions exist.[15]

Thanks to this law, the government has given away more than $245 billion in mineral reserves through patenting or royalty-free mining.[16] In 2000 alone, almost $1 billion worth of minerals was extracted, with no royalties paid to taxpayers. Indiscriminate mining has done serious, permanent damage to public lands. According to the Environmental Protection Agency, mines have polluted more than 40 percent of the headwaters of Western watersheds. More than 55,000 hardrock mines have been abandoned across the country, at a possible clean-up cost of $32 billion to $72 billion. No wonder the Green Scissors organization, which monitors government waste, has labeled the law the "granddaddy of subsidies."[17]

"I consider [the 1872 General Mining Law] the most egregious thing that the Senate turns its back on every year," former Senator Dale Bumpers has commented.[18] In 2001, Congress renewed a 1994 moratorium on patenting of public lands, but patent applications filed before 1994 may still proceed. Why has Congress tolerated such wastefulness and environmental degradation year after year? The mining industry, a powerful force on Capitol Hill, has blocked reforms to the law time and again, typically by putting strong pressure on congressional members from Western states. In 2000, mining companies spent a total of $7.52 million on lobbying activities.[19] Is the magnitude of mining subsidies surprising? We expect that most people would answer "yes." Yet the continued degradation of the environment remains a predictable outcome. Political forces stand in the way of a lasting solution.

Civil Aviation

In chapter 2, we detailed how the U.S. airline industry successfully resisted government-mandated aviation security improvements for decades, through its lobbying and campaign funding. Evidence suggests that Vice President Al Gore's decision to back away from tough new security proposals in 1997 may have been motivated by his desire to appease the airlines as his 2000 presidential campaign approached.

But Al Gore is hardly the only politician who has catered to the airlines in recent years. Mark Green recounts a similar story in his book *Selling Out: How Big Corporate Money Buys Elections, Rams Through Legislation, and Betrays Our Democracy.* In 1999, the airline industry registered its most dismal performance ever; passengers filed more than twice as many complaints with the Department of Transportation than in 1998, and the number of canceled and delayed flights rose to new heights.[20] In response, Senators John McCain and Ron Wyden introduced the Airline Passenger Fairness Act, which would authorize the Department of Transportation to require the airlines to deliver improved customer service. The airlines donated $200,000 in soft money to the two major political parties during February and March 2000, the months when discussion of the bill was most feverish. Three months later, the airlines dumped $225,000 into party coffers *in one week*—the week leading up to the vote. On June 23, the Senate Commerce Committee voted to water down the McCain-Wyden bill, leaving consumer service in the hands of the airlines' trade group, the ATA. According to Mark Green, "the original legislation was essentially dead."[21] A lone senator—Ron Wyden, the bill's cosponsor—refused, on principle, to sign the bill. Senators and airline executives alike were pleased: Thanks to the new Act, they could trumpet their dedication to "passenger fairness" without incurring the airlines' wrath. The only loser was the average consumer, who faced the same delays, cancellations, and sub-par service as before.

For those familiar with the airlines' long track record for audacity, it came as no surprise that the industry came running to Congress in the aftermath of September 11, 2001—ignoring the fact that their decades of resistance to security improvements had contributed to the attacks. Equally unsurprisingly, Congress gave the industry a $15 billion bailout and passed legislation protecting the airlines from law-suits. It did so *before* addressing the nation's aviation security crisis—which was now impossible to ignore—with passage of the Aviation and Transportation Security Act.[22]

Accounting

In chapter 3, we documented the accounting industry's 2000 fight against then-SEC Chairman Arthur Levitt's proposed conflict-of-interest rules. The clamor against reform was vociferous and backed by significant campaign contributions to the political parties and members of Congress. It was not the first time the accounting industry, by putting its clients' preferences ahead of its own impartiality, contributed to a predictable surprise. In the mid-1990s, the Financial Accounting Standards Board (FASB) proposed closing an accounting loophole that permitted companies to keep from listing stock options on their balance sheets. The FASB viewed the absence of stock options from financial statements as a deceptive distortion of companies' net worth. After all, stock options were an expense, already reported for tax purposes, just like executive salaries; the failure to account for them meant that investors were being kept in the dark about a company's actual liabilities.[23]

The accounting industry and corporate America joined forces to oppose the FASB. High-tech companies in particular had come to depend on stock options to lure and reward executives, and they fore-saw catastrophe if options were put on the books. According to a Merrill Lynch study, expensing stock options would have cut profits among the leading high-tech firms by an average of 60 percent.[24]

In 1994, Senator Joe Lieberman (D-Conn.) organized a nonbind-ing resolution condemning the FASB's proposal.[25] Years later, Arthur Levitt, SEC chair at the time, recalled the stock-option battle in an interview with the PBS show *Frontline*:

There was no question in my mind that campaign contributions played the determinative role in that Senate activity.
Corporate America waged the most aggressive lobbying campaign I think that they had ever put together on behalf of this
issue. And the Congress was responsive to that. . . . All the arguments used by the business community were the ones set
forth by Senator Lieberman in his opposition.[26]

Fearing a congressional backlash would destroy the FASB if the
proposal passed, Levitt urged the Board to back off, a decision he
later regretted.[27]

Connecticut, Lieberman's home state, has a large concentration
of *Fortune* 500 companies, many of which have financially backed his
political campaigns. During the 1993–1994 election cycle, Lieberman received $62,100 in direct contributions from the accounting in-
dustry, making him the fourth-highest Senate recipient.[28] "The insurance companies are in Connecticut and the accountants are heavily
based in Connecticut," commented Sarah Teslik, executive director
of the Council of Institutional Investors, which represents pension
funds. "FASB is in Connecticut. Both Senator Lieberman and Senator [Chris] Dodd have historically been very protective of accountants and very protective of executives, even though they talk a good
liberal Democratic line."[29]

Following the 2002 high-tech bust and financial scandals, accountants and dot-com executives were suddenly viewed as public
enemies, and many of their most staunch supporters felt compelled
to temper that support. For Lieberman in particular, his position on
stock options came back to haunt him. "I continue to believe that
stock options are a good idea," he said at an October 2002 fund-raiser,
as reported by the *New Yorker,* a few months before he announced his
intention to run for president in 2004, "but they were abused by
greedy and unethical executives. That wasn't clear to me then."

Academia

Not all of the organizations that accept handouts from Congress are
for-profit corporations. For fiscal year 2002, Congress earmarked a
record $1.359 billion to fund research projects at more than six hundred

universities and colleges.[30] On the surface, encouraging potential breakthroughs in health, science, and technology may appear to be a worthier cause than supporting the degradation of national lands, or giving tax breaks to companies that will thrive without them. But these research projects can be just as nonsensical and wasteful as legislators' other pet projects.

Traditionally, federal research funding is granted through the National Science Foundation (NSF) and the National Institutes of Health (NIH), each of which has a rigorous review process in which scientists assess the merits of proposed projects and designate funding accordingly. By contrast, when putting together the federal budget each year, members of Congress and their staffs rely on their own judgments when choosing grant recipients. Not only are they lacking in professional expertise but they are strongly influenced by their personal loyalties and by lobbyists hired by universities and colleges.[31] Such academic grants are closely tied to political clout; eight of the ten states that were given the most earmarked funds for 2002 were represented by Congress members who led appropriations committees or subcommittees in 2001, according to the *Chronicle of Higher Education*.[32] For some schools, appealing to Congress for handouts is a better use of time and money than having their faculties write detailed NIH and NSF proposals that may be rejected.

President George W. Bush's budget director, Mitchell Daniels, learned just how entrenched academic earmarks had become in Washington when, in 2001, he challenged Congress on the issue. "Their motto is, 'Don't just stand there, spend something,'" he said, speaking of lawmakers who supported the projects. "This is the only way they feel relevant."[33] Daniels' complaints were met with howls of protest and personal taunts from Congress. Daniels backed off, saying in July 2002, "We think [earmarking] does lead to poor decision-making, but enough said. We do have bigger fish to fry."[34]

And so research projects continue to be funded based on influence rather than merit. In 2002, earmarks included $700,000 given to the University of Idaho to study historic jazz, $250,000 to the University of Georgia to develop pungency tests for Vidalia onions, and $198,000 to the University of Florida to study the cultivation of ornamental fish.[35] While the results of these projects may turn out to be interesting and beneficial, it is impossible for lawmakers and their aides to judge their worthiness with any degree of accuracy. Academic earmarks should be eliminated altogether. If these research projects truly deserve millions of taxpayer dollars, Congress should increase the budgets of the NSF and NIH to accommodate them.

A SHORT HISTORY OF SPECIAL-INTEREST GROUPS IN THE UNITED STATES

The cycle of give-and-take between politicians and special-interest groups in the United States dates back to the early years of the republic. Years before the first presidential election, as Mark Green points out in *Selling Out*, George Washington, in his 1758 campaign for the Virginia House of Burgesses, resorted to questionable tactics to attract votes. Attempting to curry the favor of the landed gentry, the voting public at the time, Washington served them copious amounts of alcohol at lavish parties, a practice known as "swilling the planters with bumbo."[36] Centuries later, all American adults are entitled to cast their vote, yet special-interest groups enjoy levels of favoritism unimaginable in Washington's day.

A contemporary history of special-interest group influence begins in 1971, with the creation of the Federal Election Campaign Act (FECA). Through the Act, Congress attempted to curb runaway campaign spending by establishing contribution and expenditure disclosure rules, limiting the amount of money politicians could spend on their own campaigns, and restricting spending on advertisements. A companion Revenue Act created a system of taxpayer-subsidized elections as a means of leveling the playing field among candidates.

This attempt at reform led indirectly to the greatest election scandal in American history: Watergate. In the grace period that preceded the 1972 FECA requirements, President Nixon's reelection campaign ramped up efforts to raise $10 million in unregulated contributions before the new Act went into effect. As John Gardner, the founder of the campaign-reform group Common Cause, noted in 1973, "The money paid to the Watergate conspirators before the break-in—and the money passed to them later—was money from campaign gifts."[37]

Vowing to clean up federal elections once and for all, Congress bolstered FECA in 1974 by adding new, tighter campaign-funding restrictions, also known as the "Watergate Reforms." The amendments prohibited individuals from contributing more than $1,000 per year to a federal candidate and more than $25,000 collectively per year to all federal candidates. While existing prohibitions on direct contributions from labor unions and corporations were upheld, groups were given the power to create political action committees, or PACs. Segregated organizations that solicit voluntary contributions from individuals, PACs seek to promote and fund candidates and communicate their political views.[38] PACs were limited to donations of $5,000 to a candidate, per election.[39]

The FECA amendments had been in place just one business day when they were challenged in court by interested parties opposed to institutional change.[40] With its 1976 *Buckley v. Valeo* decision, the Supreme Court tore holes in the reforms, primarily by striking down campaign spending limits as a violation of the right of free speech. Asserted the court, "virtually every means of communicating ideas in today's mass society requires the expenditure of money."[41] *Buckley v. Valeo* loosened restrictions on congressional campaign spending, personal campaign spending by candidates, and "independent expenditures," or spending by individuals and PACs not directly linked to a candidate or an election campaign. In addition, by establishing a loophole for the funding of political ads on TV and radio, *Buckley v. Valeo* created a distinction between "express advocacy," or ads that directly encouraged a vote for or against a candidate, and "issue advocacy," or ads that attempt to guide public opinion on candidates or issues without directly encouraging or discouraging a vote for a particular candidate.[42] By freeing up restrictions on the funding of issue ads, *Buckley v. Valeo* has allowed PACs to blanket the airwaves during election seasons with ads that mention—and often ruthlessly attack—a particular candidate by name.

In his dissenting opinion to *Buckley v. Valeo*, Chief Justice Warren Burger sharply criticized the majority's decision to equate money with free speech:

> The Court's piecemeal approach fails to give adequate consideration to the integrated nature of this legislation. . . . All

candidates can now spend freely; affluent candidates, after today, can spend their own money without limit; yet, contributions for the ordinary candidate are severely restricted in amount. . . . I cannot believe that Congress would have enacted a statutory scheme containing such incongruous and inequitable provisions.[43]

As might have been predicted, *Buckley's* loosening of campaign spending limits led to an explosion in PACs. Between 1974 and 1984, the number of PACs grew from 608 to 4009, and their contributions to congressional candidates climbed from $22.6 million to $111.6 million.[44] A clear-cut predictable surprise, the savings-and-loan disaster of the late 1980s is directly linked to the size and influence of PAC dollars. Common Cause estimates that S&L-related PACs and individuals contributed almost $12 million to federal campaigns during the 1980s, in pursuit of industry deregulation. A deregulation bill was promptly passed, giving bankers free rein to gamble away billions in their clients' investments. The American people ended up paying the price of Congress's folly: The S&L bailout cost $500 billion in taxpayer funds.

Five senators saw their reputations permanently tarnished by their cozy relationship with a major player in the S&L industry.[45] The senators, along with the California Democratic Party, had received $1.4 million in campaign contributions from the director of Lincoln Savings and Loan, Charles Keating, and his family and associates. Keating asked the senators to intervene in a federal banking investigation of Lincoln. Working behind the scenes, Senators John McCain (R-Ariz.), Dennis DeConcini (D-Ariz.), Alan Cranston (D-Calif.), John Glenn (D-Ohio), and Don Riegle (D-Mich.) convinced federal regulators to stall their investigation for several months. Lincoln proved to be the biggest failure among the S&Ls, losing $3.4 billion; Charles Keating was sentenced to twelve years in prison for wire and bankruptcy fraud, though he was released early on a technicality. The shame of ethical scandal was enough to convert Senator John McCain to the cause of campaign reform.

Another substantial contribution to the trend of campaign-finance abuse at the end of the twentieth century was the Federal Election Commission's 1978 creation of the "soft money" loophole.[46]

Billed as a means of promoting citizen involvement in elections, soft-money donations were supposed to be designated for state and local party-building activities, such as voter registration drives and ads supporting party platforms rather than a particular candidate. No limits were placed on the amount of soft money that individuals and groups could donate.

Soft money began pouring into presidential campaigns in 1980. The Dukakis campaign first exploited the loophole, followed by the George H. W. Bush campaign. Soft-money donations quickly dwarfed hard-money limits; gifts of $100,000, $250,000, or even $1 million became common. During the 2000 presidential campaign, the Democratic and Republican national party committees raised a record $457 million in soft-money donations, nearly twice the $231 million they raised during the previous presidential election cycle.[47] Fewer than 1 percent of Americans give more than $200 to political candidates; the vast majority of the soft money raised by the national parties is donated by a tiny minority of U.S. citizens and organizations.[48]

With a wink and a nudge, candidates and parties assert that soft money is spent within the limits of the law. In fact, it is federal candidates who solicit soft money, most often from individuals, corporations, and unions that have already reached their annual limit in hard-money donations. These donations are funneled to state parties, which use them for voter registration drives and on "issue ads" that often *do* espouse a viewpoint toward a federal candidate, as any TV viewer during an election season can attest. Though this spending occurs at the state level, federal parties and candidates are pulling the strings.

Many business leaders have grown weary of the never-ending soft-money shakedown. "The business community, by and large, has been the provider of soft money," said Charles Kolb, president of the nonpartisan Committee for Economic Development (CED), a group of influential businesspeople advocating campaign-finance reform. "These people are saying: We're tired of being hit up and shaken down. Politics ought to be about something besides hitting up companies for more and more money."[49] In September 1999, Senator Mitch Mc-Connell (R-Ky.), the most vociferous opponent of campaign-finance reform in Congress, sent CED members a letter accusing them of trying to "eviscerate private sector participation in politics" through "anti-business speech controls."[50] Many of the executives, whose companies were facing important legislation in Congress, took the letters as a form of intimidation. "I think most of the people at CED have figured out just how corrupt the campaign-finance system is, and this letter is just an example of what they already knew," said member Edward A. Kangas.[51]

Within Congress, John McCain and Democrat Russell Feingold of Wisconsin teamed up in 1995 to fight for campaign-finance reform. The original McCain-Feingold bill called for bans on PACs and soft money, a requirement that senatorial candidates raise 60 percent of their money in their home states, and free television time and mail discounts to candidates who consented to spending limits.[52] The senators could not have known that their struggle would become a seven-year odyssey, during which their bold reforms would be watered down drip by drip. The ban on PACs fell away, as did the proposed free air-time and subsidized mailings. In 1997, when it appeared that the weakened bill would pass the Senate, antireformers Majority Leader Trent Lott (R-Miss.) and Mitch McConnell worked furiously to kill it via "poison pill" amendments they knew the bill's supporters could not accept; filibusters buried McCain-Feingold in late 1997.[53] A parallel bill, Shays-Meehan—named for sponsors Christopher Shays (R-Conn.) and Martin Meehan (D-Mass.)—faced similar obstruction in the Newt Gingrich–led House of Representatives, but it eventually passed in 1998. When campaigning for president, George W. Bush criticized McCain-Feingold's ban on soft money as "unilateral disarmament," a reform that would put Republicans at a competitive disadvantage. (In fact, in the 2000 campaign, soft money accounted for about half of the $520 million raised by the Democratic Party, as compared to one-third of the Republican Party's $716 million in contributions.[54])

It was only in 2001, following the 2000 elections, that the reformers finally secured enough votes to push their bills through both houses of Congress. Shays-Meehan won final passage in the House in a 240-to-189 vote; the Senate passed McCain-Feingold in a vote of 60-to-40. By 2002, President Bush had apparently seen the writing on the wall. He signed the bill into law on March 27. Notably, concurrent with McCain-Feingold, the Senate passed a separate resolution that allowed Mitch McConnell to be the lead plaintiff in a court challenge to the bill, and also waived gift rules so that congressional proponents and opponents in future court cases could accept free legal help.[55]

McCain-Feingold contained the following major provisions:

1. Soft-money donations to national parties are banned. State and local parties can collect up to $10,000, but the donations cannot be used to pay for ads supporting federal candidates.

2. Outside groups (including corporations, unions, and non-profits) cannot use soft money to pay for ads that use a candidate's name within thirty days of a primary or sixty days of a general election. Before these deadlines, groups airing such ads (a) cannot coordinate with candidates, (b) must only use hard money, and (c) must abide by reporting and disclosure laws.

3. The limit on hard-money individual donations was raised from $1,000 to $2,000 per election (in part to account for inflation since 1974). Individuals can contribute up to $95,000 per two-year election cycle, indexed for inflation. The limits are extended for candidates running against wealthy, self-financed opponents.[56]

"It is only the beginning," said Russ Feingold after the bill passed. "It is modest reform."[57] Scott Harshbarger, president of Common Cause, agreed: "[McCain-Feingold] is only an incremental step. If this becomes the final step, we have failed." While a clear improvement to the existing system, the reforms are far less significant than those originally proposed by McCain and Feingold back in 1995. They also could have a number of unintended consequences. McCain-Feingold increases individual limits on hard-money donations to presidential candidates but leaves the percentage of federal matching funds given to these candidates constant. For this reason, the law is expected to have the unintended effect of encouraging presidential candidates to opt out of the public financing system and state spending limits.[58] In the tradition of George W. Bush in his 2000 campaign, candidates who opt out of public financing are free to raise as much cash as they like.

McCain-Feingold could bring about a more seismic shift in the nature of political campaigns. Those on both sides of the campaign-finance reform issue expect that the new law will significantly weaken the national parties while strengthening the influence of PACs. While the law prevents political parties from raising and spending soft money, PACs retain the ability to raise as much soft money as individuals, corporations, and unions will give them. PACs can spend soft money aggressively to influence federal elections, as long as they operate independently of campaigns, refrain from explicitly calling for a particular candidate's election or defeat, and cease airing ads within the new deadlines.[59] Already a formidable special-interest bloc, as the new source of big campaign bucks, PACs are poised to become the biggest movers and shakers in Washington—just behind the elected officials themselves, of course. The Democratic and Republican parties will be relegated to the sidelines, the theory goes, left to watch the PACs solicit and spend their growing riches. "The question for the Democratic Party is, how do we capture all of this money out there and keep it in the system?" said Simon Rosenberg, president of the New Democrat Network, speaking openly of his moderate, business-oriented PAC's newfound power in the post–McCain-Feingold era. "We see this as a responsibility to step up to the plate, and as an opportunity."[60]

If the national parties do indeed lose power and influence to PACs, the change will reverberate throughout the election process. Neither the Democratic nor the Republican Party deserves our sympathy. But the fact that their power may be usurped by a new wave of special-interest groups reflects the limitations of McCain-Feingold. Rather than flushing money from the system, the reforms may merely redirect the flow of dollars, with little net change in influence peddling or corruption.

Reformers can take comfort in the fact that PACs are now restricted from running attack ads funded with soft money in the days preceding an election. But even this reasonable measure may not stand. Immediately after the passage of McCain-Feingold, Senator Mitch McConnell launched a court battle to strike down limits on campaign ads and on soft-money fundraising in general.[61] In a May 2, 2003, interim decision on McCain-Feingold, a three-judge federal court issued a lengthy and often conflicted opinion that upheld most of the law, including the ban on the raising and spending of soft money by or for federal candidates as well as the ban on issue ads. At the same time, the court allowed political parties to raise and spend soft money for other purposes, such as funding state and local candidates and financing voter-mobilization drives.[62] The Supreme Court heard the case and, in a 5-to-4 decision in December 2003, upheld all of the major provisions of the campaign-finance law, including the ban on soft money and restrictions on political advertising close to elections. "As the record demonstrates, it is the manner in which parties have sold access to federal candidates and officeholders that has given rise to the appearance of undue influence," Justices John Paul Stevens and Sandra Day O'Connor wrote in the majority opinion.[63] The justices also predicted, pessimistically, "Money, like water, will always find an outlet."[64]

Meanwhile, chipping away at McCain-Feingold is the Federal Election Commission (FEC), which the *New York Times* has called "a supposedly independent body that actually dances like a puppet to the tune of the parties it is supposed to regulate."[65] Charged with enforcing federal election laws, the FEC more often interprets them as loosely as possible. In June 2002, the commission of three Republican and three Democratic political appointees, "most of them proudly hostile to campaign reform," the *Times* asserted, voted 5-to-1 to approve exemptions to the law that seemed designed to ensure that soft money would continue to pour into the political system, especially to state and local political parties. The one dissenter to the final vote, Democratic Commissioner Scott E. Thomas, told some of the other commissioners, "You have so tortured this law, it's beyond silly."[66] Through its rules, the FEC

- allowed the national parties to establish "independent" groups that were still able to raise and spend soft money up until November 16, 2002, the day the law went into effect,

- allowed state and local parties to use restricted soft-money contributions to raise more soft money that could be spent on activities that affect federal elections, such as voter registration and get-out-the-vote drives,

- did not explicitly ban federal candidates and officeholders from "suggesting" that donors make soft-money contributions to state parties, as opposed to "soliciting" soft money, and

- allowed federal candidates to raise soft money at state and local party fund-raisers.[67]

The *New York Times* declared, "These rules and exemptions are nothing less than an abuse of power by unelected bureaucrats pushing a corrupt agenda of favoring special-interest money over the voices and votes of citizens."[68] Senator John McCain and other reformers quickly began a drive to undo the commission's sabotage through legislative action and a lawsuit.[69] But these abuses are a predictable surprise that will continue to explode until our society takes campaign-finance reform more seriously.

LUNG CANCER: THE MOST OBVIOUS PREDICTABLE SURPRISE

The leading preventable cause of death and disease in the United States, tobacco consumption, takes more than four hundred thousand American lives each year.[70] Common sense tells us that if more Americans start smoking, many of them will develop lung cancer, and many of them will die. The fact that almost one in five deaths in the United States is related to smoking still has the power to shock and surprise, as does the fact that, each day in the United States, *three thousand* children under age eighteen become regular smokers. Indeed, the majority of Americans support strong action to alleviate the crisis through actions such as giving the Food and Drug Administration (FDA) authority over the manufacture, marketing, and sale of tobacco products and holding the industry legally accountable for deception and wrongdoing.[71] The FDA and the Medicare program spend tens of millions each year to enforce underage smoking laws and treat those afflicted with lung cancer and emphysema. Groups such as the American Lung Association work diligently to educate children about the dangers of nicotine addiction. In recent years, members of Congress and President Clinton fought several battles to hold the tobacco

industry accountable for deceptively and illegally promoting and prof-
iting from its deadly products. Yet through their political favors, far
more powerful and better-funded special-interest groups thwart
these efforts and the will of the American people.

Thanks to certain members of Congress, tobacco farmers have
come to rely on government quotas as a cushion against falling demand and crop disasters, adding up to tens of millions of dollars in
annual giveaways. In July 1997, Representative Nita Lowey of New
York proposed an amendment to the 1997 Agriculture Department
spending bill to eliminate crop insurance and noninsured crop disaster
assistance for tobacco farmers. One might have expected that a substantial majority of representatives would recognize the absurdity of
supporting farmers to produce a crop that kills more than four hundred
thousand Americans each year—yet the amendment was defeated by
a 216 to 209 vote. The top nine House recipients of campaign contributions from tobacco PACs and employees during 1997 and 1998 *all*
voted against cutting the subsidies. These representatives served to-
bacco-growing states (Kentucky, North Carolina, and Virginia), and
during this one election cycle they received hard-money donations
ranging from $16,900 to $45,000.[72] In the years that followed, tobacco
quotas fell by as much as 50 percent for some farmers. Rather than
treating this fluctuation as a healthy sign of decreased demand for a
deadly crop, Congress chose to prop up the industry with $340 mil-
lion in handouts.[73] More recently, the Agricultural Assistance Act of
2003 passed by Congress and signed by President Bush provided $53
million in direct payments to tobacco growers and quota holders.[74]

In 1998, the major cigarette manufacturers, facing liability suits
with more than forty states for concealing the health risks of cigarettes, sought to cut their losses through a "global settlement." When
Congress took up the matter, however, the companies began to fight
the legislation with all of their lobbying and financial might. The anti-
smoking bill sponsored by Senator John McCain of Arizona would
have settled all of the states' smoking-related lawsuits; it also included a groundbreaking provision to allow the FDA to regulate
nicotine as a drug. With a majority of senators supporting the bill,
Senators Trent Lott and Mitch McConnell organized a filibuster in
June to delay a vote indefinitely. Supporters of the McCain bill fell

three votes short of the sixty needed to end the filibuster; a minority of forty-two senators was able to kill the bill. "What Senator Lott and his colleagues have done today is public health malpractice, plain and simple," declared former U.S. Surgeon General C. Everett Koop following the vote. "Ignoring the advice of every health professional in America, they have chosen to listen only to a handful of television ads and a lot of PAC committees."[75]

McCain attributed the defeat to the tobacco industry's use of "protection money" in the form of campaign contributions.[76] The numbers support his claim. The forty-two senators who opposed the McCain bill had accepted an average of $17,902 in hard money from the tobacco industry in the two years preceding their last elections, while the fifty-seven who supported it had received significantly less, an average of $4,810.[77] Senator McConnell, who so vigorously fought against funding the lawsuit, was the third highest Senate recipient of contributions from tobacco PACs and individuals who work in the industry between 1993 and 1998. McConnell was given $86,575 during this period; only Jesse Helms and Lauch Faircloth, the two senators from tobacco-rich North Carolina, received more ($118,950 and $117,486, respectively, from 1993 to 1998).[78] The industry didn't take any chances in its fight to beat the bill. Lobbying expenses rose from $38.2 million in 1997 to $67.4 million in 1998, moving the tobacco industry up from eighth in spending in 1997 to fourth in 1998. Industry leaders British American Tobacco and Philip Morris ranked first and second as the biggest individual spenders among *all* industries in 1998.

In 1999, President Clinton filed a $20 billion civil suit against the tobacco industry to recoup federal healthcare funds spent treating veterans, federal employees, and Medicare patients afflicted with tobacco-related diseases. In a 215-to-183 vote, a rare defeat for the tobacco industry, the House of Representatives agreed to fund the suit. The 183 dissenting members received seven times more hard money from tobacco interests than those who voted for the bill ($10,715 versus $1,539). When George W. Bush took office the following year, he infuriated antismoking groups by quietly settling the suit with the tobacco industry. Bush had received $6.5 million in soft money and PAC contributions from tobacco interests during his presidential campaign.[79] The tobacco industry pumped a total of $8.3 million into the 2000 federal elections, including $5.2 million in soft-money donations, $2.4 million in PAC contributions, and $670,000 from individual tobacco company executives and employees.[80] The companies and their lobbyists also routinely provide members Congress with favors such as subsidized air travel, funding for political conventions, and fund-raisers.

The lengths to which some members of Congress will go to protect the tobacco industry from reasonable reforms may not be any greater than the steps they take to shelter other business groups, such as airlines, auditors, and farmers of other crops. But one factor distinguishes tobacco from most other U.S. industries: It is a proven killer. How long will the American people allow the federal government to support an industry directly responsible for an ongoing predictable surprise—the deaths of hundreds of thousands of citizens each year?

IS HOMELAND SECURITY BEYOND CORRUPTIBILITY?

In chapters 2 and 3, we offered evidence of the role of special interests in the September 11, 2001, disaster. Americans were horrified to learn of the extent to which the airline industry had succeeded in weakening security standards, leaving the country vulnerable to the 9/11 attacks and, quite possibly, to future ones as well. The need for improved homeland security rose to the forefront of public consciousness. Could it be that, finally, an issue had emerged that was beyond special-interest group maneuverings and party politics?

In November 2002, a full year after its $15 billion bailout of the airline industry, Congress passed legislation creating a new Department of Homeland Security. The bill attracted wide bipartisan support and was heralded as a sweeping and decisive effort to prevent future terrorist surprises. Yet even within the life-and-death realm of homeland security, the hand of special interests appeared. With enthusiasm mounting over this major structural change in U.S. government, two paragraphs mysteriously were added to the bill at the last minute. Did they contain language aimed at protecting borders or airports?

No. Did they counterbalance changes to law enforcement with new civil liberty or First Amendment protections? No. Did the paragraphs have anything remotely to do with the issue of homeland security? No. Instead, the paragraphs protected the pharmaceutical company Eli Lilly and Company from lawsuits filed by parents seeking financial retribution for a Lilly vaccine that has been linked to autism. The provisions limited damages to $250,000 and shifted the burden of payment from Eli Lilly to the U.S. taxpayer.

What does the vaccine have to do with Homeland Security? Absolutely nothing!

The Lilly vaccine contains thimerosal, which in turn contains mercury. In the last few years, there has been rising concern that mercury may cause neurological damage in infants. While studies are still inconclusive, the American Academy of Pediatrics and the Public Health Service have urged drug companies to stop using thimerosal.[81] We do not claim to have the medical and legal expertise to render a decision on whether the vaccine is dangerous. But we do know that Congress is the wrong place for our society to decide the merits of the case. The fact that elected officials used homeland security legislation to protect a drug company that is alleged to be poisoning children is not only troubling, but disrespects those who lost their loved ones on September 11.

Perhaps even more disturbing than the paragraphs themselves was the secrecy behind them. Earlier in 2002, Senator Bill Frist (R-Tenn.) attempted to sneak legal protection for Lilly into a bill whose primary objective was to increase the availability of vaccines. A spokesperson for former House Majority Leader Dick Armey (R-Tex.), a leader in the fight against campaign-finance reform, told the *Washington Post* that the White House had requested the insertion of the Lilly protection in the homeland security bill. The White House claims to have no idea where the provision came from.

It is impossible to say with certainty who slipped the Lilly protection into the bill. But it may be relevant that President George H. W. Bush, President George W. Bush's father, was on the board of Eli Lilly in the 1970s. It may be relevant that Mitch Daniels, the White House's budget director, is a former Lilly executive, or that Sidney Taurel, Lilly's chairperson, is an adviser to George W. Bush. It may also be relevant that Eli Lilly donated $1.6 million to political candidates in 2002, more than any other drug company.[82] It may also be notable that in January 2004, months after the Lilly provision came to light, personnel from Lilly were included in a group of nearly seventy Republican lobbyists and executives hand-picked to attend a closed-door "State of the Union Briefing" just hours before President Bush delivered his speech to the nation.[83]

It could be that these cozy relationships, financial favors, and backstage passes have nothing to do with the Lilly protection. It's impossible to know for sure, since the politicians who finalized the legislation have failed to come forward with the truth. We might suspect that the beneficiary of this perk, Eli Lilly, would know something about the origin of those two paragraphs. But Lilly spokesperson Rob Smith claimed, "It's a mystery to us."[84]

The final vote for the Homeland Security bill was overwhelmingly positive and bipartisan. But congressmen from both sides of the aisle were offended by the gross corruption of the system embodied by the Lilly paragraphs. "This language will primarily benefit large brand-name pharmaceutical companies," said John McCain (R-Ariz.). It is hard to believe that corruption and the creation of new predictable surprises would be so blatantly spelled out in a piece of legislation created to cope with 9/11, but the evidence is impossible to ignore.

THE FALSE SEARCH FOR A FEW BAD APPLES

What caused the fall of Enron? Was it a system that rewarded executives for claiming profits that didn't exist? Was it the failure of the U.S. government to require the expensing of stock options, as any reasonable accounting analysis would demand? Was it Arthur Anderson's desire to overlook corrupt accounting to order to sell auditing services and even more lucrative consulting services? Or was it a case of a few bad apples taking advantage of the system? The answer is obvious: all of the above. Yet politicians have focused only on the last cause, and in doing so, they have revealed their own inherent biases.

Most complex failures, including September 11 and the fall of Enron, are caused by a confluence of factors. Occasionally, the media picks up on multiple causation; such was the case with the storm that hit the coast of Massachusetts in October 1991 and inspired Sebastian Junger's book *The Perfect Storm*, in which a number of human decisions interacted with three distinct weather patterns. More often, the human mind wraps around a single cause. As noted earlier, in debates about high rates of teenage pregnancy, the right wing argues that the cause is promiscuity, while the left claims that the cause is a lack of access to birth control.[85] In fact, most reasonable people would agree that that there is no biological mystery here: Teenage pregnancy results from promiscuity in the absence of birth control. Nonetheless, the partisans rally around single-cause explanations.

After the fall of Enron, Americans demanded to know how and why the disaster occurred. The clamor for an explanation only increased as other firms followed the same path. Predictably, following the lead of the accounting industry, most elected officials responded by pointing to a single cause: corruption. If you blame the system, that means it needs to be reformed, which could mean sacrificing campaign dollars and other perks. Much simpler, and politically safer in the short term, just to blame the bad apples.

Nervousness about campaign funding is not the only reason our leaders acquiesce, time and again, to the desires of special-interest groups. In fact, the human mind naturally attributes blame to individuals rather than to complex interactions within a system.[86] Systems are remote and difficult to pin down. Villains, whether ruthless killers such as Osama bin Laden or symbols of corporate greed like Jeffrey Skilling, are much more likely to attract public attention. The problem is that, even if we can find and punish the villains, the underlying problem will remain. Systemic change is necessary to eliminate the basic causes of any predictable surprise. We have no problem with locking up the bad apples. In fact, we hope to see more bad apples put away. Rather, we oppose the simpleminded, politically expedient quest for one explanation for any given problem.

In December 2002, whistleblowers Sherron Watkins, Coleen Rowley, and Cynthia Cooper were named *Time* magazine's "Persons of the Year" for the huge professional and political risks they took in exposing the corruption and incompetence of Enron, the FBI, and WorldCom, respectively. *Time* lauded these women for reminding us what "American courage and American values are all about."[87] In a letter in the summer of 2001, months before the company's collapse, Enron Vice President Watkins warned Chairperson Ken Lay about financial wrongdoing and the possibility of a meltdown. Coleen Rowley, an FBI staff attorney, wrote to FBI Director Robert Mueller about the national bureau's failure to follow up on the Minneapolis office's suspicions about Zacarias Moussaoui, later indicted as a 9/11 coconspirator. And Cynthia Cooper, vice president of internal audit at WorldCom, blew the cover on fraud at her company by alerting the board to the executive cover-up of $3.8 billion in losses. All three risked their careers to provide incontrovertible evidence of flawed decision-making in their organizations.

Sherron Watkins has been heralded as a hero and a patriot for her courage in blowing the whistle on Enron. So why isn't Kenneth Lay in jail? Surely wrapping up the evidence on an executive who oversaw massive corruption should be an easy task, particularly for a president eager to crack down on "bad apples." But it seems that even when it comes to dealing with bad apples, the Bush administration has its limits. Kenneth Lay, after all, was a longtime Bush family friend and a key adviser to Vice President Dick Cheney; *The Nation* magazine has documented how Lay helped craft many of the key policy recommendations for the Bush-Cheney energy task force. Cheney himself went to extraordinary lengths to hide records of the Bush energy policy from the American public, causing the GAO to take the unprecedented step of suing the executive branch to obtain information. (The GAO dropped the suit after a U.S. District Court judge ruled that the agency lacked sufficient grounds to compel Cheney to release the records.) Kenneth "Kenny Boy" Lay and Enron were the largest contributors to George Bush's campaign. Lay was one of the first to become a Bush "Pioneer" by raising $100,000; he also held a $21 million fundraiser for Bush (a record at the time), made Enron jets available to the Bush family and campaign aides, and helped to fund the 2000 Republican convention, the vote recount in Florida, and Bush's inauguration.[88] For those most cynical about the link between money and power in Washington, it was hardly a surprise that former Enron employees, advisers, and consultants were given top leadership roles in the Bush White House, including chief economic advisor (Lawrence

Lindsey), U.S. trade representative (Robert Zoellick), chairman of the SEC (Harvey Pitt), and secretary of the Army (Thomas E. White). (Lindsey and Pitt were both forced to resign in 2002, their ineptitude having become an embarrassment to Bush. White resigned in 2003.)

Searching for a few bad apples may be a fine way to appease the public, but it is no way to protect against future predictable surprises. When you can't manage to prosecute the worst apples in the barrel, you reduce your credibility and fail the public on all counts. To avoid repeating past failures, we must look more closely at both the bad apples and the system.

WHAT NEXT?

The United States is the world leader in many spheres. It is second to none in the development and proliferation of technology and medical breakthroughs. Its institutions of higher education are admired globally, and its system of democracy has been widely imitated with great success. Yet many nations have advanced far beyond us in the pursuit of Lincoln's ideal of "government of the people, by the people, and for the people."[89] In the United States, elections and elected officials have been bought and sold at levels unmatched by the rest of the democratic world. The corporate financial scandals that exploded in recent years are a symptom of this disease. Behind the specific government systems that allowed these predictable surprises to erupt lies a corrupt political process.

In the United States, grumbling about corruption in Washington is practically a national pastime. So why has the American public consistently overlooked the value of reforming its elections? Why did so few heed the rallying cry of 2000 presidential candidates John McCain or Bill Bradley for campaign-finance reform? One reason is that campaign-finance reform is an issue that only indirectly influences the vivid concerns of voters. That is, campaign-finance reform is viewed as a boring issue, too abstract and indirect to trigger passion in the voting public. A 1997 Pew Research Center poll found that just 28 percent of American voters believed finance reform should be an important campaign issue, listing it sixteenth on their list of priorities, well behind goals that would have an immediate and vivid effect on one's community, such as reducing crime and improving public schools.[90] Voters will insist that they want honest elections and politicians who pay more attention to their constituents' opinions than to PAC donations. Yet campaign-finance reform has not been able to compete for the public's attention in the way that direct issues such as education, welfare, social security, and prescription drugs can. Ironically, through their influence on all of these issues and many more, special-interest groups injure citizens on all of these fronts. But quite predictably, human judgment focuses on vivid issues and pays scant attention to boring ones. Child abduction by strangers became a vivid issue following the violent kidnapping of Elizabeth Smart in 2002, and rightfully so. Yet the media and the public alike continue to pay scant attention to the thousands of children who are quietly abducted by relatives and acquaintances each year. Paradoxically, the issues affected by the lack of campaign-finance reform overshadow campaign-finance reform itself in the competition for public attention.

Another reason that campaign-finance reform fails to attract much public notice is that it is a process issue, not an outcome issue. Campaign-finance reform affects the process of politics, which in turn affects all other issues. To value campaign-finance reform, people need to think through this process. But psychological research suggests that people do not intuitively think multiple steps ahead.[91] Negotiators often fail to think about how their opponents will respond to their next move, and they fail to develop contingency plans in the event that the other side rejects their proposal. The skill of thinking multiple steps ahead may be a necessary prerequisite of valuing campaign-finance reform.

As we described in chapter 4, people generally require vivid evidence of the need for change. The corporate collapses of 2001 and 2002 were caused in part by broken systems that were in place as a result of the corruption of the political process. As it became clear that Enron and other dishonest companies had profited from their ties to elected officials, the drumbeat for reform grew louder, and the McCain-Feingold bill finally passed into law. Of course, the bill had been significantly watered down to make it palatable to politicians who depend on the existing system, and it has been further eroded by the FEC.

What other reforms are necessary to clean up the system? In *Selling Out,* Mark Green advocates four reforms that would "restore our electoral democracy by elevating voters over donors." First, he supports the instatement of meaningful spending limits through the overturning of *Buckley* v. *Valeo,* which loosened contribution limits by distinguishing them from expenditure limits. While Green acknowledges the difficulty of persuading the Supreme Court to reverse one of its decisions, he points out that it did so memorably in 1954, when *Brown* v. *Board of Education* overturned *Dred Scott.* Green sees signs that the current Court recognizes the mistakes of *Buckley* and may soon act to correct them.

Second, Green supports public financing of congressional elections, on the grounds that it "enhances speech, promotes competition, levels the playing field, and reduces the reliance on special-interest money." For such "Clean Money" laws to achieve widespread support and effectiveness, Green advocates a generous matching rate of 4-to-1 financing, such that each proposed maximum individual contribution of $250 would be matched by $1,000 in public funds. Candidates would face "reasonable qualifying thresholds"—enough money raised from residents of their districts to prove their viability. They would also be subject to inflation-adjusted spending limits for the primary and general elections, which would have to be carefully calibrated to encourage underfunded candidates to enter the race and to keep deep-pocketed candidates from opting out of the voluntary system. Green also advocates reducing funding inequalities between wealthy, self-funded candidates and their poorer opponents; subjecting PACs to the types of contribution limits placed on individuals and other groups; imposing "fund-raising blackouts" that would shorten election seasons; and tax refunds for small campaign contributions to encourage citizen participation and increase the pool of matching funds.

Third, like John McCain and other reform advocates, Green seeks an overhaul of the FEC. Fred Wertheimer, former president of Common Cause, advocates replacing the FEC's six commissioners with a single head who could operate as an independent enforcer.[92] Green would increase the FEC's budget, reinstate its ability to conduct random audits of political campaigns (a responsibility revoked by Congress in 1979), increase the FEC's ability to seek out and eliminate loopholes (rather than promulgating them), change the number of commissioners from an even to an odd number to eliminate deadlock, and improve the selection process to ensure the appointment of qualified and experienced candidates.[93]

Fourth, like Russ Feingold, Green supports one of the reforms that fell by the wayside during McCain-Feingold's long journey: giving candidates free or reduced-cost television advertising time as a means of reducing campaign fundraising.[94] Under the provisions of the Federal Communication Act of 1934, broadcasters are obligated to serve "the public interest, convenience, and necessity" in exchange for their free federal licenses.[95] Television and radio networks have never met this responsibility. Green puts forth Walter Cronkite's 1982 market-based proposal of free broadcast vouchers that could be granted to all qualifying candidates and traded like commodities to ensure efficient distribution. The vouchers should be limited to candidates who accept spending limits, Green says. He also believes that those candidates who accept public funds should be required to debate their opponents.

While Green offers a number of concrete strategies to reduce the political barriers to surprise prevention, these ideas more broadly serve as a call for executives to ask themselves, "What are the political barriers to surprise prevention in our organization?" In most organizations, one reason that executives fail to respond to predictable surprises is that some group of individuals will thwart an effective response in order to protect their self-interest. For example, we view the failure of many corporations to expense employees' stock options on their balance sheets as a predictable surprise.

A core problem is that the decision-makers who must to act to prevent the surprise are benefited, at least in the short-term, by the failure to expense stock options. Preventing predictable surprises requires changing traditional approaches to problems, and change inevitably creates winners and losers. Yet when the gains far exceed the losses, change should occur. The challenge to leaders is to block the destructive political behavior of those who will be negatively affected by the change—even if these people are the leaders themselves. In addition, the challenge is for leaders to be courageous, and to stand up to special interests. We continue to believe that Clinton and Gore would have easily won reelection in 1996 without the support of the airline industry, that they should have had the courage and vision to make the needed changes, and to communicate these changes effectively to the public.

PART III

Preventing
Predictable
Surprises

In chapters 7, 8, and 9, we develop a prescriptive framework that focuses on three core surprise-avoidance tasks: recognition, prioritization, and mobilization (RPM). To prevent predictable surprises, leaders must enhance the capacity of their organizations to recognize emerging threats, prioritize action, and mobilize available resources to mount an effective preventative response. Leaders must begin with an assessment of the adequacy of their organizations' systems for recognition, prioritization, and mobilization using the process illustrated in the following figure.

To illustrate the application of this framework, think of a significant surprise that recently erupted in your organization or another one with which you are very familiar. Ask yourself the following questions:

The Recognition-Prioritization-Mobilization Model

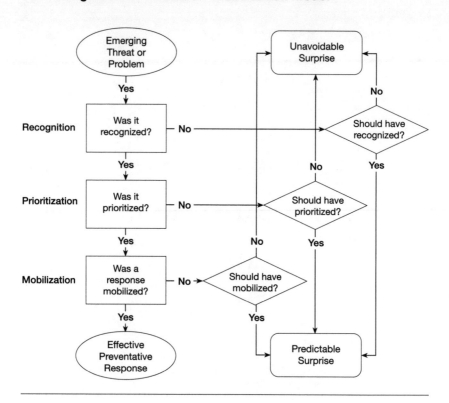

- *Recognition.* Should the threat have been recognized?

- *Prioritization.* If recognized, was the emerging threat prioritized appropriately?

- *Mobilization.* If prioritized, did the organization mobilize effectively to deal with the problem?

As we have stressed throughout this book, not all surprises are predictable. If a preventable problem was not foreseeable, or if leaders did all they reasonably could to prevent it, then they should be held blameless. At the same time, when a surprise is foreseeable and preventable, we want to hold leaders' feet to the fire. This means setting a standard for the "responsible leader" that is akin to the "reasonable person" in legal negligence cases. Could a responsible leader have been reasonably expected to recognize, prioritize, and mobilize to avoid the problem? If yes, then a serious failure of leadership materially contributed to a predictable surprise. If no, then we let the leader off the hook.

This is a high standard. To avoid predictable surprises, leaders must strive to identify the weakest links in their organizations and work to strengthen systems for recognizing emerging problems, setting appropriate priorities, and mobilizing effective preventive responses.

A prerequisite for surprise prevention is the personal involvement of the organization's leaders in providing focus, energizing the organization, exercising judgment, and having the courage to take unpopular stands. But while strong personal leadership is essential, it is not sufficient. The organization itself must be made more responsive and resilient.

In the three chapters that follow, we explore what it takes to prevent predictable surprises. We focus, in turn, on the barriers to successfully recognizing, prioritizing, and mobilizing against surprises, and we discuss proven techniques that leaders can employ to strengthen their organizations' capacity to perform these critical tasks.

7

Recognition

Identifying Emerging Threats Earlier

I n the spring of 2000, Johnelle Bryant, an employee at the Homestead, Florida, office of the U.S. Department of Agriculture, came face to face with Mohammed Atta, the leader of the 9/11 Al Qaeda terrorists.[1] Bryant processed applications for loans to support the regional agricultural industry, and Atta had shown up with a request for a $650,000 loan. "He wanted to finance a twin engine, six-passenger aircraft," Bryant remembered after the September 11 attacks. "He said he was an engineer, and he wanted to build a chemical tank that would fit inside the aircraft, and take up every available square inch of the aircraft, except for where the pilot would be sitting. And run the spray nozzles along the wingspan. And use it as both a crop duster plane, and as a charter plane."

When Bryant informed Atta that she could not simply hand him $650,000 in cash, he at first charged discrimination and then became threatening. Pointing to an old black safe behind her, he asked, "What would prevent [me] from going behind your desk and cutting [your] throat, and making off with the millions of dollars of cash in that safe?" After Bryant informed Atta that there was no money in the safe and that she was trained in karate, he backed down, and then asked her where she got her training.

Noticing an aerial photograph of Washington, D.C., that Bryant's colleagues had given her, Atta offered to buy it. "He said it was one of the best he'd seen of Washington. . . . He started throwing money on my desk. . . . I said it was a gift . . . that it was not for sale," Bryant recounted. Atta then reportedly began quizzing Bryant about major Washington landmarks: "He asked about the Pentagon and the White House, and I pointed them out. . . . And the Capitol, the photograph encompasses all that as well as the Smithsonian and the monuments too. . . . He also told me he wanted to go to New York and visit the World Trade Center." Bryant recalled that Atta was quite open about his background and affiliations, including living in Afghanistan and the engineering training he had received in Germany. "He mentioned Al Qaeda," Bryant said. "He mentioned Osama bin Laden. And when he mentioned it, I didn't have a clue what he was talking about. . . . Could have been Obi-Wan Kenobi for all I knew."

There was, of course, no way that Johnelle Bryant could have predicted the devastating attacks that Mohammed Atta would launch more than a year later on Washington and New York. In the years before September 11, 2001, few Americans were aware of the threat posed by Osama bin Laden and his Al Qaeda terrorist network. It is only in retrospect that Bryant was able to "connect the dots." Her story is not one of individual negligence. Rather, it is but one of many examples of information possessed by people in the U.S. government that, collectively, could have revealed the identity and intent of the 9/11 attackers in time to prevent the attacks. That this information was never assembled and integrated illustrates the critical role that individual and organizational factors can play in preventing the recognition of predictable surprises.

Some disasters can't be foreseen. No one, for instance, could have predicted in the 1960s that the HIV virus would jump the species barrier from monkeys to infect humans on such a vast scale. But in examining the unforeseen disasters that have stricken organizations, we have found that the vast majority should have been recognized. Recognition failures are caused by some combination of the cognitive and organizational vulnerabilities discussed in chapters 4 and 5. Cognitive biases may blind individuals to emerging threats, while organizational factors may prevent the necessary integration of information until it is too late.

To avoid recognition failures, leaders must strive to mitigate the impact of biases and to ensure that organizational resources are appropriately allocated. One way to determine whether a recognition failure occurred is to assess whether leaders marshaled adequate resources to scan the environment for emerging threats. That means determining whether leaders did a reasonable job of directing the organization to gather, analyze, and interpret available data. If not, the organization's systems for recognizing emerging threats must be strengthened.

INDIVIDUAL RECOGNITION FAILURES

Individual recognition failures occur when organizational leaders remain oblivious to an emerging threat or problem. Positive illusions, self-serving biases, and the tendency to discount the future may prevent people from acknowledging that a problem is emerging. If their state of denial is strong enough, they may not even "see" the storm clouds gathering. Even if they do, they may downplay the likelihood and significance of ominous developments.

Predicting the September 11 Attacks

In her testimony before Congress, Eleanor Hill, the staff director of the Joint Senate-House Inquiry into the cause of the 9/11 attacks, noted that the Intelligence Community (IC) in the United States was surprised by the location of the Al Qaeda attacks—striking within the United States rather than at overseas interests—but not by their timing.[2] Hill's congressional testimony documents a growing wave of information pointing to an imminent attack in the summer of 2001. But there was a widespread belief within the IC that bin Laden was unlikely to strike within the United States and, consequently, that an attack would be directed at foreign targets.[3]

This belief strongly shaped the IC's scanning and threat-assessment activities, contributing to its failure to appreciate the implications of unfolding domestic events. As Director Hill noted at several points in her testimony, this belief persisted in spite of strong evidence that bin Laden wanted to attack the United States.[4] Why didn't the IC anticipate the domestic threat? There is evidence that noise, a key contributor to recognition failures, played a role in masking the threat of a U.S. attack. Hill noted in her congressional testimony that reports of domestic threats were lost amid a much greater volume of reports pointing to attacks on overseas targets.[5]

The GE-Honeywell Merger

Recognition failures can plague even the most seasoned executives. After European Commission (EC) regulators refused to approve General Electric's $42 billion acquisition of Honeywell in 2001, GE CEO Jack Welch was quoted as saying, "You are never too old to be surprised." Welch is a famously hard-nosed executive, and if anyone could be expected to do his homework, it would be him. But was Welch correct in viewing the decision as a true surprise, an event that couldn't have been foreseen? The evidence suggests he was not. *The Economist* reported at the time that there were many warning flags of the EC's intent to scuttle the deal.[6] For some time, the magazine pointed out, a philosophical gap had been widening between Europe and the United States over the regulation of mergers. And Mario Monti, the recently appointed head of the EC's competition authority, was widely believed to be looking for an opportunity to assert European independence.

It seems that Welch was surprised because he simply didn't recognize critical environmental threats to the deal. According to the Associated Press, when Welch and his counterpart at Honeywell, Michael Bonsignore, were rushing to close the deal (United Technologies was also eager to acquire Honeywell), they "reportedly never held initial consultations with their Brussels lawyers who specialize in European competition concerns."[7] Welch appeared to assume that the merger would sail through the antitrust review. But while it did pass easily through the U.S. review—no doubt further reinforcing his confidence—it ran aground in Europe. Had Welch recognized the potential for a negative decision ahead of time, he almost certainly would have managed the merger negotiations and antitrust consultations differently—and Honeywell might well be a part of GE today.

ORGANIZATIONAL RECOGNITION FAILURES

While individuals may recognize key pieces of the puzzle, failures of environmental scanning and information integration may prevent the organizations they belong to from perceiving dire emerging threats. As we discussed in chapter 5, organizations often possess all of the information they need to recognize emerging problems, but fail to "connect the dots" among employees and departments. Information systems may not be adequately resourced, or they may not be tuned to the domains where the predictable surprises lurk. Alternatively, different divisions of an organization may possess separate pieces of the puzzle, while the organization as a whole lacks the personnel and systems necessary to integrate and distill them into actionable insights.

Predicting the September 11
Terrorist Attacks, Revisited

There is considerable evidence that systemic and well-recognized organizational weaknesses contributed to rendering the United States vulnerable to a large-scale domestic attack by Al Qaeda.[8] In particular, resource constraints appear to have reduced the effectiveness of IC scanning.[9] As Hill notes, "A lack of counterterrorism resources has been a repeated theme. . . . I believe that the Staff, the CIA, and the FBI are all in agreement that the resources devoted full time to Al Qaeda prior to September 11 paled by comparison to the levels dedicated to that effort after the attacks. As a CIA officer testified . . . both CIA and FBI personnel working on Bin Laden were 'simply overwhelmed' by the workload prior to September 11." While the IC established high-level priorities, various agencies appear to have been devoted insufficient resources to ensuring that integration occurred.[10]

Barriers to effective information integration also severely impeded IC efforts to anticipate the 9/11 attacks. Given the large number of agencies (more than a dozen) involved and the complexity of the task of collecting and analyzing intelligence, it would be surprising if information integration were not a major challenge for the IC. Unfortunately, this challenge was far from being met. As Representative Jane Harman (D-Calif.), a member of the House Permanent Select Committee on Intelligence, bluntly put it, "To date, the term 'Intelligence Community' has been an oxymoron. The community is really a collection of stovepipes working separately—often in conflicting or self-interested ways."[11] Former Congressman and House Intelligence Committee Chairman Lee Hamilton echoed this theme in his testimony: "[The term] 'Intelligence Community' is intriguing. It demonstrates how decentralized and fragmented our intelligence capabilities are."[12]

Joint Inquiry Director Hill's testimony likewise reveals the surprising extent to which integration failures within key agencies prevented them from "connecting the dots" among pieces of information concerning the 9/11 hijackers themselves.[13] These problems are starkly illustrated by the handling of the so-called Phoenix memo, one of three key developments in the United States in the months prior to the 9/11 attacks that were not connected to each other or placed in the broader context of escalating reports of threats.[14]

The "Phoenix memo" refers to an electronic communication sent on July 10, 2001, by a special agent in the FBI's Phoenix division to headquarters outlining his concerns that terrorists were being trained at U.S. flight schools.[15] The agent noted that there were an "inordinate number of individuals of investigative interest" attending this type of training in Arizona. He further speculated that the training reflected an effort to establish a corps of individuals who could be drawn upon to conduct terrorist activity in the future.[16] The memo requested that key units in Headquarters—the RFU [Radical Fundamentalist Unit] and UBLU [Usama bin Ladin Unit]—implement four specific recommendations:

- Headquarters should accumulate a list of civil-aviation university/colleges around the country.

- FBI offices should establish liaisons with the schools.

- Headquarters should discuss the Phoenix theories with the intelligence community.

- Headquarters should consider seeking authority to obtain visa information on individuals seeking to attend flight schools.[17]

Unfortunately, the Phoenix agent's memo did not result in any action. The communication did not raise any alarms at FBI headquarters or in the New York office, which had key responsibility for terrorist investigations. About a week after its receipt, lower-level headquarters personnel determined that no follow-up action was warranted. No managers at FBI headquarters took part in that decision or even saw the communication before September 11, 2001.[18] According to Hill, the personnel who received the memo "were not aware of the prior reporting on terrorist groups sending aviation students to the United States and did not know that FBI headquarters had undertaken a systematic effort in 1999 to identify Middle Eastern flight students in the United States."[19]

According to FBI personnel interviewed by Joint Committee staff, this lapse reflected a systemic problem of information sharing. Director Hill noted that "agents often will only be familiar with cases on their own squad and will not know about investigations on other squads." She further noted that the incident "illustrates the Intelligence Community's strengths and weaknesses."

The FBI field agent in Phoenix perceived, amidst a profusion of cases, that terrorists could use the well-developed system of flight-training education in the United States to prepare an attack within the country. The agent understood that it was necessary to go beyond individual cases and to undertake an empirical analysis broader than the geographic limits of a single field office. He submitted his hunch to FBI headquarters, where, for a variety of reasons, it generated almost no interest. First, no one gleaned from the FBI's own records that others at the Bureau had previously expressed concerns about possible terrorists at U.S. flight education institutions. Second, the FBI had not devoted significant effort to the task of anticipating future threats. Third, the highest levels of the IC had not communicated effectively to its personnel the critical importance of analyzing information in light of the growing awareness of an impending terrorist attack in the summer of 2001. Finally, FBI management did not perceive the potential value of alerting others within the agency to the danger perceived by the field agent.[20]

Robert Shapiro and Monsanto

The corporate world is by no means immune to recognition failures. A leading life-sciences company, Monsanto suffered a near-death experience in the late 1990s as the result of systemic recognition failures on the part of CEO Robert Shapiro and his advisers. Betting the company on a "life sciences" vision, these top executives sought to pursue the vast commercial opportunities of genetically modified organisms (GMOs). In doing so, they sold or spun off Monsanto's traditional chemical businesses and moved aggressively to acquire seed companies.

Shapiro convinced himself that producing and marketing genetically modified (GM) food would not only benefit his company but benefit society by reducing hunger worldwide. Yet he and his U.S. advisers failed to devote significant attention to the goal of winning public acceptance of genetically modified foods.

This was an especially dangerous mistake in Europe, which was still reeling from mad cow disease, reports of dioxin-contaminated chicken, and numerous other food-related concerns. Since 1980, Europe had been protesting the use of hormones to promote lean-muscle development in U.S. beef exported to the continent. In 1989, the European Union (EU) banned the import of any hormone-treated beef, despite the use of similar and even less safe hormones among domestic producers. As early as 1993, a survey of more than twelve thousand EU residents showed that consumers were wary of biotechnology, and that the media was the public's main source of information about novel foods and GMOs. A survey conducted for Britain's Department of Trade and Industry in the spring of 1999 found that only one in a hundred Britons thought that genetically modified food was good for society, and that relatively few trusted the government to make scientific decisions on this issue on their behalf. Consumers were more likely to trust consumer groups, environmental groups, and doctors than the government on this matter.[21]

In 1998, after winning EU regulatory approval for its genetically modified soybeans, Monsanto launched a $5 million advertising campaign aimed at educating European consumers about genetically modified foods. In one open letter, Monsanto wrote:

> Biotechnology is relatively new to the European consumer, even though we have been doing research in it for over twenty years. . . . Today, the benefits of biotech agriculture are primarily to farmers and the environment. . . . Tomorrow, biotech agriculture will provide more food for the developing world's increasing population more affordably.[22]

Such missives infuriated many European consumers, who felt the company was talking down to them and brushing aside their concerns. Yet Monsanto plowed ahead with its product launch.

The result was a public relations disaster. The British food retailer Iceland removed GM products from its shelves in early 1999 and announced that it would distribute only GM-free private-label foods—a move some felt was taken out of greater concern for market share than for consumer health. The major British food chains—Tesco, Co-op, and Sainsbury—soon followed Iceland's lead. Because 60 percent of products on supermarket shelves contained some form of genetically modified products, the companies' stance created a huge demand for conventional cereals and soybeans. Europe went from importing 27 percent of the U.S. soybean meal exports in 1998 to 7 percent in 1999.[23]

By the end of April 1999, Unilever, Nestlé, and Cadbury had all announced that they would phase out their genetically modified products. By late 1999, Deutsche Bank had advised its investors to divest their shares of GM-related companies. Eighty-two percent of Germans who were aware of genetically modified foods said they would be less likely to purchase such products than conventional ones; more than 75 percent of the French agreed. One-third of Britons saw "no advantages" to the foods, citing safety and health concerns.[24]

Monsanto's failure to account for the interests and opinions of its European consumers was surprising, but also quite predictable. One consultant who tried to help Monsanto reach an understanding with its critics later said, "We have never come across a company where the barriers were so strong. . . . [T]here is a barrier to really listening to what people are saying."[25] CEO Shapiro had no effective intelligence-gathering system that would help him predict the stance and behavior of European consumers, and therefore no warning of the approaching storm.

By focusing almost exclusively on technical and strategic challenges and overlooking the difficult work of winning hearts and minds, Shapiro ultimately lost his company. He was forced to sell Monsanto to Pharmacia & Upjohn, which was interested only in Monsanto's pharmaceutical division, valuing its agricultural biotechnology operations essentially at zero.[26]

SURPRISING SUCCESSES

Given the high levels of noise in the environment, the blindness and inertia engendered by cognitive barriers, and the weaknesses of organizations, one might conclude that individuals and organizations have little chance of ever recognizing and avoiding novel threats. Fortunately, this is not the case. Many far-seeing leaders and effective organizations have successfully recognized and avoided predictable surprises. Two stories, one from public policy and the other from the business realm, illustrate how this goal can be achieved.

Cooperative Nuclear Threat Reduction

Following the collapse of the Soviet Union in 1989, nuclear weapons, materials, and expertise sited in former Soviet republics risked being scattered to the winds. Recognizing the potentially catastrophic consequences of such a dispersal, Russian President Mikhail Gorbachev asked the U.S. government for assistance in dismantling Soviet nuclear weapons. Guided by intelligence assessments of the threat, the administration of President George H. W. Bush put forward a broad proposal to assist in the location, dismantlement, and destruction of these weapons in the former Soviet republics.

The result was the Cooperative Threat Reduction Program, enacted by Congress as the Soviet Nuclear Threat Reduction Act of 1991. Named for its sponsors, Senators Sam Nunn (D-Ga.) and Richard Lugar (R-Ind.), the Nunn-Lugar legislation asserted that assisting the Soviet Union and its potential successor states would advance the national security interest of the United States by addressing the threat of nuclear weapons proliferation. Experts assessed this threat as comprising three elements: (1) substandard materials protection, control, and accounting measures in the former Soviet Union that could contribute to nuclear accidents; (2) the possibility of nuclear weapons components falling into the hands of terrorists; and (3) potential transfer of weapons or weapons-related knowledge to rogue nations.[27] The Act allocated $400 million in Department of Defense funds for the elimination of these threats in early 1992. An additional $400 million was allocated in October 1992 to establish the Safe and Secure Dismantlement (SSD) Talks under the Former Soviet Union Demilitarization Act.

Between 1991 and 2003, the Cooperative Threat Reduction Program achieved some remarkable accomplishments.[28] The program resulted in the deactivation of 5,990 Soviet nuclear warheads, the sealing of 194 nuclear test tunnels, and the destruction of 479 ballistic missiles, 435 ballistic-missile silos, 97 bombers, 336 submarine-launched missiles, 396 submarine missile launchers, and 24 strategic missile submarines. The third, fourth, and eighth largest nuclear arsenals in the world—located in Ukraine, Kazakhstan and Belarus, respectively—were also removed. Roughly 22,000 former Soviet scientists assisted in these threat reduction endeavors, which helped to prevent them from being recruited into clandestine weapons-development activities by rogue states.

The program also supported covert operations in the former Soviet Union that disrupted active efforts by terrorist groups or rogue nations to acquire nuclear materials. In 1994, Project Sapphire removed from Kazakhstan 600 kilograms of highly enriched uranium, a quantity that could have been used to make up to thirty nuclear weapons. In 1997, twenty-one nuclear-capable MIG-29C attack aircraft were acquired from Moldova before they could be purchased by another country. And in 1998, Operation Auburn Endeavor removed

8.8 kilograms of highly enriched uranium from the former Soviet state of Georgia.[29]

The success of the Cooperative Threat Reduction Program is particularly notable given that it took place in the immediate aftermath of the Cold War, a period of almost forty years of hostilities between the United States and the Soviet Union. That the states were able to transition so quickly from high-stakes escalation to cooperation is a testament to the leadership and foresight of Bush and Gorbachev.

Edward Jones

Even in realms far removed from the drama of superpower politics, the ability to recognize and prevent predictable surprises is central to leadership success. The investment firm Edward Jones proved this to be true by emerging unscathed from the collapse of the Internet bubble in late 1990s and the economic downturn of 2000 to 2002. While its rivals became enmeshed in Internet mania and were bloodied by subsequent revelations concerning conflicts of interest and even active fraud, the firm of Edward Jones remained above the fray.[30]

Although hardly a household name, Edward Jones rose to become one of the largest investment advisers in the United States. The firm was founded 1871 as the investment house of Whitaker & Co., which subsequently merged in 1943 with the St. Louis brokerage Edward Jones (founded in 1922). In the subsequent fifty years, the firm honed its strategy of decentralization, creating an extensive network of over eight hundred local offices and affiliates providing client-focused investment advice throughout the United States. Beginning in 1994, the company initiated targeted international expansion in Canada (575 branch offices) and the United Kingdom (100 offices).[31]

In the late 1990s, other investment firms allowed themselves to be seduced by the Internet bubble by hawking to their brokerage clients the initial public offerings (IPOs) of companies that their investment arms were underwriting; by marketing in-house mutual funds in ways that created conflicts of interests for brokers; or by failing to maintain the independence of their analysts. Edward Jones resisted these trends and remained true to its strategy and principles.

The firm's success rests upon a simple set of strategic and organizational design principles that immunized it against the predictable surprises that have infected other investment firms:[32]

- Edward Jones is the only major financial services firm that exclusively serves individual investors, including small investors. By not seeking business from other firms, the company avoids being ethically compromised by the pressure to retain large clients.

- Edward Jones will not sell what it assesses to be risky products, including options, commodity futures, penny stocks, and initial public offerings. The company's stock analysts won't recommend a company that is less than ten years old. While this policy may cost Edward Jones adventuresome clients, it also prevents it from becoming entangled in faddish and fraudulent investments, and it keeps complexity at manageable levels for its clients.

- Edward Jones follows a long-term, "buy and hold" investment strategy, rather than moving rapidly in and out of investment instruments. This strategy reduces the perceived risk to target customers and helps protect the company from allegations regarding the questionable timing of market trades that have plagued many firms.

- Unlike firms that offer "in-house" products such as mutual funds, Edward Jones sells only products offered by other institutions. In doing so, the company avoids the conflicts of interest that arise when firms favor their own products over those of other companies.

- Edward Jones eschews online trading and other forms of centralized investment in favor of relationship-based selling. Individual firm representatives serve clients in their own community, thereby reinforcing the focus on the customer and placing long-term relationships at the core of the business.

- As a privately held company, Edward Jones is less subject to the short-term profit and growth demands experienced by publicly traded firms. For this reason, the firm is less vulnerable during bubbles, when public firms scramble herdlike to achieve unrealistic expectations, as well as during busts, when Jones's conservative strategy prevents it from being exposed to potentially ruinous losses.

The company's business model approach has yielded excellent results over the long run. In 2002, for the tenth consecutive year, Edward Jones was ranked the number one brokerage by *Registered Representative* magazine. In 2003, for the second year in a row, the firm was also ranked number one on *Fortune* magazine's list of "Best 100 Companies to Work For in America." Edward Jones was ranked number one among full-service brokers by *Kiplinger's Personal Finance* magazine in 2002, and tied for first place in J.D. Power and Associates' first survey of customer satisfaction among full-service investors in 2002. The firm also placed at eighty-one in *Forbes'* 2002 list of the United States' largest privately held companies.

While Edward Jones's long-term success is rare in the investment business, it is no accident. The company's long and illustrious history flows from a business strategy that, whether implicitly or explicitly, recognizes the threats posed by predictable surprises.

TOOLS FOR ENHANCING
PROBLEM RECOGNITION

"Prediction is very difficult," physicist Niels Bohr once noted, "especially about the future." Difficult, yes. Impossible, no. To increase their likelihood of recognizing emerging threats, leaders must establish and institutionalize effective early-warning systems in their organizations. The good news is that there are proven techniques for overcoming biases and barriers and for strengthening your organization's problem-recognition capabilities. The four techniques that follow can be used to improve your odds of recognizing looming predictable surprises in time to take corrective action:

1. *Measurement system redesign:* Redefine what the organization measures to focus attention on potential problem areas.

2. *Intelligence network building:* Establish units within the organization devoted to environmental scanning and integration of internal knowledge.

3. *Scenario planning:* Employ structured processes for identifying and educating the organization about potential future events or trends.

4. *Disciplined learning processes:* Institutionalize systems for capturing lessons-learned from surprises that have emerged in the past and for preserving this critical knowledge.

Technique #1. Measurement System Redesign

Leaders put measurement systems in place to track the performance of their organizations. Such systems consist of (1) a set of measures or specific variables that are collected and reported on a regular basis, and (2) a set of procedures concerning measurement methods and frequency, information dispersal, action triggers, and the nature of the response.

Measurement systems exert a powerful influence on human behavior in organizations. As the old adage goes, "You can't manage what you don't measure." A corollary is that organizational members tend to focus too narrowly on whatever the organization measures, especially when these measures are used as a basis for individual rewards. A second corollary is that people tend to ignore, and perhaps not even "see," that which the organization does not measure, especially if they have no incentives to pay attention to these unknown quantities.

Measurement therefore plays a critical role in focusing organizational attention. If a measurement system directs people to focus on issues or domains in which predictable surprises are likely to emerge, then it will contribute to the surprise-avoidance process. If not, it will tend to divert attention away from emerging problems until they rise to a crisis level.

A number of common measurement problems contribute to predictable surprises:

• The organization puts too much emphasis on measuring internal performance (such as product quantity, production costs, and compliance) and not enough on external performance (perceived quality, customer satisfaction, and client retention). As a result, the organization can miss critical signals regarding growing customer dissatisfaction.

- The organization focuses too much on measuring outputs (such as the quality of finished manufactured goods or customer satisfaction with service) and not enough on measuring the performance of key processes (the precision of manufacturing processes or the average time it takes to answer a customer's call). This means that the organization may not recognize very serious process problems until they have become evident to customers or have resulted in costly rework.

- The organization engages in measurement activities either infrequently or too frequently. In the former case, lack of measurement may keep the organization from being adequately warned about a predictable surprise. This is especially true as "information cycle time"—the time it takes to process and present results to decision-makers—increases. By contrast, overly frequent measurement can mask the magnitude of changes that are occurring because each incremental rise or fall appears to be small and creates a new baseline.

- The organization has inadequate triggering and response procedures. If the organization does not establish appropriate thresholds, or rules that determine when changes in key measures trigger action, it risks either underresponding to significant changes or overresponding to statistically insignificant fluctuations.

The implication of these pitfalls is that leaders should (1) refocus organizational attention on areas in which they believe predictable surprises may be lurking, including internal and external problems, outputs, and processes; and (2) carefully decide upon measurement frequency and triggering thresholds.

The goal of refocusing attention on problem areas can be achieved by defining new metrics and disciplining the organization to pay attention to them. In his classic article "Control in an Age of Empowerment," Robert Simons shows how skilled managers use formal control systems as levers of strategic change and renewal.[33] If an organization has become too focused on internal, process-related measures of performance, for example, then a move to external benchmarks, perhaps focused on customer satisfaction or competitor behavior, can increase the likelihood that predictable surprises will be recognized in time to be avoided.

Measurement systems can be systematically redesigned to detect predictable surprises. Robert Kaplan and David Norton's "Balanced Scorecard" approach is an excellent example of a structured methodology aimed at redesigning a company's measurement system.[34] As illustrated in figure 7-1, the Balanced Scorecard impels managers to

FIGURE 7-1

The Balanced Scorecard

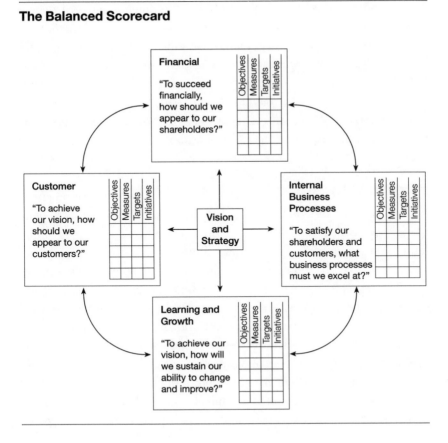

view their organization from several complementary perspectives. While it includes traditional measures of a company's financial performance, the Balanced Scorecard also adds operational measures of customer satisfaction, internal process efficiency and effectiveness, and the organization's ability to learn and improve. By focusing attention on nonfinancial measures, the Balanced Scorecard enhances an organization's ability to recognize and respond to emerging problems with customers, processes, and organizational sustainability, and therefore to avoid predictable surprises in those areas.

Technique #2. Intelligence Network Building

While it is impossible to eliminate all of the internal barriers to information sharing within an organization, it is possible to mitigate their impact by establishing cross-company intelligence-gathering networks. To do so, leaders should establish one or more dedicated cross-functional teams responsible for collecting and synthesizing relevant information from all corners of the organization. As Elizabeth Vitt, Michael Luckevich, and Stacia Misner write in their book *Business Intelligence,* "Cross-functional and business-unit applications are essentially about decision making and strategic issues that are paramount to protecting and enhancing competitive advantage; they have potential for the greatest payoff and are more advanced forms of business intelligence."[35]

Dedicated intelligence-gathering organizations need not be large, as long as they can effectively tap into the distributed insights of people whose work gives them firsthand knowledge of emerging problems. This group typically includes "boundary spanners"—employees who interact with people outside the company, such as customers, distributors, and suppliers.[36] It also includes people who are embedded in key processes within the organization, and who can provide early warnings of erosion of the organization's core capabilities.

To effectively avoid surprises, executives must also focus on building networks for personal intelligence-gathering and analysis. Too often, leaders' beliefs about the potential challenges facing their organizations are based solely on their intuition. By assembling a set of knowledgeable advisers from both inside and outside the company, leaders can test and refine their early impressions and help counter their own unconscious biases.[37]

Technique #3. Scenario Planning

Scenario planning is a structured technique for envisioning and analyzing alternative visions of the future and the implications of these visions for the organization. Scenarios are "derived from shared and agreed-upon mental models of the external world," notes Kees van der Heijden in his book *Scenarios: The Art of Strategic Conversation*. Scenarios benefit companies by creating "internally consistent and challenging descriptions of possible futures" that are meant to represent "the range of possible future developments and outcomes in the external world."[39] The goal of scenario planning is to help organizations identify and quantify risk, so that they neither take on unrecognized risks nor, critically, become overly risk-averse.

At its simplest, scenario planning can be an informal process. Try this experiment: Ask yourself and your colleagues, "What predictable surprises are currently brewing in our organization?" This may seem like an obvious question, but the fact is that it's rarely asked. From the top to the bottom of an organization, members are often aware of approaching storms but choose to keep silent, often out of fear of rocking the boat or being viewed as troublemakers. By actively encouraging people to speak up, leaders can bring to the surface problems that might otherwise go unmentioned. Anonymous polls can also be used within an organization to help uncover emerging problems.

In a formal scenario-planning process, a knowledgeable and creative group of people from inside and outside (to keep the insiders honest) the organization is convened to review organization strategies, digest available information on external trends, conduct interviews, and identify alternative futures and potential discontinuities. Based on this analysis, the group constructs a plausible set of scenarios—positive and negative—that could emerge in a given period of time (say, two to three years) both inside and outside the organization. These scenarios form the basis for the design of preventive and preparatory measures. Participants in these exercises should be instructed to develop some scenarios that, while relatively unlikely, would have a profound, detrimental impact on the organization if they occurred. Experts in scenario planning recommend that such exercises be conducted annually and that formal updates of changes in the organization and its environment be scheduled every quarter.

Technique #4. Disciplined Learning Processes

Not all emerging threats are novel; often the organization has confronted some version of the problem before. If the organization is effective at learning and at preserving institutional memory, emerging patterns may trigger early recognition of looming problems in time to mount an effective preventative response. Organizations that suffer from learning disabilities or disabling memory loss are less likely to recognize emerging threats. In this case, the organization may be doomed to fall prey to the same kind of problem over and over again: a predictable surprise.

Each surprise provides an opportunity for organizational learning. But organizational barriers can impede this learning, and institutional mechanisms must be in place for it to occur. Ian Mitroff notes in his book *Managing Crises Before They Happen*:

> Unfortunately few organizations conduct postmortems of crises and near misses, and those that do either do not perform them correctly or do not implement their findings. . . . [E]xcept in cases of criminal malfeasance or negligence, blame and fault finding are not to be encouraged. The main emphasis should be on no-fault learning. That is, it should be on the key lessons that need to be learned as well as those that have not been learned in the past, and why.[39]

Leaders can strengthen their organization's early-warning capabilities by institutionalizing organizational learning and memory preservation systems. After any significant unexpected event or crisis, a thorough "after-action" review should be conducted. The questions guiding such reviews should be: Why did the surprise occur? What were the highlights and drawbacks of the organization's response to the surprise? What are the key lessons learned? What changes need to be made to the organization's procedures and support resources to prevent a reoccurrence? The results of this postmortem must then be integrated into the organization's management practices. In many cases, it is helpful to document the results in a short report or memo to all personnel, to ensure that lessons-learned are disseminated throughout the organization.

Organizations can also take steps to reduce their vulnerability to crippling memory loss. Responsibility for environmental scanning might be assigned to specific individuals, who would develop expertise and relationships. Of course, this knowledge disappears with the employees when they (predictably) leave the organization or take new positions within it. Cross-training or rotation of personnel among key positions can help mitigate the impact of losing any one individual. Likewise, organizations that give responsibility for key tasks to teams, rather than individuals, are less vulnerable to knowledge loss. If the organization is redesigned to keep a nucleus of key teams intact, important knowledge can be preserved. The bottom line is that the most crucial organizational knowledge must be identified and preserved to the greatest extent possible.

FROM RECOGNITION TO PRIORITIZATION

Recognition is the first essential link in the chain that leads to the prevention of predictable surprises. Once recognized, however, leaders must make preventative action a priority in the midst of a noisy environment rife with competing priorities. The potential for emerging threats to be recognized but not prioritized is considerable. After any significant surprise, there are always those who correctly admit that they saw the disaster coming. In the next chapter, we consider how leaders can make prevention an individual and organizational priority.

8

Prioritization

Focusing on the Right Problems

In 1997, Douglas Ivester was promoted from chief operating officer to CEO of Coca-Cola after the sudden death of Roberto Goizueta, who had led Coke since 1981.[1] To outside observers, Ivester appeared to be the perfect candidate for CEO. "The real challenge [for Coca-Cola]," wrote one Paine Webber analyst "is not becoming a casualty of their own success. And I think with the current lineup at Coke, starting with Doug Ivester, they're not too likely to become complacent."[2] *Fortune* had named him the "prototype boss for the twenty-first century."[3]

An accountant by training, Ivester had spent nearly twenty years rising through the ranks at Coke. Appointed CFO of Coke in 1985, at age 37, he made his mark spearheading the 1986 spin-off of the company's bottling operations, Coca-Cola Enterprises. As president of European operations he oversaw the company's expansion into Eastern Europe in 1989. Ivester was named president of Coke USA a year later and became the president and COO of the entire company in 1994.

Despite his stellar credentials, Ivester had trouble making the leap to CEO. The result was a series of missteps, none fatal on its own, which cumulatively sapped Ivester's credibility. His clumsy treatment of European regulators contributed to Coke's failure to acquire Orangina in France and drastically reduced the value of Coke's acquisition of Cadbury Schweppes's brands. Ivester was also widely viewed as having mishandled a crisis involving contamination of Coke bottled in Belgium in 1999. He alienated other potential allies by failing to respond effectively to a racial discrimination suit in Coke's Atlanta headquarters and by applying too much pressure to Coke's already overtaxed bottlers over concentrate pricing and inventories.

By 1999, just two years into his tenure as CEO, Ivester resigned, having lost the confidence of Coke's board of directors. His departure came, paradoxically, at a time when the company appeared to be on the way to recovering from the impact of the Asian financial crisis and was performing as well as other leading consumer products companies. "The job of running a giant company like Coca-Cola Co. is akin to conducting an orchestra," the *Wall Street Journal* wrote, "but M. Douglas Ivester, it seems, had a tin ear. . . . [He] knew the math, but not the music required to run the world's leading marketing organization."[4]

At its core, Ivester's failure was not in misapprehending key challenges, but in ineffectively prioritizing those challenges. For many years, he had observed firsthand the leadership roles that his predecessor had effectively assumed. But Ivester either didn't view these roles to be crucial, or didn't make learning about them a priority.

Prioritization failures arise when leaders and organizations recognize potential threats but do not deem them sufficient to warrant serious attention. The cognitive and organizational barriers to effective prioritizing action are formidable. On the cognitive side, positive illusions and the tendency to discount the future, and thus to underestimate the likelihood and impact of potential problems, loom as major barriers to effective prioritization. On the organizational side, the tendency to maintain the status quo, often exacerbated by collective action problems or conflicts of interest, renders key people unwilling or unable to embrace the right set of priorities, with predictable results.

How can leaders prioritize emerging threats, given that they are beset by competing demands on their attention? How can they possibly distinguish the surprise that will happen from the myriad potential surprises that won't? Of course, they can't make such distinctions with 100 percent accuracy. Uncertainty always exists—high-probability disasters sometimes do not occur, and low-probability ones sometimes do. Therefore, if an organization undertakes careful cost-benefit analyses and gives priority to those threats that would inflict the highest costs, its leaders should not be held accountable for a failure of prioritization. If they fail to take these steps, they must concentrate on strengthening the systems for setting priorities.

INDIVIDUAL PRIORITIZATION FAILURES

Given the level of background noise—the many potential distractions that bombard senior executives each day—prioritization is arguably the biggest challenge they face. The key is to identify and focus on critical priorities and investigate them in an open and disciplined manner. Asked about her strategy for winning her third U.S. Open championship in 1986, tennis star Martina Navratilova replied, "I just try to concentrate on concentrating."[5] All too often, organizational leaders fail to follow this advice. In this section, we look at prioritization failures at the individual level, continuing our analysis of Douglas Ivester's failed tenure as Coca-Cola's CEO and examining the predictable surprise that awaited Defense Secretary Donald Rumsfeld in postwar Iraq.

Douglas Ivester at Coca-Cola

Ivester and his predecessor, Roberto Goizueta, had been a well-matched team. The extroverted, charismatic Goizueta had effectively played the role of visionary and strategist. A marketer by training, he made the safeguarding of the Coke brand a personal priority. As CEO, he also created and sustained relationships with key external constituencies.

Ivester, by contrast, was introverted, intensely driven, and highly detail oriented—qualities that served him well as chief operating officer. His finance and operations experience and his tactical and execution skills positioned him to be an effective internal disciplinarian. His focus was necessarily on achieving financial and operational results, goals that became his personal priorities. As COO, he focused on running the company's inside operations and, with the exception of making presentations to analysts, eschewed public duties such as government and press relations.

Ivester had long envisioned occupying the role of Coca-Cola's CEO. But the promotion also represented a crossroads in his life as a leader, one that demanded that he exercise different skills and, critically, take on new priorities. To succeed he would have had to move out of his comfort zone and learn new skills.

Instead of embracing these challenges, Ivester became more of a "super-COO" than a CEO. He refused to name a replacement for his old position, even under strong pressure from Coke's board of directors. His extraordinary attention to detail, which had been a virtue in his finance and operations roles, now proved to be a hindrance. He maintained daily contact with the sixteen people who reported to him and remained intimately involved in operational details. Mired in day-to-day business, Ivester appeared to neglect the strategic and visionary responsibilities demanded of an effective CEO of Coca-Cola.

Ivester fell prey to a classic prioritization failure: He expected to be successful in his new job by continuing to do what he did in his previous job, only more of it. "They put me in the job because of my skills and accomplishments," this reasoning goes. "So that must be what they expect of me now." This thinking proved destructive for Ivester. By performing his familiar tasks, he avoided his new responsibilities. This strategy left him vulnerable to being predictably surprised by the host of large-scale problems that Coca-Cola faced during his tenure.

Donald Rumsfeld and Postwar Planning for Iraq

When he appointed Donald Rumsfeld to be his secretary of defense in 2000, President George W. Bush tapped one of the most experienced and innovative leaders in the U.S. Defense establishment.[6] The former Navy pilot (1954–1957) had served as a U.S. congressman (1962–1970), U.S. Ambassador to NATO (1973–1974), chief of staff to President Ford (1974–1975), and Ford's secretary of defense (1975–1977). In 1977, Mr. Rumsfeld was awarded the nation's highest civilian award, the Presidential Medal of Freedom. This highly intelligent, forceful, and focused leader went on to serve as CEO and then chairman of the pharmaceutical firm Searle (1977–1985), chairman and CEO of General Instrument Corporation (1990–1993), and chairman of the U.S. Ballistic Missile Threat Commission (1998).

In 2000, Rumsfeld took on the role of defense secretary determined to transform the U.S. military into a more mobile, lethal, and technology-intensive fighting force. He pressed through his strategy change by altering acquisition commitments and appointing like-minded leaders in the uniformed ranks. In the process, he succeeded in alienating much of Congress and many high-ranking members of the military. Indeed, Rumsfeld appeared to be on his way out the door when the attacks of September 11, 2001, occurred. Rumsfeld's rapid response to the attack on the Pentagon, followed by his broader plan for war in Afghanistan, quickly transformed him into a leading national figure and ensured his position within the Bush administration.

Rumsfeld became a leader within the defense establishment in pushing the war on terrorism into Iraq. He pressed the Joint Chiefs of Staff to adopt a lean, rapid war plan that is sure to serve as a textbook case of effective planning and prioritization. In just a few short weeks, a relative small, highly mobile force defeated the army of Saddam Hussein and liberated Iraq.

If the war-fighting plan was comprehensive and brilliant, the postwar plan for ensuring stability and peace in Iraq was flimsy and shot through with false assumptions. Tragically for those members of the U.S. military and Iraqi civilians who may have lost their lives unnecessarily, it later emerged that a comprehensive postwar planning effort had been undertaken by the Department of State and then thrown away.[7] The Future of Iraq Project, launched in the spring of 2002 under the leadership of diplomat Thomas Warrick, systematically tapped into the diplomatic, peacekeeping, and Iraqi exile communities to create a comprehensive plan for occupation and transformation. The project assigned working groups of ten to twenty members to address postwar challenges in seventeen key policy areas, including democratic principles and procedures, economy and infra-structure, education, public finance, oil and energy, free media, and migration.[8]

The comprehensive, thirteen-volume findings of the working groups accurately predicted many of the "surprises" that would await the United States in Iraq, including the mass looting that followed the collapse of Hussein's regime.[9] Senior Iraqi exiles expressed the same concerns to Rumsfeld and his key staff in Pentagon debriefings. Massoud Barzani, leader of the Kurdistan Democratic Party and a longtime ally of the United States, commented to the *New York Times*, "On many occasions, I told the Americans that from the very moment the regime fell, if an alternative government was not ready there would be a power vacuum and there would be chaos and looting. Given our history, it is very obvious this would occur."[10]

It appears that the senior Pentagon civilians—Rumsfeld, his deputy Paul Wolfowitz, Douglas Feith, and key advisers such as Richard Perle—effectively threw away the findings and recommendations of the State Department's Future of Iraq Project, in part due to a fundamental ideological conflict. The Pentagon civilians were highly critical of the Department of State's multilateral approach, believing that it shackled U.S. power. Against this background, as the war itself became a foregone conclusion, the two departments clashed over important tactical questions. Pentagon civilians pushed for Ahmad Chalabi, the head of the Iraqi National Conference, a key exile group, to lead postwar Iraq. The Department of State was suspicious of the information Chalabi was feeding the Pentagon and believed that he was siphoning off money intended to help the resistance. (Chalabi had also been convicted, in absentia, of bank fraud in Jordan.)

Rumsfeld also ignored warnings about the size of force required to secure Iraq after the fall of the Hussein regime.[11] On February 25, 2003, just weeks before the start of the war, the Army's chief of staff, General Eric Shinseki, warned Congress that controlling Iraq would require "several hundred thousand" U.S. troops. Rumsfeld, Wolfowitz, and other civilian officials at the Pentagon denigrated his assessment. Testifying before Congress soon after, Wolfowitz called Shinseki's number "wildly off the mark," saying, "It's hard to conceive that it would take more forces to provide stability in post-Saddam Iraq than it would take to conduct the war itself and secure the surrender of Saddam's security force and his army."[12]

Effectively winning the political battle with the Department of State, as well as the support of Congress, the Pentagon established the Office of Reconstruction and Humanitarian Assistance (ORHA) on January 20, 2003, eight weeks before the invasion of Iraq. Once major operations had ceased, however, it soon became clear that post-war planning had been, at best, an afterthought. The U.S. military's failure to cope with widespread looting, to quickly restore essential services such as electricity, and to anticipate attacks by resistance groups undercut Iraqi support for the U.S. ouster of Hussein.

Lieutenant General Jay Garner, the retired Army officer whom Rumsfeld put in charge of planning the reconstruction, later revealed that he had been instructed to ignore the Future of Iraq Project.[13] Garner, who was later replaced by Ambassador Paul Bremer, also said that his superiors denied his request to have Thomas Warrick added to his staff.

"We should have tried to raise a government a little faster than we did," Garner, said in an interview with BBC Radio.[14] "If we did it over again, we probably would have put more dismounted infantrymen in Baghdad and maybe more troops there."

What caused this massive prioritization failure? One explanation is simply resource scarcity: The Pentagon may have had enough time and resource to plan for war, but not enough to plan for the postwar period. A second, more plausible explanation is less benign. Determined to press forward with his downsizing of the U.S. military, Rumsfeld could not afford to make the postwar reconstruction of Iraq a planning priority. A clear examination of the facts would have revealed that the small, mobile force used to prosecute the war wouldn't be sufficient for the postwar phase of the operation. But such an admission was unacceptable to Rumsfeld both before the war and after it, as it would have undercut his broader agenda. A third explanation is that Rumsfeld's prioritization failure resulted from bureaucratic politics, specifically the competition for influence and resources that occurs in divisions of any organization when goals and responsibilities are not clearly defined.

ORGANIZATIONAL PRIORITIZATION
FAILURES

If individuals can fall prey to prioritization failures, it should come as no surprise that organizations, whether made up of dozens or thousands of members, are even more susceptible. As discussed in chapter 5, incentive systems, collective-action problems, and conflicts of interest can lead members of organizations to pursue the wrong priorities, and set the stage for predictable surprises.

Predicting the September 11, 2001, Terrorist Attacks, Revisited

In chapter 7, we described Joint Inquiry Staff Director Eleanor Hill's congressional testimony regarding the causes of the September 11, 2001, attacks on New York and Washington. The Joint Inquiry staff found that the highest levels of the Intelligence Community (IC) were aware of the growing threat of domestic terrorism, but that this conclusion was not translated into priorities for action at lower levels. Hill concluded that leaders in the IC failed to clearly communicate beliefs and priorities, resulting in the misdirected focus on overseas targets.[15]

For example, poor communication of threat assessments and priorities from senior leadership to analysts resulted in a failure to allocate resources to the scanning of aircraft-related threats. Following the August 1998 bombings of two U.S. embassies in East Africa, IC leadership recognized the extent of the danger posed by Osama bin Laden's Al Qaeda network. In December 1998, Director of Central Intelligence George Tenet provided written guidance to his CIA deputies declaring "war" against bin Laden. Tenet wrote: "We must now enter a new phase in our effort against bin Ladin. . . . We are at war. . . . I want no resources or people spared in this effort, either inside CIA or the Community."[16]

But the Joint Inquiry's investigation found that, "despite the DCI's declaration of war in 1998, there was no massive shift of resources to focus on the threat." At numerous points in her testimony, Hill noted that there were indications that bin Laden might try to use aircraft to attack U.S. targets (see chapter 2).[17] Despite clear indications that terrorists might use airplanes as weapons, the Joint Inquiry staff found that the IC did not organize to produce any specific, integrative assessment of the likelihood of such an attack.[18]

Similar prioritization failures occurred at the Federal Aviation Administration (FAA). In August 1998, the IC learned that a group of unidentified Arabs planned to fly an explosive-laden plane from a foreign country into the World Trade Center. The information was passed to the FBI and the FAA. In working-level interactions between the agencies, the FAA assessed the plot as highly unlikely given the state of the unnamed foreign country's aviation program. They also believed that a flight originating outside the United States would be detected before it reached its intended target inside the United States.[19] They reached this conclusion despite the fact that assessments by higher-level FAA officials incorporated into the National Intelligence Estimate (IE) on terrorism pointed out dangerous weaknesses in U.S. aviation security.[20] In a mandated December 2000 classified report to Congress, the FAA and the FBI downplayed the threat to civil aviation:

> FBI investigations confirm domestic and international terrorist groups operating within the U.S. but do not suggest evidence of plans to target domestic civil aviation. Terrorist activity within the U.S. has focused primarily on fundraising, recruiting new members, and disseminating propaganda. While international terrorists have conducted attacks on U.S. soil, these acts represent anomalies in their traditional targeting which focuses on U.S. interests overseas.[21]

And so, as Hill noted, erroneous assumptions led FBI investigators to discount evidence that terrorists could be training at U.S. flight schools. It also led investigators to fasten on to alternative explanations, such as the theory that bin Laden needed pilots to move men and material within Afghanistan.[22] A year before 9/11, notwithstanding intelligence information to the contrary, the FBI and FAA assessed the prospects of a terrorist attack on domestic civil aviation to be relatively low.

That the FBI did not "connect the dots" prior to September 11 can also be partially attributed to the incentives that shaped the behavior of the agency's most critical members, the special agents operating in its many decentralized field offices. In her testimony, Eleanor Hill noted that the agency's culture and reward systems gave field agents strong incentives to focus on their own cases and not on broader, crosscutting issues:

The FBI handling of the Phoenix EC [the July 10, 2001, electronic communication alerting FBI headquarters that terrorists were possibly being trained at U.S. flight schools, described in chapter 7] is symptomatic of a focus on short-term operational priorities, often at the expense of long-term, strategic analysis. . . . [T]he case-driven, law enforcement approach, while important and extremely productive in terms of the FBI's traditional mission, does not generally "incentivize" attention to big picture, preventive analysis and strategy. This is particularly true where there is no direct and immediate impact on an ongoing criminal prosecution.[23]

In his congressional testimony, the special agent who authored the Phoenix memo echoed this conclusion, stating that he did not believe that the FBI devoted sufficient resources to counterterrorism despite its status as a "Priority 1" program. In the agent's words, counterterrorism and counterintelligence have always been considered the "bastard stepchildren" of the FBI; unlike programs focused on catching violent criminals and drug dealers, these programs did not generate tangible results.[24] The FBI's misguided focus is a classic incentive failure, of the type discussed in chapter 5. The best predictor of how organizational members will behave is what they have incentives to do. If, like the FBI, they are incented to focus on individual, local issues, it should come as no surprise if they don't pay attention to broader, collective ones.

The Great Blackout of 2003

The electrical blackout of August 2003, which began on August 14 and ended for most regions on August 15, affected more than fifty million people in portions of the U.S. Northeast and Upper Midwest, and Ontario, Canada (see the box "August 14, 2003, Blackout: Sequence of Events" for the area affected).[25] The blackout was the culmination of thousands of line disconnects and other malfunctions across the high-voltage generation and transmission systems of Ohio, Michigan, New York, and Ontario. More than a hundred power generation facilities (including nine nuclear plants) operated by sixteen utilities shut down. New York City remained black for twenty-nine hours. The power failure shuttered airports and businesses throughout the affected region and cost the U.S. economy billions of dollars.

To understand why the blackout occurred, one must comprehend the structure and dynamics of the electrical power grid. One prime benefit of electricity is that it can be generated in one place, transmitted over a substantial distance, and consumed in another area. Many sources of electricity and many consumers of electricity can be connected to a distributed "grid," or network, of high-voltage, high-capacity transmission lines. Over time, progressively larger regions across North America have been linked in this manner.

The entire system is designed to maintain a balance between demand and supply. As load on the system increases, so does electricity generation. If load begins to approach the capacity of available generation, additional generators are connected. As demand and supply begin to follow a balance, the system increases and decreases generation. Blackouts occur when a system is unable to compensate for imbalances, either because there's not enough generation available, or because constraints in the transmission lines make it impossible to transmit enough power. Naturally, there is some redundancy in the system; if one transmission line fails, power is diverted automatically to other lines—a system that works as long as those lines are not themselves overloaded. Likewise, if a generator shuts down, other generators normally increase their output to compensate. But if other transmission lines are overloaded as well, the result can be a cascading set of disconnections and shutdowns. The blackout of 2003 was the result of just such a cascading system failure, triggered by events in Ohio. The rough sequence of events is summarized in "August 14, 2003, Blackout: Sequence of Events."

The blackout was not caused by failures of recognition. The U.S. power grid's increasing vulnerability, due principally to increasing loads and lack of capital investment, was well recognized. But fixing the grid had never been a priority for industry. In a February 2002 report, "Transmission Expansion: Issues and Recommendations," the North American Electricity Reliability Council (NERC) noted:

AUGUST 14, 2003, BLACKOUT:
SEQUENCE OF EVENTS

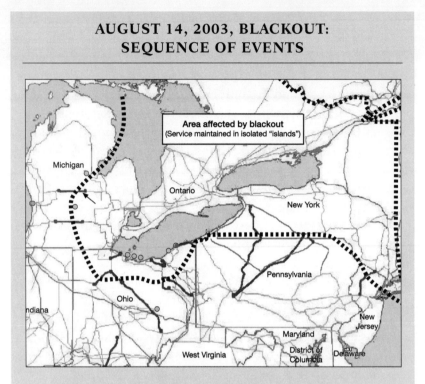

1. Between 3:05 and 3:41 P.M., three transmission lines connecting eastern Ohio and northern Ohio disconnected. The first of these lines disconnected itself when it came in contact with a tree. A second line had disconnected and reconnected twice earlier in the day for unknown reasons. The net effect was a reduction in the effectiveness of power transmission from eastern to northern Ohio. Power began to flow on other lines, which became overloaded, triggering automatic disconnection of load in northern Ohio.

2. Between 3:45 and 4:09 P.M., the two remaining transmission lines connecting eastern and northern Ohio disconnected. To compensate, power began to flow into northern Ohio from other parts of the state, as well as from Pennsylvania and Michigan. The Detroit area became more reliant on lines running east–west across Michigan.

3. At about 4:09 P.M., additional disconnections blocked the flow of power from southern and western Ohio into northern Ohio and eastern Michigan, leaving northern Ohio and eastern Michigan connected only to the immediate region.

4. In the next 30 seconds, transmission lines across Michigan and northern Ohio disconnected, and twenty generators along Lake Erie shut down. Power flows increased into northern Ohio and eastern Michigan along the remaining paths, which included the east–west transmission lines across Michigan, which then disconnected. As a result, eastern Michigan became connected to the grid only through Ontario and northern Ohio. Voltage plummeted and Detroit went dark.

5. Power was sucked into Ontario from upstate New York and transmitted into Michigan. The result was a massive reversal of the normal flows of power around Lake Erie.

6. Transmission lines between Pennsylvania and New York disconnected to protect the Pennsylvania system. Additional transmission line disconnections and generator outages resulted in a loss of power to northern Ohio. The New York–New England transmission lines also disconnected, protecting New England. Ontario separated from New York and blacked out. At about 4:13 P.M. New York City went dark and the cascading sequence was essentially complete.

Source: Adapted from "Causes of the August 14th Blackout in the United States and Canada: August 14, 2003, Outage Sequence of Events," U.S.-Canada Power Outage Task Force, November 2003.

The deregulation of wholesale electricity supply in the electric industry has led to a number of changes, including the restructuring of the electric industry, and has created many new challenges for all market participants. In part, as a result of deregulation, a rapid expansion of one portion of the electric system—generation supply—has occurred. However, the expansion of the transmission systems has not been well coordinated with the generation expansion in all regions. The failure to expand transmission on a regional basis has led to congestion in various parts of the North American transmission systems, preventing the electricity market from working as efficiently at it might.[26]

Like many electricity providers, FirstEnergy, the Ohio-based company whose failed power lines triggered the blackout, lacked incentives to invest in transmission-line capacity.[27] According to the *Wall Street Journal*, as of 2003, FirstEnergy had experienced heavy losses caused by operational problems, including shutdowns of troubled nuclear facilities. On August 5, the company restated its 2002 earnings, cutting them by $67 million, and also issued a profit warning for 2004 and 2005.[28]

More generally, fundamental incentive issues contributed to the predictable surprise, as summarized in the NERC's 2002 report.[29] These shortcomings included:

- Transmission systems designed primarily for traditional local and regional reliability fell short of the needs of competitive electricity markets.

- The expansion required to meet state mandates or retail choice overwhelmed the transmission planning process, leaving little time to develop optimal transmission plans.

- Economics increasingly became the focus of project commitment decisions, apart from reliability concerns. Short-term interests and a lack of long-term service commitments drove the decisions of power companies.

- Efforts to connect power-generation systems are complicated by regional differences in processes and procedures.

This final point highlights well-recognized flaws in controlling the transmission grid that appear to have fanned the Midwest power failure into a widespread blackout.[30] Grid operators in many parts of the country maintain central control over power lines in their regions, thereby allowing them to respond quickly to developing problems. But because the agency ostensibly responsible for controlling the

Midwest grid, the Independent System Operator (ISO), lacked this central control, it had to communicate with and coordinate the actions of thirty-three separate utility companies.[31] Utility companies and politicians in some Midwestern states who opposed the trend toward deregulation had combined forces to keep the Midwest ISO weak. The federal government had not made it a priority to fix this shortcoming. As a result, the small failures in monitoring equipment at FirstEnergy, and later ones at the Midwest ISO, triggered an irreversible cascade.

The consequences of catastrophic loss of power were recognized, but those with the authority to head off a predictable surprise—politicians and bureaucrats in some Midwestern state governments and in U.S. Congress—did not make corrective action a priority.

Interestingly, the blackout of August 2003 also demonstrated how some organizations had anticipated this predictable surprise and made prevention a priority, while others had not. The blackout impacted numerous organizations. Many were caught unprepared, but some were not. Organizations in some communities weathered the blackout without disruption, while their counterparts in other regions suffered serious setbacks. Consider the following examples:

- In New York City, most of the water system continued to function, operating on backup power supplies. In Detroit and Cleveland, water supplies were cut off, creating contamination that forced residents to boil water once the power was restored. "This wasn't supposed to happen," Cleveland Mayor Jane Campbell said. "We need to make sure this doesn't happen again."[32]

- Following severe disruptions in the aftermath of September 11, 2001, the New York Stock Exchange invested in backup facilities and power systems. As a result, the NYSE was able to shut down its systems on the day of the power outage without losing data and it opened the next day without a hitch. The NASDAQ also open for business at 9:30 as usual on Friday, August 15, but power problems delayed the opening of the American Stock Exchange, also located in New York City.[33]

- The major U.S. airports were open for business the morning after the blackout, but Air Canada temporarily suspended operations throughout Canada on August 15 when primary and secondary power systems at its control center failed.[34]

- While land-line telephone service held up well throughout the affected areas, cellular service was badly disrupted. The high volume of calls was exacerbated by power failures at cellular transmitters.[35]

- The blackout posed few problems for firms with strong information technology operations such as data and customer-service centers. Whether in preparation for Y2K or in the aftermath of 9/11, many of these firms had installed backup systems, diesel generators, and secondary data centers.[36]

- Officials in New York City quickly activated a security plan developed after 9/11. Police manned an alternate police command site in the Bronx, which had been designed to prevent high-level operations from being disrupted by an attack on departmental buildings. More than two thousand additional officers were put on the streets, bringing the total to more than 9,000. There was only one reported incident of looting in New York.[37] In Canada, by contrast, more extensive looting was reported in Ottawa and Toronto.[38]

Organizations hoping to respond effectively to predictable surprises can learn a great deal from these successes and failures. In the next section, we offer a set of tools to help you successfully set priorities and avoid predictable surprises.

BEYOND RECOGNITION: STRENGTHENING PRIORITIES

To successfully move from recognition to prioritization, leaders must focus their attention as individuals on setting priorities and, critically, they must institutionalize tools within their organizations for "concentrating on concentrating," in the words of Martina Navratilova.

The following techniques can help provide a foundation for these organizational priority-setting tasks.

1. **Structuring dialogue:** Set up decision-making processes that foster inquiry into critical issues or problems rather than advocating the positions of interested constituencies. In doing so, increase information sharing and engage in disciplined option generation and evaluation.

2. **Decision analysis:** Adopt a rigorous means of defining decision options and potential outcomes by assessing the probabilities, costs, and benefits associated with different courses of action.

3. **Incentive system redesign:** To the greatest extent possible, align the interests of individuals with those of the organization. Mitigate or eliminate potentially dangerous conflicts of interest.

Technique #1. Structuring Dialogue

Appropriate priorities emerge from healthy debate within senior management teams in organizations. Unfortunately, the barriers to productive debate are considerable. The courses of action that would prevent predictable surprises often create winners and losers in organizations; budgets must be expanded in some areas and cut in others, favorite projects must be shelved, and the distribution of power among organizational units and individuals inevitably shifts.

When an effective response is likely to generate winners and losers, debate unfortunately tends to degenerate into unproductive advocacy of the positions of entrenched constituencies. In a *Harvard Business Review* article, David Garvin and Michael Roberto described the dangers of the advocacy model of decision-making and contrast it with an approach they call "inquiry":

> When a group takes an advocacy perspective, participants approach decision-making as a contest, although they don't necessarily compete openly or even consciously. Well-defined groups with special interests—dueling divisions in search of budget increases, for example—advocate for particular

positions. Participants are passionate about their preferred solutions and therefore stand firm in the face of disagreement. That level of passion makes it nearly impossible to remain objective, limiting people's ability to pay attention to opposing arguments.[39]

The result of such positional bargaining is either deadlock—and consequently a failure to take any action—or agreement on a lowest common denominator, a "solution" that fails to prevent a predictable surprise.

To shift the decision-making process from advocacy to inquiry, Garvin and Roberto advise leaders to purposefully impose structure on debates over alternatives. One such approach, "dialectical inquiry," involves dividing a team into two subgroups that develop alternative courses of action. The groups then come together to debate the merits of each plan. Under the "devil's advocacy" method, the team's leader can assign an individual member to observe and critique advocates' positions on different courses of action. Such methods help ensure that even low-status team members can express their views.[40]

In 1962, when spy planes spotted Soviet missiles in Cuba, U.S. military leaders urged President Kennedy to authorize an immediate attack. Fresh from the bruising failure of the Bay of Pigs, Kennedy instead set up a structured decision-making process to evaluate his options.[41] In a precursor of the Devil's Advocacy method, Kennedy established two groups, each including government officials and outside experts, to develop and evaluate the two main options—attack Cuba or set up a blockade to prevent more missiles from reaching its shores. Based on the groups' analysis and debate, Kennedy decided to establish a blockade. The Soviets backed down, and nuclear war was averted. Recently available documents suggest that if the United States had invaded Cuba, the consequences would have been catastrophic: Soviet missiles that had not been located by U.S. intelligence could still have struck several U.S. cities.[42]

Technique #2. Decision Analysis

"The only proven way to raise your odds of making a good decision is to learn to use a good decision-making process—one that can get you the best solution with a minimal loss of time, energy, money, and composure," write John Hammond, Ralph Keeney, and Howard Raiffa in their book *Smart Choices: A Practical Guide to Making Better Life Decisions*.[43] Rigorous decision analysis combines a systematic assessment of the probabilities of future events with a hard-headed evaluation of the costs and benefits of particular outcomes. As such, it can be an invaluable tool in helping organizations overcome the biases that hinder them in estimating the likelihood of unpleasant events.

Decision analysis begins with a clear definition of the decision to be made, followed by an explicit statement of objectives and explicit criteria for assessing the "goodness" of alternative courses of action, by which we mean the net cost or benefit as perceived by the decision-maker. The next steps involve identifying potential courses of action and their consequences. Because these elements often are laid out visually in a decision tree, this technique is known as "decision tree analysis." Finally, the technique instructs decision-makers to explicitly assess and make trade-offs based on the potential costs and benefits of different courses of action.[44]

To conduct a proper decision analysis, leaders must carefully quantify costs and benefits, their tolerance for accepting risk, and the extent of uncertainty associated with different potential outcomes. These assessments are inherently subjective, but the process of quantification is nonetheless extremely valuable; it forces participants to express their assumptions and beliefs, thereby making them transparent and subject to challenge and improvement.

The decision tree shown in figure 8-1 illustrates an analysis of a straightforward decision that an individual faces: buying a new car or keeping an existing one. The new-car option imposes a 100 percent certain new expenditure of $3,000 per year on the decision-maker (certain because the new-car warranty and insurance keep the costs from rising higher). By contrast, the option of keeping the existing car is fraught with uncertainty. This uncertainty is quantified in terms of three options—no problems with the old car, some problems, and major problems—with associated probabilities and costs. Analysis of the costs of the two decision options reveals that, on an expected-value basis, it will cost the decision-maker less to keep the existing

FIGURE 8-1

Decision Tree Analysis

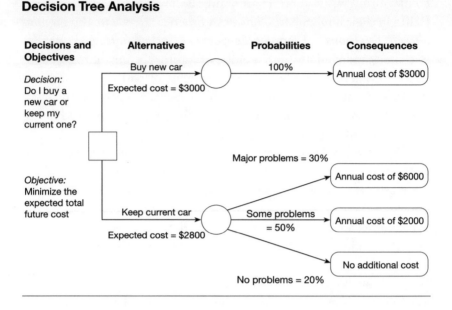

car than to buy a new one.[45] But for a risk-averse decision-maker of limited means, the 30 percent probability of being socked with $6,000 in repairs may loom large, and may lead him or her to pick the less risky new-car option.

Decision analysis is particularly beneficial in focusing decision-makers' attention on outcomes that are low in probability but very high in potential costs, such as a complete meltdown at a nuclear plant or the release of a dangerous pathogen from a tightly controlled laboratory. In the absence of rigorous quantification of costs, benefits, and probabilities, biases such as positive allusions, self-serving assessments, and the tendency to discount the future lead decision-makers to downplay these low-likelihood yet potentially catastrophic events. Decision analysis also compels groups to discuss and reach consensus on the decision to be made and its associated objectives, alternatives, consequences, trade-offs, and risks. As such, it is a natural complement to scenario planning, which, as we have discussed, helps to identify potential outcomes or events that might not otherwise have been recognized. Decision analysis provides a sound basis for assessing the implications of various scenarios and planning preventative action.

Hammond, Keeney, and Raiffa note that an effective decision-analysis must include an awareness of the decision biases that affect the decision-making process, lest biased inputs result in a biased analysis. Leaders seeking to prevent predictable surprises should review the biases presented in chapter 4.

Technique #3. Incentive Systems Redesign

An understanding of what needs to be done to avoid a predictable surprise does not necessarily translate into preventive action. As discussed in chapter 5, key members of an organization may either lack the incentives to take action or, as described in chapter 6, their self-interest may lead them to contribute directly to the genesis of a predictable surprise. For these reasons, leaders must pay close attention to the design of organizational incentive systems.

Richard Thorpe and Gill Homan note in their book *Strategic Reward Systems*:

> There is no one payment system or form of incentive that can achieve all [objectives] for all groups of staff in an organization, so managers are necessarily required to weigh up the advantages and disadvantages of any system before making judgments based on a balanced assessment of all likely outcomes. Moreover, it is not an area in which doing nothing is an option, simply because all employers have to have some form of mechanism, however ad hoc in nature, in order to pay their employees.[46]

According to the basic principles of incentive-system design, organizational members should have the incentive to make decisions that are good for the organization as a whole rather than decisions that benefit only particular individuals or members of specific units. In addition, conflicts of interest involving people outside the organization (advisers and other interested parties) should be identified and eliminated.

These seemingly straightforward principles become complicated in execution. Individual incentives can never be completely aligned with the best interests of institutions or society, to the extent that those interests can be defined at all. Likewise, it is impossible to completely eliminate conflicts of interest for all of the people who permeate the boundary of an organization. Rather than striving for perfection, effective incentive systems seek to achieve the maximum possible incentive alignment by combining meaningful carrots and sticks with cost-effective monitoring of employee conduct. Collective action problems such as the global fishing crisis can be approached through a combination of incentives: positive ones, such as reasonable returns for a sustainable number of fishers and assistance for others to enter new lines of work; and negative ones, such as severe penalties, including fines. Such rewards and punishments must be backed up by a system for monitoring conduct and disciplining offenders. Weaknesses in any part of the incentive system will likely lead to failure.

Conflicts of interest can be addressed in similar ways. In the case of the U.S. auditing industry, for example, it would be best if auditors were not compensated financially by those whose books they oversee. But the political barriers to the creation of a large regulatory agency to police public accounting are great, and this solution is unlikely to be adopted. The next-best solution is a system that would allow accounting firms to make reasonable returns, while punishing and deterring outright fraud through a system of monitoring and penalties (a combination of the market and the SEC). A better system would also manage incentives by enacting rules aimed at circumventing the insidious effects of auditor bias. Such rules would include rotating auditing firms among companies and barring auditors from providing any other services to their clients and from taking jobs with their clients. These legislative changes would reduce the likelihood that other auditing firms will go the way of Arthur Andersen.

In organizations, the issue of whether to reward individual or group performance and whether to provide fixed or incentive-based rewards looms large. When success depends heavily on group cooperation, an organization that rewards individuals can run into trouble. Hand out too many bonuses, and individuals may do whatever it takes to "hit the numbers." Of course, employees who lack adequate incentives can become a drain on a company. Designing incentive-systems that effectively calibrate this delicate scale is a challenge, but failing to do so can be fatal.

Success in moving from recognition to prioritization sets the stage for the final element of the RPM model—mobilization. Leaders seldom have the direct authority to translate their priorities into action. Therefore, if they are to prevent predictable surprises, they must persuade, negotiate, and build coalitions. In the next chapter, we turn our attention to these methods of influence.

9

Mobilization

Building Support for
Preventative Action

In February of 1998, a coalition of thirty-nine American and European pharmaceutical companies sued the government of South Africa over its attempt to reduce the cost of antiretroviral drugs used to treat HIV/AIDS.[1] In 1997, the government had passed the South African Medicines Act, which legalized parallel importation of medicines and permitted substitution of generic equivalents for patented drugs. Parallel importation would allow South Africa to import otherwise costly drugs from countries with lower prices instead of purchasing them from the manufacturers' local subsidiaries. Generic substitution effectively allowed the country to ignore patents and purchase drugs directly from low-cost manufacturers of equivalent pharmaceuticals.

With more than one in ten of its citizens infected with HIV, and faced with some of the highest drug prices in the world, the South African government understandably wanted to reduce costs and increase the availability of life-saving medicine. But some in the pharmaceutical industry argued that, with its new initiatives, the government was seeking to shift attention away from its own failed public health policies. The government of President Thabo Mbeki had been slow to acknowledge the problem of HIV/AIDS, or even to admit that it was a sexually transmitted disease.[2] In addition, the state of the country's health infrastructure was dire; its ability to reliably enforce the onerous daily drug regimen required to suppress the disease, and therefore to avoid creating resistant strains, was very much in question.

For their part, the pharmaceutical companies feared that South Africa would set an undesirable precedent. If patents for HIV/AIDS drugs were effectively gutted in South Africa, the slope could be very slippery indeed. Ultimately, the companies feared, the situation in South Africa could undermine their control over critical intellectual property throughout the developing world.

In May 1997, Aldridge Cooper of Johnson & Johnson and Harvey Bale of the Pharmaceutical Research and Manufacturers of America began writing U.S. Trade Representative (USTR) Charlene Barshefsky and Commerce Secretary William Daly, asking them to oppose South Africa's Medicines Act.[3] Many other drug company representatives and members of Congress also wrote to Barshefsky and other U.S. government officials criticizing South Africa. Members of Congress pressed the Clinton administration to intervene. In response, the USTR placed South Africa on the Special 301 "watch list" in 1998, putting the country at risk for U.S. sanctions.

In February 1998, the pharmaceutical company coalition, represented by South Africa's Pharmaceutical Manufacturers Association (PMA), filed their suit in Pretoria against the Medicines Act. The crux of their argument was that the Act was unconstitutional because it gave the health minister excessive power, violated international agreements on trade in intellectual property, and discriminated against the industry.

Meanwhile, in the United States, political pressure grew to increase access to AIDS drugs in South Africa. In June 1999, the AIDS organization ACT-UP began shadowing Vice President Al Gore's presidential campaign, accusing him of "medical apartheid."[4] These protests were heard loud and clear within the U.S. government. In September 1999, the U.S. and South African governments reaffirmed their shared goal of fully protecting intellectual property rights under

international agreements while addressing the health issues identified by South Africa. A few months later, USTR removed South Africa
from the special 301 watch list.[5]

The industry pressed forward its lawsuit in South Africa, however.
Arguments opened in March 2001, sparking international outrage;
press reports throughout the world were highly critical of the industry's tactics. Frustrated, the pharmaceutical companies continued to
argue that patent protection was vital to maintaining their current
and future research and development expenditures. But in juxtapos-
ing profit margins and research investment against the urgent need
for medicines for the dying, the industry was fighting a losing battle.
Soon after, the suit was withdrawn.

The story did not end there. The industry's suit helped catalyze a
coalition of developing countries and nongovernmental organizations
(NGOs) determined to carve out large public health exceptions to existing international law governing trade in intellectual property, laws
that the pharmaceutical industry had worked long and hard to
achieve. Led by the governments of South Africa and India and
NGOs such as Health Action International, Treatment Access Campaign, and Médecins Sans Frontières (MSF), the coalition launched
an international campaign to increase the availability of "essential
medicines," arguing that one-third of the world's population lacked
access to much-needed drugs.[6]

The "essential medicines" coalition chose as its battleground the
Doha Ministerial, a November 2001 meeting intended to start up
a new round of international trade negotiations. By threatening
to bring the talks to a standstill—a particularly alarming prospect
given the failure of the Seattle WTO ministerial meeting in late
1999—the coalition won broad public health exemptions in the
Doha Declaration.

The pharmaceutical industry's failure to effectively address the
concerns of governments, NGOs, and citizens regarding their drug
policies in AIDS-ravaged Africa was a classic case of inadequate mobilization leading to a predictable surprise. Mobilization failures
occur when leaders recognize impending predictable surprises and
acknowledge that action to avoid the surprise should be a priority, but
fail to do their utmost to mobilize a preventative response.

As discussed in chapters 5 and 6, potent organizational and political barriers impede the mobilization to forestall predictable surprises. Organizations tend to embrace continuity and stability—often for good reasons, such as employee and customer loyalty.[7] But pernicious incentives, collective action problems, or simple inertia can stand in the way of needed action, rendering the organization vulnerable to a crisis. On the political side, people with vested interests will predictably organize to defend their perquisites, creating coalitions and lobbies that seek to block action. It is very difficult to realize broad but modest benefits for many (such as access to affordable, life-saving drugs) in the face of opposition from an energetic few who stand to lose a great deal (such as the pharmaceutical industry). The strength of these barriers should not be underestimated; nor should the extent to which people will go to resist change. A leader's efforts can be undermined not only by open resistance, but by people who withhold their support or cut off resources such as talent and information.

When an emerging threat has been determined to have serious potential consequences, leaders must mobilize to prevent it. This means marshaling support, educating important external constituencies, focusing the attention of key people in the organization, and making surprise prevention a personal priority. If leaders embrace the challenge of mobilization and exert effort commensurate with the risks involved, they should not be held accountable if a surprise occurs. If they fail to do so, they must strengthen their capacity for mobilizing effective responses.

ORGANIZATIONAL MOBILIZATION FAILURES

Some organization mobilization failures result from *inaction* on the part of leaders. Others, such as the pharmaceutical industry's confrontational response to the challenge posed by the South African government and the HIV/AIDS crisis, are the result of *misguided mobilization*—energetic efforts to confront serious problems that go badly awry.

Shell and Greenpeace, Revisited

The case of Shell and its attempted sinking of the Brent Spar, recounted in chapter 5, provides examples of both effective mobilization—on the part of Greenpeace—and ineffective mobilization—on the part of Shell. Greenpeace's tactics in confronting Shell are a classic example of the use of asymmetrical means by "weaker" organizations against "stronger" ones. As such, the story illustrates what David Yoffie and Mary Kwak have described as "judo strategy," or the use of speed and flexibility to overcome deficits in size.[8]

Greenpeace's objective was to create and sustain a crisis for Shell. It did so by occupying the Brent Spar, thereby creating an initial focal event that attracted free media attention. By continually threatening to reoccupy the Spar, Greenpeace put Shell on the defensive. Like any guerrilla organization, Greenpeace hoped that Shell would overreact and lash out in ways that would build the story, sustain media attention, and catalyze opposition. Greenpeace seemed to understand that, too often, companies that are targets of negative media attention help to prolong the damage. By using water cannons to prevent the activists from reboarding the platform and by allowing Greenpeace to provide the only media communication links from the Spar, Shell ensured a steady stream of damaging images and stories for the world press. Shell's solution—to defend the Spar with water cannons—was technically effective but politically tone deaf. The spectacle of Greenpeace running its rubber rafts into the gauntlet provided media outlets worldwide with compelling daily video footage and ample opportunities for anti-Shell spin.

Greenpeace was effective in framing the debate in terms that resonated with the public. By comparing the dumping of the Spar in the North Atlantic to "the car being dumped in the village pond," Greenpeace made Shell's plans understandable and offensive to the average citizen. Meanwhile, Shell's rational engineering mind-set apparently blinded the company to the importance of framing and emotions.

Greenpeace also effectively shifted the battlefield in ways that exploited weaknesses in Shell's organizational structure. Rather than confront Shell head-on where it was strongest, such as with legal or political challenges, the activists hit the company where it was weak. It was Shell UK that planned to sink the Spar, and Shell UK that worked with the British government to gain approval for the sinking. But, of course, many other countries surround the North Sea, where the Spar was anchored, including Germany. Greenpeace knew that the Northern European public was more sensitive to environmental issues than the British public. Shell, which had large operations in Germany and elsewhere on the continent, should also have been aware of these regional differences in Europe. But other Shell units had not been consulted in the decision to sink the Spar.

In addition to media coverage, Greenpeace used timing as a tool as well, by occupying the Spar just before a major summit on the North Sea environment. Its actions led to a full-blown boycott of Shell in Germany and to pressure on Shell UK from the German government. This, in turn, turned up the political and economic heat on Shell in Germany, to the point where its leaders began to press their British colleagues and the Shell board to cancel the dumping.

How might Shell have better mobilized to respond to Greenpeace's occupation of the Brent Spar? Rather than prolonging the crisis by lashing out at the Greenpeace protestors, Shell could have put the dumping on hold and announced plans to engage the British government in further dialogue on the matter. This strategy would have left Greenpeace with a bunch of protestors bobbing uncomfortably on an aging structure in the North Sea. Lacking a "Shell strikes back" story, the media would have rapidly departed. An earlier decision to put disposal plans on hold could therefore have prevented the crisis from escalating by denying Greenpeace its high-profile issue and audience.

The Pharmaceutical Industry and South Africa

In contrast to the outright failure of Shell to mobilize to meet the threat posed by Greenpeace, the pharmaceutical industry engaged in energetic, but misguided mobilization in its dealings with South Africa and HIV/AIDS drugs. The industry was very much, as Shakespeare might have put it, "hoist with its own petard." It not only failed to mobilize support for its point of view, but predictably catalyzed the formation of an opposing coalition—a phenomenon called *reactive coalition building.*[9]

This is but one example of a broad range of situations in which leaders actually set themselves up for predictable surprises through misguided mobilization efforts. The George W. Bush administration's pattern of international diplomacy—threatening unilateral military action to mobilize collective action—provides a rich array of examples in this vein. In situations ranging from the invasion of Iraq to the undercutting of the Kyoto protocols to the imposition of steel tariffs to the preferential granting of postwar reconstruction contracts to allies, the administration's reflexive unilateralism and reliance on hard power arguably squandered the United States's enormous reservoir of international goodwill and soft "values" power. (Of course many argue that the Clinton administration squandered the hard power of America by miring the country in the swamp of multilateralism.)

From these mistakes, a straightforward and general lesson emerges for leaders hoping to prevent a predictable surprise: Avoid taking actions that could contribute more to the opposition's mobilization than to mobilization of support for your own cause. What might the pharmaceutical industry have done differently in South Africa? Abandoning its court case, establishing charitable foundations, and donating the drugs—notably, what it ended up doing anyway. By failing to take these cooperative actions early on, the industry was viewed as having undertaken them reluctantly, only as a last resort. An opportunity to generate goodwill—as well as to direct focus to the South African government's shortcomings—was lost.

POLITICAL MOBILIZATION FAILURES

In the political realm, special-interest groups described in chapter 6 contribute to predictable surprises by resisting mobilization, for entirely understandable reasons:

- *Loss of a comfortable status quo.* People grow comfortable with their current situation, with its power and perquisites, and fight to preserve it.

- *Threats to self-defining values.* Needed changes may challenge traditional notions of what is valuable. As a result, people may fear that they will have to behave in ways that are antithetical to their self-image.

- *Loss of a sense of competence.* People fear they will feel incompetent in postchange environments and will be unable to perform as required.[10]

The Great Blackout of 2003, Revisited

As we described in chapter 8, control over the power grid in many regions of the United States and Canada is vested in "independent systems operators" (ISOs). As the electricity sector was deregulated throughout the 1990s, these operators were established as quasi-independent organizations. ISOs are charged with overseeing grid operations, matching supply and demand of electricity, and safeguarding the condition of the grid.

In 1992, the Congress passed the Energy Policy Act, setting the stage for electric-utility industry deregulation and restructuring. The Energy Policy Act vested decisions about the form and timing of deregulation to state legislatures.[11] The Midwest ISO, which played a critical role in the August 2003 grid failure, was established in February 2002 as the result of an agreement among state governments to monitor portions of fifteen states. At the time of the blackout, it was one of the most recently established grid operators. Unlike most other ISOs in the country, however, the Midwest organization was not given authority to run the regional electric market. As a result, there was no unity of control over how electricity was bought and sold in the region. Critically, the Midwest ISO was not given the authority to buy additional power in order to bolster reliability. Instead it had to coordinate with thirty-three utilities in the region that collectively retained control.[12]

The weak ISO that resulted from negotiations among state governments in the Midwest represents a classic political mobilization failure. In spite of clear recognition of the dangers of decentralized control, the Midwest ISO was hobbled at birth by political disputes between Midwestern states that favored deregulation and states that opposed it.[13] Seeking to preserve the power of local utilities, the latter coalition of states successfully watered down the plan to create the ISO. The U.S.-Canada Power System Outage Taskforce concluded that confusion and a lack of coordinated response to the anomalies of August 14, 2003, contributed materially to the blackout.[14]

Given the economic costs of the blackout and the clear evidence that the weakness of the Midwest ISO contributed to the crisis, one would reasonably expect that this problem would be addressed as quickly as possible to prevent another predictable surprise. Amazingly, however, a coalition of regional groups lobbied, successfully as of late 2003, to prevent the grid from coming under federal jurisdiction and having control shifted from utilities to federal and regional authorities.[15]

In the aftermath of the blackout, the Federal Energy Regulatory Commission (FERC) developed an ambitious plan to restructure control of the grid, placing control of 150,000 miles of transmission lines in the hands of four or five regional authorities, rather than the 130 distinct operators. The plan also called for standardization in the rules governing electricity markets and interstate transfers of power. The intent, in part, was to address the market manipulation that afflicted California in 2002 as well as to increase reliability.

Opposing these efforts were constituencies in the Southeast and Northwest U.S. that had long enjoyed the benefits of low-cost power. Blessed with ample hydroelectric power and with a history of using low-cost electricity to spur development, these regions had made only halting steps toward market deregulation and regional control. For them, the FERC plan represented a major loss of local control.

Led by Senator Maria Cantwell (D-Wash.) and supported by companies such as Southern Co., an owner of monopoly utilities serving over four million customers in four Southern states, the coalition successfully lobbied to insert language into the Bush administration's controversial 2003 energy bill. This language would have modified the FERC plan, giving utilities first right of refusal to use their transmission lines even if they were nominally under ISO control and effectively gutting the reform arrangement.[16] According to data from the Center for Responsive Politics obtained by the *Wall Street Journal*, Southern Co. has been the second largest contributor to current members of the House Energy and Commerce committee, giving them $481,500 since 1989.[17]

And so reforms needed to address a critical weakness in the national infrastructure fell afoul of special-interest politics. In late November 2003, a coalition of Democrats and six Republicans joined forces to prevent an array of provisions in the energy bill from coming up for a vote in the Senate.[18] These provisions included:

- Subsidies that would double the production of ethanol

- Liability limits for the makers of the gasoline additive MBTE

- Tax breaks for the oil and gas industry

- Expansion of exploration on public lands

- Exemptions from provisions of existing environmental laws for owners of aging coal plants

This move in the Senate delayed enactment of the FERC reforms until at least 2004. If the reforms are not enacted in a timely manner, no one should be surprised if the nation suffers additional damaging blackouts. They are predictable, if not surprising; the only surprise has been the failure to mobilize to address them.

HIV/AIDS in South Africa

While the government of South Africa eventually embraced a vigorous strategy of providing antiretroviral medicines to those infected by HIV, this turnaround came very late in the evolution of the epidemic. The government in general, and President Thabo Mbeki in particular, failed to exercise leadership in the late 1990s through 2002. During this period, the extent of HIV infection rates—more than one in ten South Africans, or close to five million people—was not in dispute in international public health circles. Nor, in the broader medical community in South Africa, was there any doubt that HIV caused AIDS and that HIV was a sexually transmitted disease.

The ongoing reluctance to mobilize had tragic consequences in 1999, when Mbeki's government refused to provide the drug AZT to pregnant women infected with HIV. In a speech on the subject in

October 1999, Mbeki stated that there was "a large volume of scientific evidence alleging that, among other things, the toxicity of this drug is such that it is in fact a danger to health."[19] He further asserted that it would be "irresponsible" not to pay attention to the "dire warnings" of researchers about the safety of AZT. Yet AZT was a standard tool used in many countries to prevent infants from being infected during childbirth; its effectiveness (a 50 percent reduction in infection rates) and safety were not in dispute among reputable authorities. AIDS activists ultimately won a court case compelling the government to provide the drug to HIV-positive mothers.

The failure of the South African government to mobilize to address the AIDS crisis had its roots in history, values, and economics. While in the U.S. and Europe, HIV/AIDS at that time primarily afflicted homosexuals, the sick in sub-Saharan Africa were overwhelming heterosexual. Transmission was facilitated by the fact that South Africans were more likely than many populations to have multiple sexual partners, a reality that many in South Africa were reluctant to acknowledge. The apartheid regime had created "homelands" in which large numbers of black families were forced to live. But the need for workers in white-controlled areas had resulted in the separation of many black men from their families. These men often had more than one sexual partner. A lack of education regarding safe-sex practices, particularly the benefit of condoms, also rendered South Africans more susceptible to HIV transmission, as did the weakened immune status of many poor blacks.

As a result of these factors, recognition of AIDS/HIV as a priority problem for South Africa did not lead the government to mobilize until very late in the game. When asked whether he was prepared to acknowledge the link between HIV and AIDS in a September 2000 interview with *Time* magazine, Mbeki continued his denial and offered this confused reasoning:

> No, I am saying that you cannot attribute immune deficiency solely and exclusively to a virus. There may very well be a virus. But TB, for example, destroys the immune system and at a certain point if you have TB you will test HIV positive because the immune system is fighting the TB which is destroying it. Then you will go further to say TB is an opportunistic disease

of AIDS whereas in fact TB is the thing that destroyed the immune system in the first place. But if you come to the conclusion that the only thing that destroys immune systems is HIV then your only response is to give them antiretroviral drugs. There's no point in attending to this TB business because that's just an opportunistic disease. If the scientists . . . say this virus is part of the variety of things from which people acquire immune deficiency, I have no problem with that.[20]

Only one of Mbeki's cabinet ministers had had the courage to break ranks. It wasn't until former President Nelson Mandela began to make blunt public statements about the epidemic, and to advocate actively for debate on AIDS policy within the African National Congress, that the winds began to shift. In the same month that Mbeki expressed the views quoted above, Mandela directly challenged them, citing "dominant opinion that prevails throughout the world" that HIV causes AIDS. Mandela asserted that he would only be persuaded otherwise if new scientific research showed "conclusively that that view is wrong."[21] In a subsequent interview with the *Sunday Times* (London), Mandela said, "We must not continue debating, to be arguing when people are dying."[22] He also made a important statement about the role of leader in preventing predictable surprises and issued a stinging rebuke of Mbeki's leadership.

In February 2002, Mbeki was still refusing to accept the known link between HIV and AIDS or to allow state hospitals to offer antiretroviral drugs to AIDS sufferers.[23] By August, however, the government ceased its opposition to providing the drugs and developed a program to make them available. But in September 2003, Mbeki provoked outrage when he said, "Personally, I don't know anybody who has died of AIDS." Asked if he knew anyone who was HIV positive, he said, "I really, honestly, don't know." This came at a time when 600 people were dying of AIDS and 250 children were being born with HIV every day.[24]

THE ROLE OF LEADERSHIP

Throughout this book, we have stressed the responsibilities of leaders to recognize, prioritize, and mobilize to prevent predictable surprises.

Of these, mobilization in the face of concerted opposition may be the most difficult task.

Courage—the willingness to, as John F. Kennedy put it, "speak truth to power"—is one leadership quality that is indispensable in efforts to mobilize to prevent predictable surprises. Many of the great figures of history solidified their reputations through their efforts to catalyze action to avoid predictable surprises, often in the face of significant resistance. Think of Winston Churchill sounding the alarm about the ambitions of Hitler, or Roosevelt finding ways to support England in its darkest hour. To quote Churchill, "when the eagles are silent, the parrots begin to jabber."[25] Kennedy, Martin Luther King Jr., and a host of others have paid the ultimate price to achieve their visions.

This is not to say, of course, that individual leadership is sufficient to address all predictable surprises. Leaders must have the wisdom to recognize when they are swimming against a floodtide and when the time is ripe for change.

The interplay of social forces and individual action in addressing predictable surprises is captured in a model of social change developed by Kurt Lewin, a pioneer in the field of group dynamics.[26] One of Lewin's fundamental insights is that social systems exist in a state of tension between forces pressing for change and forces resisting change. When driving forces and restraining forces are roughly in balance, the system may fluctuate within some set of narrow limits, but no further.

As the forces driving for change mount, so too do the forces that resist change, at least at first. But if the pressure becomes great enough, the system may become ripe for "revolution," leading to the establishment of a new equilibrium. At this crucial point, the presence or absence of what Lewin calls *channel factors* becomes important. "Small but critical facilitators" of change, channel factors are those pivotal individuals and events that catalyze change.[27] In his study of the genesis of European revolutions, for example, historian Charles Tilly notes that the timely acts of a single rebel—in other words, a channel factor—may signal the possibility of successful rebellion to others, leading to the coalescence of latent opposition:

> The unpunished defection of one visible member [of a ruling coalition] sends a whole barrage of signals: the very possibility of defection, the decreasing capacity of the central executive

to maintain its commitments and keep others in line, the opportunity to seize assets formerly under central control, the chance for cooperation with other defectors, and the probable increased costs of loyalty to the center.[28]

In this way, courageous leaders "tunnel through" residual barriers to change, initiating chain reactions that lead to seemingly disproportionate results.

TOOLS FOR ACCELERATING MOBILIZATION

While essential, individual courage is rarely sufficient to head off a predictable surprise. Leaders must also be relentless in raising awareness and building support for needed action. As lawyer and civil rights activist Florynce Kennedy so aptly put it, "Don't agonize. Organize."[29] Leaders can adopt a number of techniques to enhance their ability to mobilize to avoid predictable surprises.

1. *Persuasive communication.* Present arguments and data in ways that raise awareness of the problem and the need for action.

2. *Coalition building.* Analyze existing political alignments, tap into existing sources of power, and build supportive coalitions.

3. *Structured problem-solving.* Set up collective learning processes that progressively enmesh people in defining the problem and developing solutions.

4. *Crisis-response organization.* Design organizations that are capable of responding rapidly and effectively to emerging crises.

Technique #1. Persuasive Communication

Persuasive communication can be viewed as the use of data, argument, and analogy to create a favorable definition of the problem to be solved and the set of potential solutions. In his book *Propaganda, Polls, and Public Opinion,* Malcolm Mitchell characterizes persuasive communication as "a burning glass, which collects and focuses the diffuse warmth of popular emotions, concentrating them on a specific issue."[30] Such communication is effective because (1) people's interests remain latent and diffuse until they are faced with a choice, and (2) people perceive their interests differently depending on how choices are posed. When delivered well, communication taps into the powerful emotional forces that influence individual choice.

For centuries, philosophers have advised leaders on how to communicate persuasively. In *Rhetoric*, Aristotle noted:

> Of the modes of persuasion furnished by the spoken word there are three kinds. The first kind depends on the personal character of the speaker; the second on putting the audience in a certain frame of mind; the third on the proof, or apparent proof, provided by the speech itself. Persuasion is achieved by the speaker's personal character when the speech is so spoken as to make us think him credible. We believe good men more fully and readily than others.[31]

Expanding on this foundation, we offer a number of classic tactics for persuasive communication:

- *Invoking the common good.* This approach involves emphasizing collective benefits, downplaying individual costs, and casting the stakes of action in terms of social responsibility.

- *Linking choices to core values.* Marketers and propagandists long ago learned the power of linking choices to the values that define self-identity. Thus, cigarette companies link smoking to independence and the freedom to choose.

- *Heightening concerns about loss or risk.* Desired courses of action should be cast in terms of potential gains or as risk reduction, and undesired choices should be cast in terms of potential losses or dangers.[32]

- *Narrowing or broadening the focus.* A choice that could be construed as setting an undesirable precedent might best be framed as a highly circumscribed, isolated situation independent of other decisions. Other choices might be better situated within the context of a higher-level set of issues.

- *Enlarging the pie.* Choices perceived as win-lose proposi-
  tions are particularly difficult to sell. Broadening the range of
  issues under consideration can facilitate mutually beneficial
  trades that "enlarge the pie."[33]

- *Repetition of resonant messages.* Simplifying the message
  makes it more memorable. Repetition, as long as it is not par-
  rotlike, helps cement messages in target audiences. This principle underlies the use of "sound bites" on television and radio.

- *Inoculating against expected challenges.* Aristotle and
  many others since have advised persuaders to inoculate their
  audiences against the arguments they expect their opponents
  to make. Presenting and decisively refuting weak forms of expected counterarguments immunizes audiences against the
  same arguments when they are advanced in more potent forms.

Based on their analysis of the intended audience, leaders can
draw selectively upon these techniques to get their message across.

Technique #2. Coalition Building

When leaders must mobilize people outside of their direct lines of
control to confront a difficult problem—as is almost always the
case—they need to build coalitions. In highly politicized environments such as Congress, coalition building is an essential component
of change. Coalitions can be just as important in the business world.
Sometimes executives have to make major organizational changes to
guard against a potential disaster. Such changes always create winners and losers and generate overt and covert resistance. To prevail,
leaders must be able to consolidate their supporters, neutralize their
opponents, and convince fence-sitters (through the use of persuasive
communication, carrots, and sticks) to back change. A prerequisite
for doing this is figuring out who wields influence both inside and
outside the organization and using this knowledge to build momentum for their cause.

Effective coalition building draws on the power of social influence. Research in social psychology has established that people prefer making choices that enable them to:

- *Remain consistent with strongly held values and beliefs.* They tend to share these beliefs with important reference groups such as peers or professional associations. People asked to engage in behavior inconsistent with their values or beliefs experience internal psychological "dissonance," external social sanction, or both.

- *Remain consistent with their prior commitments.* They do so because failure to honor commitments tends to incur social sanctions. People prefer not to make choices that require them to reverse themselves or that overtly constrain their future choices by setting undesirable precedents.

- *Preserve their sense of control.* Choices that threaten one's position in a social hierarchy and sense of control are likely to provoke anxiety.

- *Repay obligations.* Reciprocity is a strong social norm; people are vulnerable to appeals for support that invoke past favors they have received.

- *Preserve their reputations.* Choices that preserve or enhance one's reputation tend to be viewed favorably, while those that could jeopardize one's reputation are viewed in a negative light.

- *Gain the approval of respected others.* These might include opinion leaders, mentors, and others to whom people look for clues about the "right" way to think.[34]

In sum, people rarely make important choices independently; most are influenced by their networks of relationships and the opinions of key advisers. Understanding these relationship networks and leveraging them to build momentum dramatically increases leaders' ability to build supportive coalitions. For this reason, leaders should identify influential individuals and groups and map their *influence networks*—patterns that show which members of a group defer to which on crucial issues.[35] Also important are *communication networks*, or the channels through which groups share information.[36] Such analysis offers clues to the identity of *opinion leaders* to whom others look for answers, and who may also exert disproportionate influence outside their own group.[37] Success in convincing these pivotal people of the need for change translates into much broader acceptance, while resistance on their part can signal a general lack of support.

A thorough analysis of these factors will help leaders develop effective coalition-building strategies. One classic tactic is *entanglement,* by which leaders convince people to make a small, seemingly innocuous commitment as the first step down the slippery slope of larger ones. Most managers can recall having been asked, "Just come to the meeting and hear what we have to say," followed by, "Just get one of your people to take a quick look into it," and so on.

Another potent tactic is *sequencing*—approaching influential parties in a carefully thought-out order, to increase the likelihood of gaining support.[38] Most managers have had the experience of coming to a meeting and realizing in the midst of it that the "real" meeting had already happened—or of finding out that to get Alicia on board for a change initiative, for example, it would be wise to get Frank's support first.

Both entanglement and sequencing are undertaken with the goal of creating momentum for change by shaping potential allies' (and adversaries') perceptions of their alternatives. A key goal is to convince people that the status quo is not sustainable, that surprise is inevitable, and that the only remaining question is what type of change is necessary.

Finally, leaders hoping to avoid predictable surprises should keep in mind that coalition *breaking* often is as important as coalition *building.* Effective assessments of the strength of opposing coalitions can help to predict—and lessen—their impact. If opposing coalitions have begun to form, how long have their efforts been under way and how strong have they become? Is the opposition united through long-standing relationships and shared interests, or by short-term opportunism? Are there "linchpins" who can be won over and whose conversion will substantially weaken resistance? Will resistance by opposing coalitions likely be active or passive, and what forms might it take? More generally, how do key people perceive their alternatives, and how might these perceptions be altered? A clear focus on such issues will aid the new leader in developing more powerful change strategies.

Technique #3. Structured Problem-Solving

In his book *Building Team Power*, Thomas Kayser asserts that there is a "need for managers at all levels . . . to learn the fundamental how-to's of a consistent, organization-wide problem-solving process capable of helping groups collaborate in identifying, analyzing, and solving business and organizational problems."[39] Structured problem-solving is one technique for fostering group learning. It consists of a set of steps and associated tools that decouples problem definition from alternative generation and evaluation:[40]

Step 1. Work to define and gain consensus. Begin by focusing on diagnosis and data collection, and then discuss what the problem is.

Step 2. Probe beyond symptoms. "Cause/effects mapping" is commonly used to support this process. The group is asked to graphically map out the connections between the presenting problem and its symptoms, contributing causes, and deeper root causes. In the process, the group is challenged to differentiate between unfounded beliefs and information about cause-and-effect relationships that is supported by data. The results are used to stimulate and focus additional diagnostic efforts.

Step 3. Establish evaluative criteria. "Multi-attribute utility theory" can be employed to quantify and define decision-makers' assessments of the relative importance of different criteria in assessing the "goodness" of outcomes. Its use permits decision-makers to clarify and debate the trade-offs that alternative courses of action represent.

Step 4. Develop broad sets of options. "Brainstorming" encourages group members to suppress their normal critical impulses in order to free up creativity. Groups are given a set period of time to generate options for dealing with the problem and are told not to worry yet about practicalities. Criticism also is specifically forbidden at this point in the process.

Step 5. Evaluate options and reach conclusions. In addition to multi-attribute utility theory, "multi-voting" techniques can be employed to winnow down the alternatives to the best few. In multi-voting, members of the group are given a limited number of votes to cast in favor of specific alternatives. This means that they do not have to advocate for a single alternative at this point, but rather can support their top few choices. Once the votes are counted, the least supported alternatives can be eliminated, and debate can continue.

Structured problem-solving can be used in tandem with techniques discussed in chapters 7 and 8. Scenario planning can help to define the problem. Decision analysis can be applied to support the evaluation of options. Structured debate techniques can help the group to reach conclusions.

Structured problem-solving is a powerful mobilization technique, as it progressively fosters deeper awareness in groups of the existence of predictable surprises. In fact, structured problem-solving can be viewed both as a common language for fostering dialogue and as a form of progressive entanglement. By focusing first on reaching consensus on "the problem" and then on its root causes, this technique makes the need for action harder to dispute. Likewise, agreement on objective criteria for evaluating options makes it difficult for special-interest groups to argue for their own narrow political agendas. By the end of such a process, people may be willing to accept outcomes they never would have accepted at the beginning.

Technique #4. Crisis Response Organization

When crises do erupt, leaders must ensure that their organizations are ready to meet them. For this reason, effective leaders put in place the organizational structures, dedicated resources, and procedures necessary to respond rapidly to crises. A rapid, centralized response requires a clear line of command and the ability to shift rapidly into what the military terms "war-fighting mode." Without such preparation, the organization will respond incoherently and ineffectively. All but the smallest organizations should devote the resources necessary to set up dedicated crisis-response facilities and other infrastructure to respond to the emergency.

Of course, crises rarely occur exactly as they did in preparation scenarios. The danger exists that plans tailored to a rigid set of planning scenarios will prove "brittle"—unable to be rapidly adapted to the circumstances at hand. For this reason, flexibility must be built into an organization's crisis-response routines. Crisis-response plans can be created as a set of "packaged" responses—modules that leaders mix and match as their first response to a crisis. When implemented effectively, this strategy buys the organization time to craft a deeper, more customized response. One example of a crisis-response module is a building evacuation plan that could be activated for many different crisis situations. Others include facility lockdowns, preset communication protocols for contacting key employees, police and fire response, press relations, and grief management. Regardless of their form, each module should provide a list of steps to be taken and resources to be summoned. A tool for assessing organizational crisis-readiness is provided in appendix B.

You might wonder why we include crisis organization as a tool for preventing predictable surprises. The reason is that the act of preparing for crises contributes to their avoidance. "One of the best ways to understand what you need to do before a crisis takes place," one leading expert in crisis response noted, "is to understand what you need to do during its occurrence."[41] Forewarned is forearmed.

A CALL TO ACTION

Consider yourself forewarned *and* forearmed. In this section of the book, we have provided leaders with the RPM model, a prescriptive framework to help them better recognize, prioritize, and mobilize to prevent predictable surprises. There should be no shortage of situations in which you can apply these ideas and tools.

10

Future Predictable Surprises

We began this book by posing the following questions:

- Does your organization have serious problems that you know won't solve themselves?

- Are these problems likely to get worse over time?

- Could they eventually flash into a damaging crisis that will take most people in your organization by surprise?

We often ask these questions of the executives we meet, whether in our classes, on airplanes, or in meetings, and find that most can rattle off a list of predictable surprises that exist in their organization. We view it as the responsibility of executives to identify predictable surprises and to follow through to prevent them. Many executives do a good job of diagnosing potential crises. But, amazingly, they routinely leave predictable surprises to develop and fester.

Throughout the book, we have focused on predictable surprises that have already caused significant damage to individuals, organizations, the natural environment, and society in general. The astute reader might argue that predicting the past is easy—the real challenge is to predict future surprises. This is a completely reasonable challenge. Indeed, we are on record predicting the U.S. accounting debacle documented in chapter 3, and we also predicted that Enron was not the end of the story. But if our concept of predictable surprises has merit, we should be able to use it to identify future surprises that will be observable to the general public, rather than merely to members of one organization. We believe that the concept of predictable surprises is up to this challenge.

In this chapter, we introduce some visible public issues that should be treated as predictable surprises. Before presenting these new issues, we have some final words regarding some of the predictable surprises discussed earlier in the book. Despite spectacular disasters, many of the surprises we documented remain unsolved; therefore, we see them as ongoing predictable surprises. These surprises include campaign-finance reform and auditor independence in the United States, and the global depletion of fish stocks. After reviewing the state of these ongoing predictable surprises, we will predict the future—or as we see it, connect the dots—to identify additional predictable surprises. These predictable surprises include government subsidies, global warming, governments ignoring future financial obligations, frequent-flyer programs, and the vague contracts that are all too common in the negotiation world.

ONGOING PREDICTABLE SURPRISES

In chapter 3, we made a strong case that the joint collapse of Enron and Arthur Andersen was a predictable surprise that resulted from the dependence of auditors on their clients for future business. We documented the compromises that went into the Sarbanes-Oxley bill and the limited impact that we believe the bill will have in preventing corporate corruption. Sarbanes-Oxley was a compromise between pro- and antireform forces; the industry that was being regulated had a heavy hand in the changes that were enacted. When "auditor rotation" was written into law, the auditing firms made sure this only meant that the individual lead auditors working for a particular client should be rotated regularly, rather than the type of change that is truly needed: rotation of auditing firms among clients. Since the bill's passage, more auditor-related scandals have emerged, and they will continue to do so in the future.

In chapter 6, we discussed the destructive influence of special-interest groups on American politics and the enduring failure to enact meaningful campaign-finance reform. We documented the long and difficult journey through Congress of the McCain-Feingold bill, which passed only after being significantly weakened, due to the influence of the very special-interest groups the bill was intended to keep in check. Between 1995 and 2002, the bill was watered down to such an extent that for many members of Congress, the costs of living with its modest provisions were lower than the costs of being on record as voting against campaign-finance reform. Unfortunately, the compromises that were necessary to pass the bill also took away its teeth. As a result, even after the passage of McCain-Feingold, the U.S. electoral system remains wide open to the influence of special-interest groups that reduce the overall benefit to society. McCain-Feingold may have temporarily weakened the national political parties, but PACs have been strengthened.

Why do we so often fail to reform our systems even after a disaster occurs? There are two main culprits. First, most people view compromise as a reasonable behavior. But in case after case, when organizations have made compromises between reform and maintaining the status quo, the status quo has had an overwhelming influence, and the corrupt system remains. When a system is broken, we need to fix it rather than making a trivial adjustment.

Second, after a predictable surprise erupts, parties engage in political behavior to ensure that they do not suffer the consequences—even when they contributed to the disaster. After September 11, 2001, the priority of the commercial aviation industry was to avoid blame (which it deserved) and to seek funding from the government for its losses. When Enron folded, the auditing industry protected its financial interests by playing a core role in "reforming" the system. And when it became clear that the McCain-Feingold bill was not going away, lobbyists contributed significant resources to make sure that their services would be needed in the future. Once an explosion occurs, we need courageous leaders to repair the damage and ensure that it never happens again. Far too often, we get compromises and corrupted decision processes instead.

In chapter 4, we documented the predictable surprise of the collapse of the fisheries in the northeast United States, in great part due to the government subsidization of high-tech fishing fleets. Across the globe, this pattern has played out again and again in recent decades. The North Sea, for example, provided Europe with a reliable source of fish for centuries. But by 2002, as a result of overfishing supported by government subsidies, European fishers had all but gutted the sea of its formerly rich supplies of cod and hake.[1] As in the United States, European scientists and environmental groups had warned the EU that fish stocks were being dangerously depleted. And as in the United States, European fishers rejected appeals for meaningful fishing quotas, accusing the scientists of being alarmists. Predictably, throughout the 1990s, the EU and national governments caved in to the vocal majority; EU fisheries ministers routinely eased the fishing quotas recommended by marine biologists and upheld fishing subsidies. As of 2002, the member states of the European Union contributed about £1 billion per year ($1.6 billion) to the EU's fishing fund.

Once the crisis could no longer be denied, the fishers' predictable response was to seek out new waters to exploit. A new trend has emerged: rich nations, having depleted their own waters, are paying poor nations to empty theirs. For more than a decade, the European Union has been paying impoverished African nations "cash for access" deals to allow European fishing fleets unfettered access to West African coasts. The conservation group WWF estimates that foreign fleets will pay €144 million ($160 million) in 2003 to fish in the territorial waters of sixteen African nations.[2]

The West African coasts are the traditional home of an abundant supply of more than 1,200 fish species. Sustainability is supposed be ensured by the United Nations Convention on the Law of the Sea, which requires that access agreements only allow the harvesting of surplus fish that the host nation cannot harvest itself.[3] In August 2001, the northwest African nation Mauritania, which has a small coastal fleet, signed a new treaty with Europe worth €430 million over five years. While the treaty specifies the number of vessels that can be allowed to fish, no limits are placed on the amount of fish the Europeans can catch, allowing them to overharvest the Mauritanian coast just as they did the North Sea. Each boat fishing off of Mauritania costs EU taxpayers approximately €350,000 (about $390,000) in access payments.[4] The EU nations with the greatest number of trawlers, such as Spain, reap the bulk of the profit, while other European countries pay hundreds of millions of Euros to allow foreign ships access to African waters.

Fishing activity off northwest Africa has risen threefold since the 1970s, yet during this period the volume of fish landed has stagnated. The livelihood of local fishermen is quickly being destroyed; their small boats don't stand a chance against state-of-the-art trawlers from Europe. Dr. Ndiaga Gueye, director of marine fishers for the Senegalese government, attributed Senegal's willingness to sign a disadvantageous agreement with the EU to the need for money to build hospitals and schools, while also citing "political and diplomatic reasons."[5] African officials dependent on European aid and debt relief may feel they have no choice but to sign whatever contracts the EU hands them.

Cash-for-access deals damage the environment, the global economy, and the European Union's reputation as a fair and ethical entity. One European commentator in the *Times* of London observed, "What is outrageous is that we are not just dumping the burden of our surplus fishermen on Africa but are exporting a discredited subsidy regime as well."[6] The predictable surprise that will result from allowing subsidized EU fishers unfettered access to African coasts is obvious: Fish stocks will be further depleted; European economies as a whole will suffer at the hands of a special-interest group; and African nations will face the loss of an invaluable natural resource. Inevitably, European fishers will then look for new coasts to exploit. But the coasts are not limitless. Drastic steps must be taken to prevent the day when there will be no new waters to fish.

Back in the North Sea, in December 2002, the EU fisheries ministers restricted cod boats to about two weeks of fishing per month— twice the number of days recommended by the European Commission, but a significant shift in policy nonetheless.[7] The subsidization of shipping boats is scheduled to be phased out by the end of 2004. These changes come too little, too late.[8] Worldwide, elected officials must take a firm stand against high-tech fishers, a special-interest group that has done much to give government subsidies a bad name.

GOVERNMENT SUBSIDIES

Subsidies are traditionally defined as government grants given to individuals and companies with the goal of assisting enterprises that are considered advantageous to the public.[9] While some subsidies do encourage actions that contribute to the public good, most help only particular people, corporations, and industries. As such, they inflict more harm than good on the public, and in many cases they create predictable surprises. Government money (your tax dollars) spent on subsidies often promotes activities and consumption that would not occur normally, from the purchase of cigarettes to the purchase of high-tech fishing trawlers. As such, subsidies inject artificiality and inefficiency into the global marketplace. They lead us to destroy our forests and virtually give away mining rights. They generally create benefit for special-interest groups at the expense of the public. If the government didn't pay U.S. tobacco farmers to grow their crop, tobacco prices would reflect true market rates, cigarettes would be more expensive, and more people would quit smoking; in addition, some farmers might switch to harvesting a less harmful crop. If fishing companies weren't paid to buy environmentally destructive boats, they might find ways to harvest fish sustainably; better yet, they might diversify to more profitable and sustainable industries.

Most of our elected officials understand these basic economic facts. They know that subsidies distort the marketplace and give certain groups an unfair advantage over others, causing overall harm to society. They also understand that, by propping up industries as destructive and mismanaged as fishing and tobacco, they are making existing problems even worse. Yet, year after year, most members of Congress continue to support old subsidies while coming up with creative new schemes for new ones. As we discussed in chapter 6, estimates on the total annual cost of corporate welfare in the United States range from $87 billion to $167 billion per year, depending on whether tax breaks are added to the sum along with subsidies.[10] Subsidies are listed in Congress's annual appropriations bills as federal outlays. Because these bills are often hammered out just before the start of a new campaign season, the temptation to write in gifts for deep-pocketed and vocal special-interest groups has proven irresistible.

We have attributed predictable surprises to a number of cognitive, organizational, and political biases. Such biases often lie at the root of government subsidies. It is likely that many politicians saw the looming crisis of overfishing, for example, but allowed special-interest group intimidation to convince them to hold overly optimistic hopes for the future. "It never ceases to amaze me how members of Congress who criticize welfare for the poor on moral and constitutional grounds see no problem with the even more objectionable programs that provide welfare for the rich," Representative Ron Paul, a Texas Republican and a foe of subsidy programs, has commented.[11] Subsidies have particularly insidious effects on the developing world, as shown in our earlier discussion of Europe's exploitation of African fish stocks. An even more monumental story is currently being played out quietly in the realm of agriculture.

Farming subsidies in Europe, the United States, and Japan have been justified for decades on the grounds of supporting a modest, traditional way of life and protecting farmland from development and abandonment.[12] But by paying wealthy farmers to produce a greater supply of crops than the world demands, these developed nations create market distortions that have a devastating effect on developing nations that depend on farming for their economic survival.

In 2002, the thirty industrial nations of the Organization for Economic Cooperation and Development (including Japan, South Korea, the United States, Canada, Mexico, and most of Europe) spent $311 billion on domestic agricultural subsidies. This figure is roughly equivalent to the gross domestic product of all of Africa, and it dwarfs the $50 billion in assistance that the developed world gave the developing world in 2002.[13] European farmers receive 35 percent of their income from government subsidies; American farmers get 20 percent. According to the World Bank, the European Union subsidizes dairy farmers at a rate of $913 per cow annually.[14] Consider this: nearly one billion people worldwide struggle to scrape by on just $1 a day, while European Union cows net an average of $2.50 per day in government subsidies.[15]

Cows are not the only ones living large. Agriculture subsidies are often touted as a means of supporting small mom-and-pop farms, yet they typically are funneled to huge agricultural corporations, or agribusinesses. In the United States, farm subsidies are an enormous corporate welfare program: Nearly 70 percent of payments go to the largest 10 percent of producers.[16] The ten-year, $171 billion farm bill that President Bush signed in May 2002, with strong backing from Congressional Democrats, ensures that these handouts will not disappear soon.[17]

Because they encourage domestic overproduction, agriculture subsidies depress crop prices abroad. Prices for coffee, cocoa, rice, and sugar fell by more than 60 percent between 1980 and 2000, a drop that has had a disastrous impact on the many developing nations that rely on these crops as their chief exports.[18] Western farm subsidies cost poor countries approximately $50 billion in lost crop exports.[19] Sugar farmers in South Africa lose $100 million in annual exports to American and European sugar subsidies.

The most grotesquely subsidized crop in the United States is cotton, at $3 billion to $4 billion annually—an amount higher than the overall value of the cotton itself. America's twenty-five thousand cotton farmers, who are guaranteed an inflated price for every pound of cotton they produce, have an average net worth of $800,000.[20] What's more, the majority of cotton subsidies are concentrated in the hands of just 10 percent of cotton farmers. Because U.S. taxpayers subsidize the sale of cotton at below-production costs, more than half the cotton grown in the United States is exported. U.S. cotton is now routinely "dumped" at prices that drive down world prices.

In the impoverished African nations of Burkina Faso, Mali, Benin, and Chad, which fall nearly dead last in global rankings of living standards, cotton has long been the primary export. A cash crop, cotton is still picked by hand on small farms. In a *New York Times* editorial entitled "Your Farm Subsidies Are Strangling Us," Burkina Faso President Blaise Compaore and Mali President Amadou Toumani Toure noted that cotton accounts for up to 40 percent of export revenues and 10 percent of GDP for their countries, as well as for Benin and Chad, while global cotton subsidies amount to a staggering $5.8 billion in the 2001–2002 production year.[21] America's cotton subsidies exceed the entire GDP of Burkina Faso. The presidents write:

> Not only is cotton crucial to our economies, it is the sole agricultural product for our countries to trade. Although African

cotton is of the highest quality, our production costs are about 50 percent lower than in developed countries even though we rely on manual labor. In wealthier countries, by contrast, lower-quality cotton is produced on large mechanized farms, generating little employment and having a questionable impact on the environment. Cotton there could be replaced by other, more valuable crops.[22]

"America wants us to comprehend the evil posed by violent anti-Western terrorism, and we do," Compaore told the *New York Times* in a separate interview. "But we want you to equally concern yourself with the terror posed here by hunger and poverty, a form of terrorism your subsidies are aiding and abetting. If we cannot sell our cotton we will die."[23] This statement is not an exaggeration: The farming subsidy programs of developed nations are causing people to die in Burkina Faso, and in many other nations.

When it comes to farming subsidies, the United States is not the biggest culprit. As of 2003, Europe was doling out $49 billion in agricultural subsidies each year.[24] This tradition of exorbitance began in the 1960s, when Europe instituted a common agricultural policy that rewards its farmers merely for doing their jobs. Because Europe's program subsidizes farmers based on the type and amount of crops they produce, European farmers have no incentive to follow basic economic principles of supply and demand. Grow more food, their governments tell them, and we'll give you more money. Predictably, the farmers have done just that, at the expense of their counterparts in poor nations, who simply cannot compete.

In the last few decades of the twentieth century, enticed by the rich nations' promises of peace and prosperity, developing nations clamored to play a role in the global marketplace. They joined the World Trade Organization (WTO) and signed global free-trade agreements such as the New Economic Partnership for African Development and the North American Free Trade Agreement. During this era, developed nations and developing nations alike struck down tariffs, quotas, and subsidies, resulting in rapid gains in global economic activity. But the concessions only went so far; protectionist policies remained in place in the Western world, and in some cases even expanded. As a result, global economic growth has stagnated, and for

many poor countries, the promises of globalization remain unful-
filled. Exports accounted for 20 percent of the world's economic activity in 2000, but fell to 18.8 percent in 2003, according to the
research firm Global Insight.[25] The Philippines has lost hundreds of
thousands of farming jobs since joining the WTO in 1995, with modest surpluses turning into deficits. Former Philippine President Fidel
Ramos, who strongly supported the nation's entry into the world market in the mid-1990s, now blames "hidden farm subsidies and other
tricks" of rich nations for the suffering of Filipino farmers.[26] "Everyone
is questioning globalization," Javier Gonzalez Fraga, the former head
of Argentina's central bank, told the *New York Times* in mid-2003.
"The virtuous circle—we were to import capital goods from the in-
dustrialized nations and they were to buy our agricultural produce—
never happened."[27]

If developing nations are to rise from poverty, they must be given
the same rights as developed nations, including the right to compete
in the world export market. This will only happen if the United States
and other nations terminate their farm subsidies, thereby allowing
commodity prices to return to realistic levels. The International Monetary Fund (IMF) estimates that a repeal of all of the developed
world's agriculture trade barriers and subsidies would improve global
welfare by about $120 billion. If Africa were able to increase its share
of world exports by just 1 percent, it would realize an additional $70
billion a year, or five times the amount the continent receives in aid
and debt relief.[28]

In the early years of the twenty-first century, the leaders of developed nations have been vocal in advertising their commitment to increasing aid to the world's poorest nations, as evidenced by President
Bush's $15 billion AIDS initiative in Africa. While the goal of alleviat-
ing poverty and disease worldwide should be applauded, it is important to note that these efforts are more than undercut by homegrown
subsidies that sustain and exacerbate misery across the globe. Until
developed nations commit to slashing agriculture subsidies from their
federal budgets once and for all, they do not deserve to claim the
moral high ground in the war on poverty.

Will Western leaders act to alleviate the crisis, or allow it to fester
into a predictable surprise? Will Western leaders learn to trust the

marketplace, or simply wait for the next African famine and blame it on a lack of rain? Will Western leaders take the lead to stop subsidizing the fishing industry, or wait until the fish are gone? The predictable surprises that come from subsidies are amazingly obvious, yet our leaders fail to hammer out the international agreements that could stop them.

A couple of small but hopeful signs indicate that the tide could turn against agriculture subsidies. In the United States, Vice President Dick Cheney interceded in February 2003 to persuade Congressional Republicans to drop plans for $3.1 billion in new farming subsidies disguised as disaster relief. Senators wanted to raise subsidies by 42 percent for farmers living in counties designated as disaster areas during the previous two years—regardless of whether the farmers had suffered losses due to drought or flooding.[29] At Cheney's insistence, the bill was revised to make aid contingent upon disaster-related loss, with reimbursement coming from existing agricultural spending. Cheney's intervention corresponded with talks in Tokyo between the United States and its trading partners on reducing and eventually eliminating farm subsidies.

In July 2003, the European Union took baby steps toward reforming its farm subsidy policy. European farmers can no longer greatly increase their subsidies by producing excess food; subsidies to the largest farms will be funneled to "rural development projects"; and environmental criteria will be factored into funding decisions.[30] These reforms do not address export subsidies and do not reduce the overall amount of EU farm aid, but they do at least contribute to the ongoing global dialogue on agriculture subsidies.

In late 2001, the World Trade Organization began a round of trade liberalization talks in Doha, Qatar, dubbed the "development round" for a planned focus on the concerns of poor nations. In August 2003, in advance of September WTO negotiations in Cancún over subsidies, the United States and the European Union agreed to reduce protection for their farmers simultaneously, though they did not set specific goals or deadlines for subsidy reduction.[31] Interestingly, some large U.S. farming groups, such as the American Soybean Association, support such reforms. Echoing the arguments of developed nations, they believe that the elimination of subsidies will benefit everyone who engages in global trade, including U.S. farmers. "We're saying let each country produce what they produce best, and not be adversely affected by the size of another government's treasury," Rick Tolman, chief executive of the National Corn Growers Association, told the *New York Times*.[32]

In their editorial, the presidents of Burkina Faso and Mali concluded, "Our demand is simple: apply free trade rules not only to those products that are of interest to the rich and powerful, but also to those products where poor countries have a proven comparative advantage. We know that the world will not ignore our plea for a fair playing field."[33] It remains to be seen whether these leaders' counterparts in the developed world will respond to this plea.

GLOBAL WARMING

The largest and most dangerous predictable surprise is also the policy issue most consistently avoided by the Bush administration, as it has been by many previous administrations—global warming. To overview this problem, we first need to provide some basic facts about the earth.

The sun's energy reaches the earth as visible light, infrared light, ultraviolet light, and other forms of radiation such as radio waves and x-rays.[34] Warmed by this radiation, the earth gives off radiation in turn, primarily infrared light. The earth's atmosphere absorbs much of this infrared light, and in the process, warms the earth's surface. The eighteenth-century physicist and mathematician Joseph Fourier termed this phenomenon the "greenhouse effect," because greenhouses also absorb light and block cold air.[35] Due to the greenhouse effect, the earth is about 58 degrees Fahrenheit warmer than it would be without any atmosphere, a warmth essential to life as we know it.

Fossil fuels such as coal, oil, and natural gas are made up primarily of carbon and hydrogen. When these fuels are burned, they combine with oxygen; in this process, hydrogen converts to water vapor (H_2O) and carbon becomes carbon dioxide (CO_2). Because these two naturally occurring atmospheric gases are effective at trapping infrared light as heat, they are known as "greenhouse gases."

As energy is created on earth, carbon is neither created nor destroyed, but transferred from one place to another. In addition to being trapped in carbonate rocks such as limestone, carbon is found in four places in widely varying amounts that we may think of as "units." First, it is a component of all living things; we can think of the carbon locked up in land-based plant and animal life as one unit; one further unit comprises the carbon found in marine plants and animals. Second, there is the earth's atmosphere, containing the equivalent of 70 units of carbon in the form of carbon dioxide. Third, about 800 more units of carbon are stored in the ground as fossil fuel, primarily coal but also natural gas and oil. Finally, an additional 4,000 units of carbon are dissolved in the ocean.[36]

When we burn fossil fuels to heat our homes, run our cars, or generate electricity, we free carbon into the air. A complex cycle eventually sends the carbon to the sea floor in the form of calcium carbonate (mainly from the shells of plankton and mollusks), which, over eons, reenters the earth. As we have pumped more and more CO_2 into the atmosphere, it has slowly built up. When researchers first began to measure this concentration in the 1950s, it stood at approximately 250 parts per million (ppm); it now stands at about 350 ppm. This buildup increases the atmosphere's ability to absorb infrared light and thus raises average temperatures.

The issue of global warming was first noted by the media in the 1930s when a prolonged period of warm weather demanded explanation. Predictably, interest in the matter waned when the warm spell ended. Today, our leaders widely accept global warming as a very real threat; nonetheless they ignore the problem. Several international scientific panels, including the Intergovernmental Panel on Climate Change and the UN Environment Program, have conducted studies that conclude that the effects of global warming are negative and will become visible as early as the twenty-first century.[37] Although scientific evidence of the ever-increasing threat of global warming continues to mount, our leaders have refused to take any definitive action to decrease the emissions of greenhouse gases. The considerable cost of reducing carbon dioxide levels would weaken economies in the short term. As a result, there is a strong desire to maintain the status quo by discounting this future threat.

The lack of acknowledgment of the issue is likely to result in a disaster of dramatically greater cost than that of prevention. The 1997 Kyoto Protocol was a landmark international agreement to stopped the doubling of CO_2 levels by nearly five years and return greenhouse emissions to their 1990 levels by the year 2000. But because the United States has refused to ratify the measure, it is unlikely that the Protocol will ever be successful. The visible effects of global warming seem imminent.

Unfortunately, scientists have been unable to make reliable predictions regarding several key aspects of global warming. The computer models used to examine the global climate are unreliable, preventing credible quantitative predictions. The amount of warming that is currently occurring cannot be known for certain, nor can the speed with which warming will affect the environment. We do know that the problem of global warming will not solve itself. By 2050, if fossil fuels continue to burn at their current rate, the amount of carbon dioxide in the atmosphere will climb to twice its preindustrial level. The effects of global warming on ocean levels and weather patterns will dramatically change the climate of some areas. Global warming will cause glaciers to melt and oceans to rise, with potentially disastrous consequences for coastal areas and low-lying countries such as Bangladesh. Some islands and coasts will become uninhabitable; dikes will have to be built to protect cities and some agricultural land. Some populations will be forced to relocate; others will have to reorganize their systems of agriculture. Current predictions suggest that the net change will hinder food production. At present, the production and distribution of crops is barely keeping pace with population growth, and global warming could upset this balance. Because plants have a limited ability to migrate, global warming will eventually lead to a decrease in forests and plant life.

Although reducing greenhouse gas emissions has some beneficial effects in the present, such as the creation of more cost-efficient energy solutions, it would help primarily to avoid a great future cost—the more destructive effects of global warming. But such action would incur significant costs on taxpayers; compliance with the Kyoto agreement would cost the world $53 billion per year in 1990 dollars.[38] Additionally, nations in the process of industrialization, such as

China and India, would suffer economically if they had to reduce their reliance on fossil fuels.

Any elected officials who support measures at combating global warming can expect a good portion of their constituency to balk at footing the substantial costs. Consequently, our leaders have been reluctant to alter the status quo by compelling industries and individuals to change the way they use energy. The natural human impulse to discount the future and avoid all costs, even minor inconveniences, prohibits the acceptance of wise trade-offs that would require the infliction of a smaller cost in the present to avoid a catastrophe in the future.

In addition, the omission bias causes people to concentrate on avoiding harm through their actions, while ignoring the harms that come from inaction.[39] Citizens and government officials alike will deny responsibility for exacerbating global warming through their neglect of the issue and excuse themselves from changing their energy-consumption habits.

Finally, certain groups will benefit from inaction—namely, corporations that would have to forgo some of their profit in order to decrease their use of fossil fuels. Accordingly, these special-interest groups are motivated to lobby elected officials not to take preventative action against global warming, solely for their own benefit. The efforts of these groups effectively bar important political bodies and potential vehicles for change such as Congress from enacting meaningful and timely reforms. Sadly, legislators will often oppose deals that are beneficial to the majority of their constituency rather than risk a backlash from a more vocal special-interest group.

The global warming issue allows us to see all of the ingredients of a predictable surprise in action. Unfortunately, it is probably the most significant and potentially destructive predictable surprise that society is currently ignoring. Our leaders know about the problem and recognize that it must be remedied, yet they are rendered immobile by cognitive and political factors. If unchecked, the threat that greenhouse gas emissions pose will only grow over time. By continuing to avoid the costs of prevention we only accumulate an infinitely larger, inescapable debt for the future. The eventual "surprise" is likely to be a disaster beyond our leaders' current imagination. When the disaster starts to occur, we can count on them to deny that they had any reason to believe that the problem could become so large.

IGNORING FUTURE FINANCIAL OBLIGATIONS: EXPLODING MEDICAL COSTS AND RETIREMENT COMMITMENTS

Most of us believe that we should prepare financially for old age. We know that we should save for retirement so that we can pay our health-care bills when we are elderly rather than placing this burden upon our children. Unfortunately, the U.S. government does not seem to grasp this basic logic. As the Baby Boomer generation reaches retirement age, the government will face rising health-care costs and a diminished ability to pay for them, due to deficits incurred during the years the government should have saved up for the Boomers' retirement.[40] In this section, we argue that the U.S. government is ignoring its future financial obligations to such a degree that a major disaster is becoming inevitable. We also argue that too many corporations have been using the U.S. government as a role model in this regard, and we describe a similar scenario that is playing out in an aging Europe.

Over the next twenty-five to fifty years, medical costs in the United States are expected not only to increase but to explode. A vast number of economic and demographic studies project a dramatic increase in the percentage of senior citizens age 65 and above in the U.S. population by the middle of the twenty-first century.[41] By 2025, the United States as a whole will have as high a percentage of elderly citizens (over 65 years of age) as the state of Florida had in 1990.[42]

Rising U.S. life expectancy can be attributed in large part to the amazing medical discoveries of recent decades, discoveries that will continue to emerge and improve our quality—and quantity—of life. Some illnesses that used to be death sentences can now be treated and cured, while other once-fatal diseases have become chronic conditions that require ongoing care and increased medical costs. But these precious extra years of life do not come cheaply. The companies responsible for medical breakthroughs expect a payback for their successful drugs and medical devices. Essentially, the average U.S. citizen is living longer (often long enough to contract more than one major disease) and getting diseases that require repeated interactions with the health-care delivery system—interactions that often require increasingly expensive technologies. The number of elderly nursing-home residents is expected to grow from 1.3 million in 1980 to 5 million in 2040; between 1988 and 2018, nursing-home costs are projected to triple from $33 billion to $99 billion.[43] In 1997, President Clinton's Council of Economic Advisors (CEA) projected the expected burden of an aging population on federal entitlement programs such as Medicare and Medicaid. Figure 10-1 provides the CEA's estimates.[44]

These increasing medical costs will occur at the same time that the ratio of retirees to workers will double. Today, we average two retirees for every ten workers; by 2030, we will be supporting almost four retirees for every ten workers. Consistent with the above, President

FIGURE 10-1

Growth in U.S. Federal Entitlement Spending

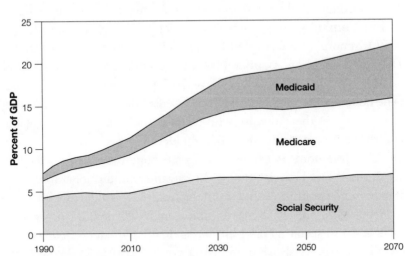

Source: "The Council of Economic Advisors on the Challenge of an Aging Population," *Population Development Review* 23, no. 2 (June 1997): 443-451.

Clinton's Council of Economic Advisers argued in 1997 that when the large Baby Boom cohort enters retirement age, federal Social Security, Medicare, and Medicaid outlays will rise sharply.[45] In 1997, expenditures on these key social programs represent less than 9 percent of GDP. That proportion is expected to rise to 19 percent by 2050 and to 22 percent by 2070.[46] In recent decades, the level of federal revenues was about 18 percent of GDP. Thus, unless reforms are instituted, the three major entitlement programs could consume all government revenues by 2050 and exceed them thereafter. If the government intends to continue to spend money on education, defense, and other popular programs, it will have to dramatically increase taxes and incur huge budget deficits, with adverse effects on economic growth and a spiraling effect on each future generation.

The U.S. government is fully aware that as Baby Boomers enter old age, they will become an unprecedented burden on federal resources. We might expect our leaders to acknowledge this mounting problem and work on creating surplus funds to cover these future costs. But as of 2003, the country had sunk into staggering levels of deficits. With the exception of a brief respite between 1998 and 2001, during which the nation enjoyed four consecutive years of budget surpluses, the nonpartisan Congressional Budget Office (CBO) reports uninterrupted federal deficits since the early 1970s. The federal debt compounded from $712 billion, or 26.1 percent of GDP, in 1980 to $3,540 billion, or 34.3 percent of GDP, in 2002. (The deficit is the annual figure that reveals how much more the government spent than took in, while debt is the total amount that the government owes, primarily to bondholders.)

This bad news is expected to get exponentially worse. In July 2003, the White House Office of Management and Budget forecast a steady increase in gross federal debt from $6.7 trillion in 2003, or 62.8 percent of GDP, to $9.4 trillion in 2008, or 68.3 percent of GDP.[47] This escalating debt burden is driven by federal deficits during the George W. Bush administration. In August 2003, the CBO predicted that federal budget deficits could total $5 trillion over the next ten years. This prediction was at odds with the Bush White House's own 2003 forecast that the budget deficit would peak at $475 billion in 2004 and fall significantly in subsequent years. Yet the

CBO based its conservative forecasts on the cost of three programs supported by Bush and Congressional Republicans, the last two supported by the Democrats as well: (1) making the 2001 and 2003 tax cuts permanent, at a cost of $1.5 trillion over ten years, (2) enacting a new $400 billion prescription drug program for senior citizens, and (3) revising the alternative minimum tax, which is expected to raise taxes for tens of millions of taxpayers as their incomes rise with inflation, at a cost of $400 billion to the government.[48]

The Bush administration's 2001 and 2003 tax cuts will significantly exacerbate the predicament of the aging U.S. population, burdening younger generations with federal debt at the same time they will be forced to finance the Baby Boomers. Bush's 2003 tax-cut proposal amounts to $674 billion, according to reported simulations conducted by nonprofit group Citizens for Tax Justice (CTJ), boosting the preexisting 2001 tax cuts by more than 50 percent over this decade. In January 2003, the CTJ released a study describing the size and distributional impacts of Bush's 2003 tax cut plans. The distributional impact is tabulated in figure 10-2.[49]

The implications of CTJ's findings are astonishing. When (and if) the 2001 Bush tax reductions are implemented, 52 percent of the aggregate $917 billion tax reductions will end up in the pockets of the wealthiest 1 percent, whose average 2010 income is forecasted to be $1.5 million.[50] In that year alone, members of this elite group will each receive average tax-cut windfalls of $85,000 each. Over the course of the decade, they will each receive average tax cuts of $342,000, which amounts to $477 billion in aggregate. The resulting distributional distortions will be exacerbated by Bush's 2003 tax-cut proposal; although lowering taxes on working families somewhat, 60 percent of these proposed tax reductions would go to the most wealthy 10 percent of American taxpayers.

In February 2003, 450 leading economists, including nine Nobel laureates, signed a statement opposing the argument that the tax cuts would stimulate the economy.[51] They maintain that the tax cuts will not spur adequate short-term job creation necessary to mitigate the ongoing U.S. economic slump of the early 2000s. Furthermore, these experts argue that the tax-cut plan was designed not to rebound the economy from a recession but to "reform" the tax system. Thus, the

FIGURE 10-2

Details of the Effects of the Bush 2003 Tax Cut Plan in 2003

Income Group	Income Range	Average Income	Average Tax Cuts from				Shares of Tax Cuts			
			Child Credit	Dividend Exemption	Rate Cuts and Other	Total	Child Credit	Dividend Exemption	Rate Cuts and Other	Total
Lowest 20%	Less than $16,000	$ 9,000	$ −1	$ −1	$ −4	$ −6	0.1%	0.1%	0.2%	0.1%
Second 20%	$16,000–29,000	22,000	−51	−7	−10	−19	7.8%	0.6%	1.4%	2.1%
Middle 20%	$29,000–46,000	35,000	−144	−27	−118	−209	22.1%	2.3%	4.2%	6.2%
Fourth 20%	$46,000–77,000	59,000	−252	−83	−323	−667	38.6%	7.0%	11.5%	14.2%
Next 15%	$77,000–154,000	103,000	−263	−288	−1,291	−1,841	30.2%	18.4%	34.4%	29.7%
Next 4%	$154,000–374,000	217,000	−35	−1,332	−2,157	−3,524	1.1%	22.7%	15.3%	15.2%
Top 1%	$374,000 or more	1,082,000	−1	−11,483	−18,643	−30,127	0.0%	48.9%	33.1%	32.4%
All		$69,100	$ −130	$ −233	$ −559	$ −922	100%	1005	100%	100%
Addendum										
Bottom 60%	Less than $46,000	$ 22,000	$ −65	$ −12	$ −54	$ −131	30.0%	3.0%	5.8%	8.5%
Top 10%	$104,000 or more	259,000	−125	−1,884	−3,568	−5,578	9.7%	80.2%	63.3%	60.1%

Source: "The Council of Economic Advisors on the Challenge of an Aging Population," *Population Development Review* 23, no. 2 (June 1997): 443–451.

Bush plan does not effectively deal with "overcapacity, corporate scandals, and uncertainty [that] have and will continue to weigh down the economy."[52] The economists emphasize that the Bush tax cuts will exacerbate the nation's long-term budget outlook by adding to the projected chronic deficits, thus endangering the government's capacity to finance benefit programs such as Medicare, Medicaid, and Social Security.

According to the Bush administration's 2003 projections, health expenditures in the United States will rise from $195 billion in 2002 to $334 billion in 2008; Medicare expenditures will climb from $230 billion in 2002 to $339 billion in 2008; and Social Security expenditures will rise from $456 billion in 2002 to $591 billion in 2008.[53] That health-care expenses are rising while the nation's ability to pay for them decreases cannot be denied. The Bush administration anticipates the exploding burden of an aging population and its associated medical costs. Yet rather than working to alleviate the problem, the administration is hastening and magnifying the crisis by increasing federal deficits and sinking the government deeper into a quagmire of federal debt. An enormous predictable surprise is in store when the federal government either defaults on its obligations to citizens or destroys the economy by spending our resources to meet these obligations, rather than spending the money to pursue true economic growth.

Any personal financial adviser would advise an individual or family facing big future expenditures, such as a mortgage or college tuition, to begin cutting back as early as possible on unnecessary expenses and start saving money. Indeed, in August 2003, the Federal Reserve Board and the Treasury Department outlined a five-step plan to help the record numbers of bankrupt and debt-ridden U.S. consumers better manage their credit. The advice included building savings, paying down debt, and understanding one's personal credit history. In interviews with the *Chicago Tribune*, budget experts pointed out the irony of Bush administration officials advising citizens on wise money management. Referring to the government's advice to "build savings to avoid high-cost debt and improve payment options," Robert Bixby, executive director of the Concord Coalition, which advocates a balanced U.S. budget, said, "I'd say the government is flunking that one. It is doing just the opposite."[54] Leon Panetta, a former federal budget director and Clinton administration chief of staff, concurred: "They are obviously not building savings, and they are borrowing to pay the bills."[55] The International Monetary Fund pointed to Bush's tax cuts as one cause of the worsening deficit, which "will make it even more difficult to cope with the aging of the Baby Boom generation, and will eventually crowd out investment and erode U.S. productivity growth."[56]

According to these experts, the government would be prudent to begin paying down its debt in preparation for meeting its future financial obligations. Instead, the Bush administration has doled out one tax cut after another, for reasons that seem to be based more on pleasing voters in the short term than on sound economic principles. In doing so, our leaders perpetuate the optimistic illusion among the citizenry that we can have our cake and eat it too—that we can see our taxes reduced now and still receive our fair share of entitlements later in life. This belief is a fantasy. The system will burst, and many people will be hurt in the process. We are burdening future generations with incredible amounts of debt, and we ourselves may fail to receive the benefits our leaders have promised. But because these costs will come long after our current leaders have served their terms of office, they feel it is in their short-term political interest to ignore the looming predictable surprise.

The phenomenon of rising health-care costs threatening to overburden the young and place governments in financial crisis is not unique to the United States. Worldwide, life expectancy has risen more over the past 50 years than over the previous 5,000 years.[57] At the same time, the average global fertility rate is falling, from about 5.0 births per woman in 1972 to about 2.5 in 2002. In the developed world today, including the United States, Europe, and Japan, one in seven people is elderly (age 65 and older); by 2030, one in four will be elderly, possibly as many as one in three.[58] Such trends will place an unprecedented burden on working-age people.

Europe in particular is aging—not just its already ancient cities, but the people themselves. Today in Europe, the median age is 38 years. By 2050, given projected fertility rates, the average European will be 52.3 years old, compared with the corresponding U.S. figure of 35.4 years.[59] Low fertility rates are contributing to Europe's rapid aging.[60]

To sustain a given population level, a minimum birth rate of 2.1 per woman is necessary. The birth rates of a number of European countries fall far below this number; German women have 1.3 births on average, and Italian women have 1.2 on average. Notably, the current U.S. fertility rate stands at about 2.0 children per woman.

As a result of the population decline in Europe, the aggregate number of workers will start shrinking by the 2020s. With this massive shift, European political and economic power will decline relative to the United States, China, India, and Latin America. The ability of many European countries to meet their obligations to retirees, in terms of pensions and health care, will be even worse than the crisis faced by the retirement of America's Baby Boom generation.[61] The graying of the European Union creates a fiscal threat that could potentially bankrupt major powers. In Europe, health-care and pension systems, like those in the United States, are largely based on the pay-as-you-go principle. In such economies, the ratio of workers, who pay taxes, to retirees, who receive benefits, is critical. In every EU nation but Ireland, the ratio of workers to retirees is shrinking dramatically.[62] Today, this ratio is approximately 3 to 1 for the developed world at large. By 2025, in most European countries, fewer than two workers will support each retiree; in Germany and Italy, the ratio is expected to drop to 1 to 1—or even less—by 2030. A decreasing number of young people will be paying into pension systems that support progressively larger numbers of people over the course of their relatively long retirements (only 39 percent of European men age 60 to 65 remain in the workforce).[63]

Unfunded pension liabilities in Germany already exceed 100 percent of GDP; France and Italy are in worse shape, with unfunded pension liabilities exceeding 200 percent of GDP.[64] In most developed countries, outlays on public pensions are conservatively estimated to rise by 4 to 6 percent of GDP over the next thirty years, but could rise by as much as 9 to 15 percent when health benefits are included.[65] So great is the impending crisis that Europe will not be able to confront it effectively through traditional belt-tightening measures, such as raising taxes, cutting spending, and borrowing more money. Indeed, in most European countries, projected senior benefit expenditures could very well crowd out all other government spending.

To meet current benefit promises, European income taxes, which already typically top 40 percent of payroll, would have to be raised by 25 to 35 percent by 2030. By 2030, Germany's payroll tax will have to exceed 50 percent, with the pension portion alone exceeding 25 percent. In Italy, by 2030, to cover the cost of caring for seniors, taxes would claim nearly 70 percent of a worker's pay. By 2030, government borrowing to finance rising health-care and pension expenditures would consume the total savings of the developed world, leaving nothing for private investment. Naturally, global capital markets would not support such a scheme.

In our overpopulated and environmentally precarious world, ecologists, medical doctors, and sociologists applaud Europe's declining fertility rates. Such trends, they note, can be attributed to Europe's prosperity, reflected in part by the wide array of career and reproductive options available to women. While this trend has its benefits, both for individuals and families in the short term and the ecosystem in the long term, it also will have unintended (though blameless) negative effects on European society. If Europe is to continue to prosper, it must come up with a solution to its demographic dilemma, lest its citizens find themselves deprived of health-care and living in societies in decay. European nations are faced with a major predictable surprise, one they cannot afford to ignore.

The most obvious solution would be to loosen immigration restrictions, thereby increasing the number of taxpayers. In fact, immigration already plays a critical role in Europe's current demographic development. Since 1989, migration has been the main component of annual population change in the European Union. In 2000, the annual net European migration rate represented about 65 percent of total population growth.[66] Notably, the populations of certain EU states, namely Germany, Italy, Greece, and Sweden, would all be in decline without positive net migration.

The European Union's pressing macroeconomic demand for immigration notwithstanding, most of the policy emphasis in European nations has been on immigration prevention and restriction, reflecting the perception of European stakeholders that the costs of immigration outweigh benefits.[67] Those who oppose loosening European borders argue that immigrants take jobs from locals; that they "don't integrate well" (a euphemism for the belief that immigrants are responsible for increased crime rates); and, conversely, that successful, hard-working immigrants cause a "brain drain" in their countries of origin. The arguments are largely unconvincing, given the economic and cultural contributions that so many immigrants have made both to European nations and to their homelands.[68]

Because their stance on immigration issues can make or break politicians' careers, immigration debates have largely remained shortsighted and nationalistic. But the problems facing an aging Europe, given its free inner market, are very much pan-European. With free movement of labor and capital among its states, the looming demographic crisis of the European Union can only be averted at the common European level. European immigration politics manifest a typical tragedy of commons: Policymakers have an incentive to think nationally and restrictively about immigration as it makes or breaks their governments. Yet officials understand that the European Union as a whole would be better off if immigration were increased to countermine the predictable surprise of an aging society. Europe must decide whether to dramatically increase levels of immigration or accept the fact that, as it ages, it will be diminished economically and sidelined in world affairs.

Shortsighted, self-interested financial strategies pervade not only governments, but organizations of all kinds, including corporations. The savings-and-loan crisis of the 1980s was built by crooked executives and aided and abetted by members of Congress seeking to placate this influential special-interest group (see chapter 6). Many of the financial scandals documented in chapter 3 were based on bad news that could be hidden only temporarily. These accounting tricks were uncovered, but because the system has not been adequately reformed, we can expect them to pop up at other companies in the future. Similarly, much of corporate America has been seeking out ways to make long-term pension deficits look smaller, in order to bolster short-term financials.[69] The federal government is doing its best to ignore the problem, which is perpetuated by many of the biggest donors to election campaigns. This predictable surprise will emerge when retirees find themselves deprived of the pension checks they were promised.

On another front, corporations have tried for a long time to avoid expensing stock options on their financial statements, in order to inflate earnings. Options give employees (and others) the opportunity, or option, to purchase the stock of a company at a preset price. Some corporations give options to employees, primarily executives, as part of compensation. And these corporations have successfully influenced accounting rules so that neither the employer nor the employee is required to recognize the expense of options until they are exercised. This creates a tax deferral for the employee; in addition, ignoring this expense serves to make the corporation's financial condition appear better than it actually is. Defenders of options argue that they cannot be expensed since no one knows what they will be worth in the future. But options are freely traded, and well-accepted financial calculations allow us to assess their worth. This accounting procedure makes corporations look good in the short-term, but eventually the predictable surprises will emerge. Transparency and honest accounting are sacrificed once again.

By focusing exclusively on short-term appearances, our government and too many corporations are creating predictable surprises for retirees and the U.S. economy in general. We must act now to correct these mistakes; if we wait until the disaster is obvious, it may be too late.

WAITING FOR YOUR MILES TO EXPLODE

In the aftermath of September 11, 2001, U.S. airlines faced significant financial challenges. Many people were newly afraid to fly, and many remain so to this day. With the 1990s financial boom over, the number of business flyers fell dramatically. The airlines lost billions of dollars in equity after 9/11, United Airlines and US Airways filed for bankruptcy, and many other airlines continue to struggle for their economic life. We expect that most of the major U.S. airlines will survive in some adjusted form. But eventually, another crisis will hit: the billions of dollars of debt that airlines owe their customers in the form of frequent-flyer miles.

The majority of the examples in this book have concerned governments and very public corporate failures. Our selection was partially based on the availability of this data, and partially due to our desire to present vivid stories that readers already know something about. Early on, we argued that predictable surprises await most organizations. However, we do not have the right to publicly announce predictable surprises based on private discussions. Thus, future corporate predictable surprises have been underrepresented in our examples in relation to governmental crises. Yet, in some cases, information about future corporate predictable surprise can be found in public sources. The future explosion of the airlines' frequent flyer programs is one such example.

In 1981, American Airlines introduced the most innovative marketing program in the history of the airline industry. The plan stated that flyers could earn miles for the flights they took and redeem these miles for travel awards. From a myopic perspective, this appeared to be a brilliant marketing strategy. The idea was to give flyers a unique reason to choose American. From a long-term financial perspective, it created a predictable surprise that is destined to explode.

Following American's lead, other major U.S. airlines hurried to create their own frequent-flyer programs. Soon they were offering double miles to their most frequent passengers, miles for hotel stays, miles for car rentals, miles for credit card use, etc. The expansion of benefits required to remain competitive in the industry resulted in significant liabilities. By 1987, various newspaper analyses estimated that the airlines owed their passengers between $1.5 and $3 billion dollars in free trips.

The programs' structures gave passengers an incentive to be frequent flyers of the airlines that flew to the largest number of cities—United and American. Despite the mounting long-term debt, American and United Airlines' frequent-flyer programs were paying off in the short-term with small gains in market share. As a result of losing ground to United and American, Delta Air Lines announced on December 15, 1987, that all passengers who charged their tickets to American Express would get triple miles for all of 1988. Delta assumed that passengers would switch their loyalty to Delta in exchange for triple miles. Instead, as Delta should have predicted, all of the major airlines announced that they too were offering triple miles, as well as a number of other new benefits.

The escalation of competition among frequent-flyer programs continued. Airline debt rose significantly, with some estimates placing it as high as $12 billion by 1990.[70] As early as 1988, Mark Lacek, then director of business-travel marketing at Northwest Airlines, lamented the escalation of mileage promotions: "It's suicide marketing. Insanity."[71] Around the same time, *Fortune* magazine concluded, "In the annals of marketing devices run amok, few can compare to the airlines' wildly popular frequent flyer plans."[72] Yet for the next fifteen years, the problem continued to grow.

Frequent-flyer programs are similar to the social dilemmas that we discussed in chapters 4 and 5. Each airline has a marketing benefit from having an attractive frequent-flyer program. But when all of the airlines have such programs, more and more flyers redeem miles for their tickets rather than paying in cash. The systems have significant operating expenses, and, most importantly, the long-term debt to customers is staggering. Collectively, all airlines have been made worse off by the frequent-flyer war. Over the past quarter century, the air carriers escalated frequent-flyer competition and made matters worse for all companies involved.

Over the years, the airlines have succeeded in making your miles less and less valuable. They have increased the number of miles needed for many routes, decreased the number of seats available for miles redemption, created "blackout" periods during which miles cannot be redeemed, and invented a host of other methods for reducing the value of miles. Despite their efforts, the debt owed to consumers remains enormous. Estimating the total debt that the airlines currently owe their customers is a tricky accounting question. It is made even trickier by the airlines' massive campaign contributions to politicians (even during bankruptcy) to influence accounting laws that allow them to understate the true amount of debt. In its broadest sense, the timing of when a contingent liability (the technical accounting term that describes the mileage awards owed) should be recorded is associated with the matching principle. That is, the liability (and corresponding reduction in income) should be recorded in the same period that any associated revenue has been earned. But what amount should be recorded as a liability? This is perhaps the biggest debate surrounding the recording of a contingent liability.

Like many contingent liabilities, reporting of the airlines' frequent-flyer obligations is made difficult by subjectivity, the different ways that the contingent liability can be assessed, and the desire of the airlines to understate their debt. There is no sure way of knowing whether and when members will redeem their accumulated miles. In addition, for passengers who do end up using their miles, it is unclear how they will redeem them. Aside from traveling for free, travel awardees can opt to use the miles for first-class and business-class upgrades and for other benefits such as hotel, rental-car vouchers, and consumer products.

We can say for sure that there is a strong market for frequent-flyer miles. Airlines sell hotels, car-rental companies, and credit-card companies miles that they can distribute to their customers. Airlines also sell miles to corporations to be distributed as they see fit. As of 2003, the going rate per mile fell to between one and two cents. Using the conservative one-cent-per-mile figure, when a customer has 25,000 miles in her frequent-flyer account, an airline would owe her $250 of value. But because of the uncertainty described earlier, it could be argued that this figure should be adjusted downward: Not everyone will redeem his or her miles. In addition, more and more passengers are using their miles in ways that create more than one cent per mile of benefit.

So, how do the major airlines account for unredeemed miles? First, they ignore the miles until they reach blocks of 25,000 miles for a specific individual (they act as if 24,000 miles has no value to you). Then, for each 25,000-mile block of unredeemed miles, they enter a liability; that is, they recognize that they owe some amount for the future use of that block of 25,000 miles. As of 2003, for Delta, Northwest, and US Airways, the liability entered ranges between $16 and $25 per ticket, to account for the cost of writing the ticket and the meal you will eat on the plane.[73] These airlines totally ignore the possibility that you or your company might have paid for a ticket with real dollars if the free miles did not exist. Thus, they are selling 25,000 miles for an amount between $250 and $500 and listing the liability at an amount less than $25. Because the airlines do not provide their rationale for the value they put on these liabilities, it can only be inferred. We must conclude that the airlines are hiding frequent-flyer debt. When we use the conservative estimate of $250 per ticket, and accept the airlines' deceptive procedure of ignoring mileage that is not in 25,000 mile chunks, the debt that the five largest U.S. airlines (American, United, Delta, Northwest, and US Airways) owe their customers exceeds $10 billion. Obviously, if we use the figure of $500 per ticket, the total debt exceeds $20 billion. Less than $2.5 billion is recognized on the airlines' books. To put this $10 billion dollar in perspective, as of August 12, 2003, the combined value of all of the stock for all five airlines fell well below $4 billion.

Eventually, most of us will decide to redeem our miles. When we do, a predictable surprise will emerge. The airlines will need to default on the debt they owe us and face legal action, or their revenue will crumble dramatically. Meanwhile, the airlines have been effective in lobbying to keep the real debt off of their books. If the real debt were listed, the predictable surprise would occur even faster.

We have spoken to many airline executives involved in the mileage programs. These executives are happy to explain the benefits created by the frequent-flyer programs, such as customer loyalty. They are also pleased with their ability to generate revenue by selling miles to hotels, car-rental companies, and so on. What they choose to ignore is that customers' loyalty to other airlines creates a real problem for them. They also prefer to ignore the huge debt that is mounting day by day, as customers rack up more and more miles. Anxious to justify their failed course of action, they ignore the strong evidence that frequent-flyer programs are a multi-billion-dollar mistake created by a series of irrational decisions. Like so many other predictable surprises, this motivated irrationality keeps executives from identifying their missteps and developing a more rational strategy for the future. Finally, the airlines have lost sight of their mission: to make a profit for their shareholders. Instead, they have falsely defined their goal as beating the other airlines. But being the best of a series of bankrupt firms is not a winning strategy.

Long ago, the airlines should have reduced the costs of their frequent-flyer programs. Promotions that are sure to be matched by competitors benefit only the customer. American should have realized when it created its program that other airlines were likely to follow suit. Delta should have considered the likely response of its competitors before announcing triple miles, and all airlines should have considered how to manage the decisions of the other parties in the industry. Instead, the airlines have chosen to bolster short-term financials and use deceptive accounting to hide their future problems. This strategy has worked for a while, but eventually the house of cards will collapse.

Our advice: Use your miles before they explode!

VAGUE CONTRACTS

As management professors, we often teach negotiation simulations to our students. In these simulations, pairs of participants assume opposing roles and conduct a negotiation. When the two parties return to the classroom, one of them writes the agreement on the board. Often, as soon as the agreement is on display, the other party shouts, "That's not what we agreed to!" How can this be true, when the two parties reached agreement just ten minutes earlier? In such cases, the parties typically made an oral agreement on an ambiguous contract, and each party then made inferences concerning the ambiguity. Not surprisingly, these inferences were self-serving: Both parties inferred the ambiguity in their favor.

In real negotiations in the workplace, it is common for two parties to reach a handshake agreement and have the lawyers write it up the next day. Typically, problems crop up at this stage. Businesspeople often claim that "lawyers destroy agreements." Lawyers counter that businesspeople have the strange tendency to shake hands before they actually agree, and then to report different deals to their respective attorneys. Only when the attorneys draft the agreement do the differences become apparent.

Disagreement about the nature of a contract is a fairly minor and common predictable surprise in negotiation. The bigger question becomes, why do so many parties with contracts they've agreed upon still end up spending enormous sums on attorney fees to handle arbitration hearings and court proceedings? What is so complicated about reading the contract and implementing its terms?

The authors have experience dealing with a pair of corporations in the same industry. Both companies are household names with excellent reputations. Both are highly profitable and are regularly written up as two of the best places to work in the country. They both employ fine people. Yet the two companies' employees hate each other.

Why? The answer lies in a poorly written contract.

Many years ago, when Company B was a start-up firm, Company A invested significant funds in Company B. In return, Company A received the rights to "certain uses" of a product invented and developed by Company B.

The product turned out to be even better than anyone expected. Suddenly, the ambiguous term "certain uses" was worth billions of dollars.

In the last decade, the two companies have spent over $300 million fighting legal battles over Company A's rights to the product. Thousands of executive hours have been lost, two fine companies have ended up hating each other, and opportunities to collaborate on other ventures have been destroyed.

Like Companies A and B, we believe that attorneys often will allow ambiguity to remain in a contract, rather than confronting an issue that might endanger the deal. But ambiguity begins with the negotiators themselves, and they are the parties most responsible for the predictable surprise of legal action.

Negotiators need to be clear about their agreement before leaving the table. Rather than just relying on a handshake, they should write down a nonbinding set of terms conditional on legal approval, and go over each one point by point. Attorneys should also ask themselves, or their colleagues, how a contract might be interpreted differently before they sign it. Reducing the ambiguity in contracts on the front end can help eliminate the need for dysfunctional, rancorous, and expensive conflict on the back end. Reducing such ambiguity will prevent many future predictable surprises in the corporate world.

CONCLUSION

We opened this chapter with the argument that the idea of predictable surprises allows us to see into the future. This is not a mystical process, but an analytic one. We hope that our evidence regarding both ongoing and likely future predictable surprises, including government subsidies, global warming, governments ignoring future financial obligations, and frequent-flyer programs, have helped convince you to care about these issues. Ideally, we hope that you will be motivated to get involved in society's debates about these issues, if you are not already, and to support political candidates who have the courage to confront predictable surprises, rather than passing on harm to future generations.

Just as important as attuning you to society's predictable surprises is the possibility that this book will inspire you to think about the predictable surprises occurring in your own organization. We hope that our discussions in part II of the book on cognitive, organizational, and political barriers to effective response will aid you in considering why your organization has ignored predictable surprises in the past, and how it can confront predictable surprises in the future. We hope that part III of the book has helped provide more specific guidance on recognizing, prioritizing, and mobilizing action when confronting predictable surprises. And we hope that these final chapters demonstrate that careful analysis can be used to identify predictable surprises before they explode in your organization.

Appendix A

General Accounting Office Reports Warning of Aviation Security Weaknesses, 1994–2001

Aviation Security: Additional Actions Needed to Meet Domestic and International Challenges (GAO/RCED-94-38, January 27, 1994).

Aviation Security: Development of New Security Technology Has Not Met Expectations (GAO/RCED-94-142, May 19, 1994).

Aviation Security: FAA Can Help Ensure That Airports' Access Control Systems Are Cost-Effective (GAO/RCED-95-25, March 1, 1995).

Terrorism and Drug Trafficking: Threats and Roles of Explosives and Narcotics Detection Technology (GAO/NSIAD/RCED-96-76BR, March 27, 1996).

Human Factors: Status of Efforts to Integrate Research on Human Factors into FAA's Activities (GAO/RCED-96-151, June 27, 1996).

Aviation Security: Immediate Action Needed to Improve Security (GAO/T-RCED/NSIAD-96-237, August 1, 1996).

Aviation Security: Urgent Issues Need to Be Addressed (GAO/ T-RCED/NSIAD-96-251, September 11, 1996).

Aviation Security: Technology's Role in Addressing Vulnerabilities (GAO/T-RCED/NSIAD-96-262, September 19, 1996).

Aviation Safety: New Airlines Illustrate Long-Standing Problems in FAA's Inspection Program (GAO/RCED-97-2, October 17, 1996).

Aviation Safety and Security: Challenges to Implementing the Recommendations of the White House Commission on Aviation Safety and Security (GAO/T-RCED-97-90, March 5, 1997).

Terrorism and Drug Trafficking: Responsibilities for Developing Explosives and Narcotics Detection Technologies (GAO/NSIAD-97-95, April 15, 1997).

Aviation Security: FAA's Procurement of Explosives Detection Devices (GAO/RCED-97-111R, May 1, 1997).

Aviation Safety: Weaknesses in Inspection and Enforcement Limit FAA in Identifying and Responding to Risks (GAO/RCED-98-6, February 27, 1998).

Combating Terrorism: Observations on Crosscutting Issues (GAO/T-NSIAD-98-164, April 23, 1998).

Aviation Security: Implementation of Recommendations Is Under Way, but Completion Will Take Several Years (GAO/RCED-98-102, April 24, 1998).

Aviation Security: Progress Being Made, but Long-term Attention Is Needed (GAO/T-RCED-98-190, May 14, 1998).

Air Traffic Control: Weak Computer Security Practices Jeopardize Flight Safety (GAO/AIMD-98-155, May 18, 1998).

Information Security: Serious Weaknesses Put State Department and FAA Operations at Risk (GAO/T-AIMD-98-170, May 19, 1998).

Aviation Safety: FAA's Use of Emergency Orders to Revoke or Suspend Operating Certificates (GAO/RCED-98-199, July 23, 1998).

Aviation Security: FAA's Actions to Study Responsibilities and Funding for Airport Security and to Certify Screening Companies (GAO/RCED-99-53, February 25, 1999).

Computer Security: FAA Needs to Improve Controls Over Use of Foreign Nationals to Remediate and Review Software (GAO/AIMD-00-55, December 23, 1999).

Federal Aviation Administration: Challenges in Modernizing the Agency (GAO/T-RCED/AIMD-00-87, February 3, 2000).

Aviation Security: Slow Progress in Addressing Long-Standing Screener Performance Problems (GAO/T-RCED-00-125, March 16, 2000).

Aviation Security: Vulnerabilities Still Exist in the Aviation Security System (GAO/T-RCED/AIMD-00-142, April 6, 2000).

Security: Breaches at Federal Agencies and Airports (GAO-OSI-00-10, May 25, 2000).

Computer Security: FAA Is Addressing Personnel Weaknesses, but Further Action Is Required (GAO/AIMD-00-169, May 31, 2000).

Aviation Security: Long-Standing Problems Impair Airport Screeners' Performance (GAO/RCED-00-75, June 28, 2000).

FAA Computer Security: Concerns Remain Due to Personnel and Other Continuing Weaknesses (GAO/AIMD-00-252, August 16, 2000).

FAA Computer Security: Actions Needed to Address Critical Weaknesses That Jeopardize Aviation Operations (GAO/T-AIMD-00-330, September 27, 2000).

Aviation Security: Additional Controls Needed to Address Weaknesses in Carriage of Weapons Regulations (GAO/RCED-00-181, September 29, 2000).

Major Management Challenges and Program Risks: Department of Transportation (GAO/GAO-01-253, January 1, 2001).

Aviation Rulemaking: Further Reform Is Needed to Address Long-standing Problems (GAO/GAO-01-821, July 9, 2001).

Appendix B

Ten Elements of an Effective Crisis-Response Plan

Effective crisis-response plans include the following ten elements:

1. *A representative set of planning scenarios.* It's essential to create a set of crisis scenarios that serve to guide planning. This need not be an exhaustive list of everything that could happen, but it should represent a broad range of potential emergency situations that your organization could plausibly face. Examples include economic dislocation and infrastructure failure (e.g., power-grid outage coupled with extreme heat or a disruption in the water supply).

2. *A flexible set of response modules.* Leaders should be able to pull combinations of preset response "modules" off the shelf. Modularizing the elements of a crisis-response plan will provide your organization with the flexibility needed to deal with unexpected scenarios or combinations of scenarios. Because real crises rarely match planning scenarios, if response options aren't flexible and modularized, novel events or combinations of events can yield ineffective or "brittle" responses.

Response modules might include backup power and activation of reserve production capacity as well as communication with media and other external constituencies.

3. *A plan that matches response modules to scenarios.* This core plan links each of the planning scenarios to the response modules that will be immediately activated. For example, a "loss of power" event triggers an immediate move to backup power, plus preset communication protocols to convene the crisis-response team and to warn staff.

4. *A designated chain of command.* One finding of research on crisis response is that decentralized organizations, which are so good at promoting innovation in normal times, prove to be woefully inadequate in times of crisis. Crisis demands a rapid centralized response, which necessitates a clear line of command. This means creating a centralized parallel organization in which the leader has a designated deputy, who in turn has a backup who could take command. It also means having a core crisis-response team of perhaps five or six people who function as the leader's staff in the parallel crisis-management organization.

5. *Preset activation protocols.* Preset signals are needed to activate and coordinate the various response modules in the event of a crisis. Clear triggers should transition your organization from "normal" to "war-fighting" mode and activate specific response modules. You must also establish "all clear" signals that shift the organization back to its normal operating mode.

6. *A command post and backup.* Select a location that can be rapidly converted for use by the crisis-response team. Depending on the crisis, requirements might include the ability to rapidly connect many lines of communication, and to gain access to external media (TV coverage) and to crisis-management plans. In addition, a backup command post should be located off-site in the event that evacuation is necessary.

7. *Clear communication channels.* Channels such as internal speakers and TV monitors must be easily activated to convey instructions to people on-site and off-site. When possible, these channels should have redundancies, including backups that are not linked to the telephone system or the Internet. Messages should be composed in advance, and there also should be mechanisms in place for rapidly locating key staff (e.g., "check in" via Web pages or phone).

8. *Backup resources.* Critical resources must be stocked and tapped if necessary. Examples include backup power generation, gas supplies, modest reserves of food and water, and medical supplies. Agreements should also be negotiated with external agencies to provide specific resources in time of crisis, such as augmented private security.

9. *Regular simulation exercises.* The best plans are worthless if they exist only on paper. Your organization's crisis-response team should regularly (at least biannually) conduct preparedness exercises, test channels, and stock inventories. To measure speed of response, these exercises should be unscheduled.

10. *Disciplined post-crisis review.* Each crisis provides an opportunity for organizational learning and revision of plans. For this reason, the crisis-response team should conduct a post-crisis review after each significant event. The guiding questions should be: What went well and what went poorly? What are the key lessons-learned? What changes do we need to make to our organization, procedures, and support resources?

Notes

Chapter 1

1. B. Fischhoff, "Hindsight Foresight: The Effect of Outcome Knowledge on Judgment under Uncertainty," *Journal of Experimental Psychology: Human Perception and Performance* 1 (1975): 288–299.

2. M. H. Bazerman, K. Morgan, and G. F. Loewenstein, "The Impossibility of Auditor Independence," *Sloan Management Review* (summer 1997): 89–94.

Chapter 2

1. J. D. Peach, "Aviation Security: FAA Needs Preboard Passenger Screening Performance Standards," *Report to the Secretary of Transportation. Resources, Community, and Economic Development Division, U. S. General Accounting Office* (GAO/RCED-87-182, 1987); K. O. Fultz, "Aviation Security: Development of New Security Technology Has Not Met Expectations," *Report to Congressional Requesters. Resources, Community, and Economic Development Division, United States General Accounting Office* (GAO/RCED-94-142, 1994); K. O. Fultz, "Aviation Security: Urgent Issues Need to Be Addressed," *Testimony Before the Subcommittee on Aviation, Committee on Transportation and Infrastructure, House of Representatives. Resources, Community, and Economic Development Division, U. S. General Accounting Office* (GAO/TRCED/NSIAD-96-251, 1996); G. L. Dillingham, "Aviation Security: Long-Standing Problems Impair Airport Screeners' Performance," *Report to Congressional Requesters. Resources, Community, and Economic Development Division, U. S. General Accounting Office* (GAO/RCED-00-75, 2000).

2. W. V. Robinson and G. Johnson, "Airlines Fought Security Changes: Despite Warnings, Companies Wanted to Avoid Delays," *Boston Globe*, 20 September 2001.

3. G. L. Dillingham, "Aviation Security: Vulnerabilities Still Exist in the Aviation Security System," *Testimony before the Subcommittee on Aviation, Com-*

mittee on Commerce, Science and Transportation, U.S. Senate; Resources Community, and Economic Development Division, U.S. Government Accounting Office (GAO/T-RCED/AIMD-00-142, 2000), 4.

4. G. L. Dillingham, "Aviation Security: Terrorist Acts Demonstrate Urgent Need to Improve Security at the Nation's Airports," *Testimony before the Committee on Commerce, Science, and Transportation, U.S. Senate; U. S. General Accounting Office Report* (GAO-01-1162T, 2001).

5. "Deregulated Airlines, Banking, Electricity, Telephones, Cable TV," *Consumer Reports* (July 2002), 30.

6. J. D. Peach, "Aviation Security: FAA Needs Preboard Passenger Screening Performance Standards."

7. Ibid.

8. M. Schiavo, *Flying Blind, Flying Safe* (New York: Avon Books, 1997), 206.

9. Ibid., 204.

10. Ibid., 206.

11. "What is the ATA?" Air Transport Association, 22 July 2002, <http://www.airlines.org> (accessed 11 March 2004).

12. G. M. Gaul, J. V. Grimaldi, and J. Warrick, "How Terror Could Break Through; At the Airports: Risks to Security Detected, Debated for Many Years," *Washington Post,* 16 September 2001.

13. Fultz, "Aviation Security: Development of New Security Technology Has Not Met Expectations."

14. Robinson and Johnson, "Airlines Fought Security Changes."

15. Schiavo, *Flying Blind, Flying Safe,* 193–194.

16. Ibid., 194.

17. S. Fainaru, "Clues Pointed to Changing Terrorist Tactics," *Washington Post,* 19 May 2002.

18. Ibid.

19. Federal Aviation Administration, Department of Transportation, *Proposed FAA Regulations on Security Profiling* (19 April 1999), 22.

20. Fultz, "Aviation Security: Urgent Issues Need to Be Addressed," 2.

21. Schiavo, *Flying Blind, Flying Safe,* 202.

22. "Lobbyist Spending: Airlines; 1997 data," Center for Responsive Politics, <http://www.opensecrets.org/Lobbyists/induscode.asp?code=T1100&year=1997&txtSort=C> (accessed 11 March 2004).

23. B. Yeoman and B. Hogan, "Airline Insecurity," *Mother Jones,* January/February 2002, 45.

24. Robinson and Johnson, "Airlines Fought Security Changes."

25. C. Eisenberg, "A Surge of Donations: Airline's Gifts to DNC Debated," *Newsday,* 16 March 1997, A4.

26. C. Eisenberg, "Split on Aviation Safety Panel: No Consensus Yet on Bag-Match Plan," *Newsday*, 11 February 1997.

27. White House Commission on Aviation Safety and Security, *Final Report to President Clinton* (1997), 5–6.

28. Ibid., 17.

29. Eisenberg, "Split on Aviation Safety Panel."

30. Ibid.

31. C. Eisenberg, "Dissent within Aviation Panel," *Newsday*, 21 February 1997.

32. "Appendix A: Commissioner Cummock Dissent Letter, February 19, 1997," White House Commission on Aviation Safety and Security, *Final Report to President Clinton* (1997).

33. C. Eisenberg, "Dissent within Aviation Panel."

34. Robinson and Johnson. "Airlines Fought Security Changes."

35. C. Eisenberg, "A Surge of Donations."

36. Ibid.

37. Ibid.

38. Ibid.

39. Gaul, Grimaldi, and Warrick, "How Terror Could Break Through."

40. B. Adair, "Gore Cultivates Close Ties to Airlines," *St. Petersburg Times*, 4 October 1999.

41. Ibid.

42. Ibid.

43. J. Pasternak, "FAA, Airlines Stalled Major Security Plans," *Los Angeles Times*, 6 October 2001.

44. Fainaru, "Clues Pointed to Changing Terrorist Tactics."

45. Ibid.

46. S. M. Hersh, "Missed Messages," *New Yorker*, 3 June 2002, 44.

47. Fainaru, "Clues Pointed to Changing Terrorist Tactics."

48. T. Rohrlich, "A Gap in Aviation Security," *Los Angeles Times*, 5 November 2001.

49. Schiavo, *Flying Blind, Flying Safe*, 293.

50. Pasternak, "FAA, Airlines Stalled Major Security Plans."

51. F. James, "Air Risks Remain, Experts Say," *Chicago Tribune*, 15 November 2001.

52. Rohrlich, "A Gap in Aviation Security."

53. Ibid.

54. Ibid

55. D. Armstrong and J. Pereira, "To Some, Profiling 'Not a Dirty Word': Airlines Revamp Method to Spot Terrorists," *Denver Post*, 24 October 2001.

56. Pasternak, "FAA, Airlines Stalled Major Security Plans."

57. Gaul, Grimaldi, and Warrick, "How Terror Could Break Through."

58. Peach, "Aviation Security: FAA Needs Preboard Passenger Screening Performance Standards."

59. Dillingham, "Aviation Security: Long-Standing Problems Impair Airport Screeners' Performance."

60. P. Eddy, "Security, What Security? How Airports Offered Terrorists an Open Door," *Sunday Times* (London), 16 September 2001.

61. Robinson and Johnson, "Airlines Fought Security Changes."

62. Eddy, "Security, What Security?"

63. L. Terrazzano and S. Adcock, "Balancing Security; Airlines: It's Government's Job," *Newsday,* 20 September 2001.

64. Pasternak, "FAA, Airlines Stalled Major Security Plans."

65. Yeoman and Hogan, "Airline Insecurity."

66. Ibid.

67. B. Morrison and G. Stoller, "Officials Warned of 'Evidence' of Strikes," *USA Today,* 12 September 2001.

68. Ibid.

69. M. Taylor, "Holes in U.S. Airports' Security; Weapons Often Get Past Guards, Experts Say," *San Francisco Chronicle,* 12 September 2001.

70. M. Grunwald, "Terror's Damage: Calculating the Devastation," *Washington Post,* 28 October 2001.

71. "Sept. 11 . . . And a Year of War, Anxiety and Questions," *New York Times,* 11 September 2002.

72. R. Halicks, "Remember 9/11: Aftermath," *Atlanta Journal-Constitution,* 1 September 2002.

73. M. Echenberg, "The Sky Is Falling: Political Negotiations and Moral Leadership Surrounding Airline Security in the Aftermath of September 11," (unpublished student research paper, Harvard Business School, 2002), 9.

74. K. L. Alexander, "Airline Losses Expected to Surge after N.Y. Crash; Analysts Say Some Struggling Carriers Could Be Forced into Bankruptcy," *Washington Post,* 13 November 2001.

75. D. Leonhardt and M. Maynard, "Troubled Airlines Face Reality: Those Cheap Fares Have a Price," *New York Times,* 18 August 2002.

76. Grunwald, "Terror's Damage: Calculating the Devastation."

77. W. Neikirk, "Federal Deficit Soars: White House Projects Record $455 Billion Shortfall This Year," *Chicago Tribune,* 16 July 2003.

78. W. M. Welch, "Experts Predict Deficits Will Last Years," *USA Today,* 20 November 2001.

79. Dillingham, "Aviation Security: Vulnerabilities Still Exist in the Aviation Security System."

80. Pasternak, "FAA, Airlines Stalled Major Security Plans"; T. Rohrlich, "Response to Terror: Aviation Security," *Los Angeles Times,* 5 November 2001.

81. B. Dedman, "Fighting Terror: Words of Caution; FAA Looking to Expand System," *Boston Globe,* 12 October 2001.

82. L. Zuckerman and J. Sullivan, "The Crash of Egyptair 990: The Safeguards; An FAA Study Shows Few Gains in Improving Security at Airports," *New York Times,* 5 November 1999.

83. G. L. Dillingham, "Aviation Safety and Security: Challenges to Implementing the Recommendations of the White House Commission on Aviation Safety and Security," *Testimony before the Subcommittee on Aviation, Committee on Commerce, Science and Transportation, U.S. Senate; Resources Community, and Economic Development Division, U.S. Government Accounting Office* (GAO/T-RCED-97-90, 1997), 2.

84. Schiavo, *Flying Blind, Flying Safe,* 210.

85. Pasternak, "Air Security: AFF, Airlines Stalled Major Security Plans."

86. White House Commission on Aviation Safety and Security, *Final Report to President Clinton* (1997), 5.

87. Terrazzano and Adcock, "Balancing Security; Airlines: It's Government's Job."

88. Robinson and Johnson, "Airlines Fought Security Changes."

89. Terrazzano and Adcock, "Balancing Security; Airlines: It's Government's Job."

90. Gaul, Grimaldi, and Warrick, "How Terror Could Break Through."

91. Terrazzano and Adcock, "Balancing Security; Airlines: It's Government's Job."

92. "Airlines: Background," Center for Responsive Politics, 1 December 2001, <http://www.opensecrets.org/industries/background.asp?Ind=T1100> (accessed 11 March 2004).

93. E. Nakashima, "President Signs Airport Security Bill; DOT Has 9 Months to Investigate, Hire and Deploy 28,000 Baggage Screeners," *Washington Post,* 20 November 2001.

94. "Press Releases: Transportation Security Administration Awards Contracts for Private Screening Pilot Programs to San Francisco International and Tupelo Airports," *Transportation Security Administration,* 11 October 2002, <http://www.tsa.gov/public/display?theme=44&content=09000519800037c0> (accessed 11 March 2004).

95. "Holes in Airport Security," *Boston Globe,* 8 June 2003.

96. M. L. Wald, "Threats and Responses: Airport Security; Boston Airport Acts Quickly to Prepare for New Rules," *New York Times,* 18 December 2002.

97. Nakashima, "President Signs Airport Security Bill."

98. Ibid.

99. Robinson and Johnson, "Airlines Fought Security Changes."

Chapter 3

1. C. Johnson, "Auditor Tells of Lawsuit Fears; Andersen's Duncan Anticipated SEC Probe," *Washington Post,* 14 May 2002, E4.

2. D. Greising, "No Accounting for Fight Against Real Oversight," *Chicago Tribune,* 23 June 2002.

3. E. A. Torriero and R. Manor, "Jury Finds Andersen Guilty," *Chicago Tribune,* 16 June 2002.

4. M. H. Bazerman, K. P. Morgan, and G. F. Loewenstein, "The Impossibility of Auditor Independence," *Sloan Management Review* (summer 1997), 90.

5. H. Smith, "Who Dropped the Ball?" *PBS Frontline Report: Bigger Than Enron,* 20 June 2002, <http:www.pbs.org/wgbh/pages/frontline/shows/regulation/watchdogs> (accessed 11 March 2004).

6. B. Sternberg, "Accounting's Role in Enron Crash Erases Years of Trust," *USA Today,* 22 February 2002.

7. J. Mayer, "The Accountants' War," *New Yorker,* 22 & 29 April 2002, 66.

8. General Accounting Office (1996), *The Accounting Profession: Major Issues: Progress and Concerns* (GAO/AIMD-96-98, 1996), 96.

9. Arthur Levitt, "Testimony Concerning: Commission's Auditor Independence Proposal, before the Senate Subcommittee on Securities, Committee on Banking, Housing, and Urban Affairs," U.S. Securities and Exchange Commission, 28 September 2000, <http://www.sec.gov/news/testimony/ts152000.htm> (accessed 11 March 2004).

10. J. K. Stewart, "Incentives Feed Audit Woes," *Chicago Tribune,* 10 March 2002.

11. Ibid.

12. Ibid.

13. F. Norris, "Accounting Firms Accept Rule to Limit Conflict of Interest," *New York Times,* 15 November 2000.

14. H. Smith, "Interview: Arthur Levitt," *PBS Frontline Report: Bigger than Enron,* 12 March 2002, <http://www.pbs.org/wgbh/pages/frontline/shows/regulation/interviews/levitt.html> (accessed 11 March 2004).

15. Ibid.

16. Arko Datta/Reuters, "Andersen's Enron Misadventure Exposes Rot at the Heart of an Old but Tainted Profession," *Toronto Star,* 26 January 2002.

17. D. Alexander and R. Kaiser, "Andersen Consulting Emphasis Questioned," *Chicago Tribune,* 27 January 2002.

18. K. Eichenwald, "Andersen Trial Yields Evidence in Enron Fall," *New York Times,* 17 June 2002.

19. Ibid.

20. H. Smith, "Enron: What's the Fix?" *PBS Frontline Report: Bigger than Enron*, 20 June 2002, <http://www.pbs.org/wgbh/pages/frontline/shows/regulation/etc/hedrick.html> (accessed 11 March 2004).

21. H. Smith, "Interview: Lynn Turner," *PBS Frontline Report: Bigger than Enron*, 5 April 2002, <http://www.pbs.org/wgbh/pages/frontline/shows/regulation/interviews/turner.html> (accessed 11 March 2004).

22. Ibid.

23. G. B. Moriarty and P.B. Livingston, "Quantitative Measures of the Quality of Financial Reporting," *Financial Executive* (July/August 2001), 53–56.

24. Ibid.

25. Smith, "Interview: Lynn Turner."

26. Mayer, "The Accountants' War," 69.

27. Smith, "Interview: Arthur Levitt."

28. T. Bliley, M. G. Oxley, and W. J. Tauzin, "Letter from House Commerce Committee," *PBS Frontline Report: Bigger than Enron*, 17 April 2000, <http://www.pbs.org/wgbh/pages/frontline/shows/regulation/congress/house.html> (accessed 11 March 2004).

29. Mayer, "The Accountants' War," 64.

30. Ibid., 70.

31. K. Lay, quoted in H. Smith, "Letter from Kenneth Lay," *PBS Frontline Report: Bigger than Enron*, 20 September 2000, <http://www.pbs.org/wgbh/pages/frontline/shows/regulation/congress/lay.html> (accessed 11 March 2004).

32. Smith, "Letter from Kenneth Lay."

33. The Center for Responsive Politics is a nonpartisan, nonprofit Washington, DC, research group that tracks money in politics. Data are available at <http://www.opensecrets.org>.

34. F. Norris, "3 Big Accounting Firms Assail SEC's Proposed Restrictions," *New York Times*, 27 July 2000.

35. Ibid.

36. Ibid.

37. J. Berardino, "Transcript: U.S. Securities & Exchange Commission Hearing on Auditor Independence," U.S. Securities & Exchange Commission, 26 July 2000, <http://www.sec.gov/rules/extra/audmin.htm> (accessed 11 March 2004).

38. Bazerman, Morgan, and Loewenstein, "The Impossibility of Auditor Independence," 90.

39. M. H. Bazerman, *Judgment in Managerial Decision Making*, 5th ed. (New York: John Wiley & Sons, 2001).

40. Bazerman, Morgan, and Loewenstein, "The Impossibility of Auditor Independence," 92.

41. M. H. Bazerman and G. F. Loewenstein, "Transcript: U.S. Securities & Exchange Commission Hearing on Auditor Independence," U.S. Securities & Exchange Commission, 26 July 2000, <http://www.sec.gov/rules/extra/audmin.htm> (accessed 11 March 2004).

42. M. H. Bazerman, G. F. Loewenstein, and D. A. Moore, "Why Good Accountants Do Bad Audits," *Harvard Business Review* (November 2002): 97–102.

43. Levitt, "Testimony Concerning: Commission's Auditor Independence Proposal, before the Senate Subcommittee on Securities, Committee on Banking, Housing, and Urban Affairs."

44. P. Spiegel, "Accountants Split over Rules on Auditor Independence," *Financial Times,* 21 September 2000, 14.

45. "The Ties that Bind Auditors," *The Economist,* 12 August 2000.

46. Mayer, "The Accountants' War," 70.

47. Smith, "Interview: Arthur Levitt."

48. S. Labaton, "Hurdles Are Seen for Audit Changes," *New York Times,* 24 January 2002.

49. Mayer, "The Accountants' War," 68.

50. Ibid., 64.

51. Ibid., 71.

52. D. Alexander and M. M. Garza, "Andersen Execs Aired Concerns," *Chicago Tribune,* 18 January 2002.

53. J. Spinner, "'You Were Right'; Lawmakers Face SEC Chief Who Warned of Auditors' Conflicts," *Washington Post,* 25 January 2002.

54. "Enron Auditor Feared He Was Guilty," Associated Press, 15 May 2002.

55. Mayer, "The Accountants' War," 71.

56. Ibid., 66.

57. Ibid., 68.

58. S. Labaton, "U.S. Favors Swift Justice, Not Slow Reform," *New York Times,* 16 June 2002.

59. D. Alexander, "Final 4 Don't Get Message," *Chicago Tribune,* 17 June 2002.

60. Smith, "Interview: Arthur Levitt."

61. M. Duffy and J. F. Dickerson, "Enron Spoils the Party: Bush Wants His State of the Union Speech to Drown Out Those Stories Linking the Disgraced Company and the White House," 27 January 2002, *Time,* <http://www.time.com/time/nation/article/0,8599,197609-1,00.html> (accessed 11 March 2004).

62. Mayer, "The Accountants' War," 70.

63. Alexander, "Final 4 Don't Get Message."

64. Smith, "Interview: Lynn Turner."

65. E. Bumiller, "Bush Signs Bill Aimed at Fraud in Corporations," *New York Times,* 31 July 2002.

66. R. A. Oppel, "Negotiators Agree on Broad Changes in Business Laws," *New York Times,* 25 July 2002.

67. "Editorial: Will Auditing Reform Die Before It Begins?" *New York Times,* 27 December 2002.

68. J. D. Glater and D. Leonhardt, "Corporate Conduct: The Impact," *New York Times,* 25 July 2002.

Part II

1. A. L. McGill, "Context Effects in Judgments of Causation," *Journal of Personality and Social Psychology* 57 (1989): 189–200; C. Winship and M. Rein, "The Dangers of Strong Causal Reasoning in Social Policy," *Society* 36, no. 5 (July/August 1999): 38–46; C. Winship, "The Dangers of Strong Causal Reasoning: Root Causes, Social Science, and Poverty Policy in Experiencing Poverty," in *Experiencing Poverty: Studies in Cash and Care,* ed. J. Bradshaw and R. Sainsbury (Burlington, VT: Ashgate, 2000), 26–54.

2. Winship and Rein, "The Dangers of Strong Causal Reasoning in Social Policy."

3. McGill, "Context Effects."

Chapter 4

1. "Here's the Catch: Order Could Be Death Sentence," *San Antonio Express-News,* 15 May 2002.

2. Material in this paragraph adapted from M. Bazerman, J. Baron, and K. Shonk, *"You Can't Enlarge the Pie": Six Barriers to Effective Government* (Basic Books: New York, 2001).

3. R. A. Myers and B. Worm, "Rapid Worldwide Depletion of Predatory Fish Communities," *Nature* 423 (15 May 2002): 280–283.

4. W. J. Broad and A. C. Revkin, "Has the Sea Given Up Its Bounty?" *New York Times,* 29 July 2003.

5. R. Tempest, "Strict New Limits on Coastal Fishing Adopted," *Los Angeles Times,* 14 September 2002.

6. M. H. Bazerman, *Judgment in Managerial Decision Making,* 5th ed. (New York: Wiley & Sons, 2002); R. Hastie and R. Dawes, *Rational Choice in an Uncertain World: The Psychology of Judgment and Decision Making* (Thousand Oaks, CA: Sage Publications, 2001).

7. S. E. Taylor, *Positive Illusions* (New York: Basic Books, 1989).

8. S. E. Taylor and J. Brown, "Illusion and Well-being: A Social Psychological Perspective on Mental Health," *Psychological Bulletin* 103 (1988): 193–210.

9. D. M. Messick, S. Bloom, J. P. Boldizer, and C. D. Samuelson, "Why We Are Fairer than Others," *Journal of Experimental Social Psychology* 21 (1985): 480–500.

10. L. Babcock and G. Loewenstein, "Explaining Bargaining Impasse: The Role of Self-serving Biases," *Journal of Economic Perspectives* 11, no. 1 (1997), 109–126; R. M. Kramer, "Self-enhancing Cognitions and Organizational Conflict," (unpublished student paper, Stanford University, 1994).

11. Kramer, "Self-enhancing Cognitions and Organizational Conflict"; Taylor, *Positive Illusions*.

12. J. Crocker, "Biased Questions in Judgment of Covariation Studies," *Personality and Social Psychology Bulletin* 8 (1982): 214–220.

13. E. J. Langer, "The Illusion of Control," *Journal of Personality and Social Psychology* 32 (1975): 311–328.

14. Kramer, "Self-enhancing Cognitions and Organizational Conflict."

15. T. C. Sorenson, *Kennedy* (New York: Harper and Row, 1965), 322.

16. Kramer, "Self-enhancing Cognitions and Organizational Conflict."

17. G. Allison, *Essence of Decision* (Boston: Little, Brown & Co., 1971).

18. K. Q. Seelye, "President Distances Himself From Global Warming Report," *New York Times,* 5 June 2002.

19. Al Gore, *Earth in the Balance: Ecology and the Human Spirit* (Boston: Houghton Mifflin, 1992).

20. Babcock and Loewenstein, "Explaining Bargaining Impasse: The Role of Self-serving Biases"; K. A. Diekmann, S. M. Samuels, L. Ross, and M. H. Bazerman, "Self-Interest and Fairness in Problems of Resource Allocation," *Journal of Personality and Social Psychology* 72 (1997): 1061–1074.

21. D. M. Messick and K. Sentis, "Fairness, Preference, and Fairness Biases," in *Equity Theory: Psychological and Sociological Perspectives,* ed. D. M. Messick and S. Cook (New York: Praeger, 1983), 61–64.

22. Diekmann et al., "Self-interest and Fairness in Problems of Resource Allocation"; Messick and Sentis, "Fairness, Preference, and Fairness Biases."

23. M. A. Neale and G. B. Northcraft, "Experience, Expertise, and Decision Bias in Negotiation: The Role of Strategic Conceptualization," in *Research on Negotiations in Organizations,* vol. 2, ed. B. Sheppard, M. Bazerman, and R. Lewicki (Greenwich, CT: JAI Press, 1990): 55–76.

24. M. Ross and F. Sicoly, "Egocentric Biases in Availability and Attribution," *Journal of Personality and Social Psychology* 37 (1979): 332–337.

25. R. Sutton and R. M. Kramer, "Transforming Failure into Success: Impression Management, the Reagan Administration, and the Iceland Arms Con-

trol Talks," in *Organizations and Nation-States: New Perspectives on Conflict and Co-operation*, ed. R. L. Zahn and M. N. Zald (San Francisco: Jossey-Bass, 1990).

26. Kramer, "Self-enhancing Cognitions and Organizational Conflict."

27. J. Rawls, *A Theory of Justice* (Cambridge, MA: Harvard University Press, 1971).

28. D. E. Sanger, "Threats and Responses: The President's Speech; Bush Sees 'Urgent Duty' to Pre-empt Attack by Iraq," *New York Times*, 8 October 2002.

29. S. J. Hedges, "Critics Urge War Inquiry," *Chicago Tribune*, 9 July 2003.

30. M. Killian and B. Kemper, "CIA Taking Blame for Iraq Claim: Tenet Says Agency Erred in Letting Bush Make Iraq Charge," *San Diego Union Tribune*, 12 July 2003.

31. D. Remnick, "Faith-based Intelligence," *New Yorker*, 28 July 2003.

32. M. Isikoff and T. Lipper, "A Spy Takes the Bullet," *Newsweek*, 21 July 2003.

33. S. Hersh, "Selective Intelligence," *New Yorker*, 12 May 2003.

34. S. J. Hedges, "All the Facts that Fit (for Now)," *Chicago Tribune*, 20 July 2003.

35. Ibid.

36. Tubke-Davidson, "Q&A: War and Intelligence," *New Yorker Online Only*, 7 May 2003, <http://www.newyorker.com/online/content/?030512on_onlineonly01> (accessed 15 March 2004).

37. R. Dreyfus, "The Pentagon Muzzles the CIA: Devising Bad Intelligence to Promote Bad Policy," *American Prospect* 13, no. 22 (16 December 2002).

38. Hersh, "Selective Intelligence."

39. K. A. Wade-Benzoni, A. E. Tenbrunsel, and M. H. Bazerman, "Egocentric Interpretations of Fairness in Asymmetric Environmental Social Dilemmas: Explaining Harvesting Behavior and the Role of Communication," *Organizational Behavior and Human Decision Processes* 67, no. 2 (1996): 111–126.

40. Ibid.

41. F. Cairncross, *Green, Inc.: A Guide to Business and the Environment* (Washington, DC: Island Press, 1995).

42. G. Loewenstein and R. H. Thaler, "Intertemporal Choice," *Journal of Economic Perspectives* 3 (1989), 197–201; D. Gately, "Individual Discount Rates and the Purchase and Utilization of Energy-using Durables," *Bell Journal of Economics* 11 (1980): 373–374; M. D. Levine, J. E. McMahon, and H. Ruderman, "The Behavior of the Market for Energy Efficiency in Residential Appliances Including Heating and Cooling Equipment," *Energy Journal* 8, no. 1 (1987): 101.

43. Gore, *Earth in the Balance*, 191.

44. Wade-Benzoni, Tenbrunsel, and Bazerman, "Egocentric Interpretations of Fairness in Symmetric, Environmental Social Dilemmas."

45. E. A. Mannix and G. L. Loewenstein, "The Effects of Interfirm Mobility and Individual Versus Group Decision Making on Managerial Time Horizons," *Organizational Behavior and Human Decision Processes* 59 (1996), 371–390.

46. *Frontline*, PBS, 21 May 1991.

47. I. Ritov and J. Baron, "Reluctance to Vaccinate: Omission Bias and Ambiguity, *Journal of Behavioral Decision Making* 3 (1990): 263–277.

48. Ibid.

49. Bazerman, Baron, and Shonk, *You Can't Enlarge the Pie,* 19.

50. D. Kahneman and A. Tversky, "Psychology of Preferences," *Scientific American* 246 (1982): 161–173.

51. W. Samuelson and R. Zeckhauser, "Status Quo Bias in Decision Making," *Journal of Risk and Uncertainty* 1 (1988): 7–59.

52. S. Benartzi and R. H. Thaler, "Naive Diversification in Defined Contribution Savings Plans," *American Economic Review* 91, no. 1 (2001): 79.

53. T. C. Schelling, "Some Economics of Global Warming," *American Economic Review* 82 (1992): 1–14.

54. "Early Deaths: Fact and Fiction," *BusinessWeek (Industrial/Technology edition)* 3677 (17 April 2000), 8.

55. A. Tversky and D. Kahneman, "Judgment under Uncertainty: Heuristics and Biases," *Science* 185 (1974): 1124–1131.

56. L. Babcock and G. Loewenstein, "Explaining Bargaining Impasse: The Role of Self-serving Biases," *Journal of Economic Perspectives* 11, no. 1 (1997): 109–126.

Chapter 5

1. This account is drawn from S. Passow and M. Watkins, "Sunk Costs: The Plan to Dump the Brent Spar (A)," Case 9-903-010 (Boston: Harvard Business School, 2003).

2. "The Battle for Brent Spar," *Public Eye,* BBC, 3 September 1995.

3. The extensive literature on organizations as information-processing systems has its origins in the work of Cyert, March, and Simon. In developing their behavioral theory of the firm, Cyert and March modeled organizations as information-processing systems and developed the important concepts of quasi-resolution of conflict, uncertainty avoidance, problemistic search, and organizational learning in *A Behavioral Model of the Firm* (Englewood Cliffs, NJ: Prentice-Hall, 1963). Herbert Simon extended that work, developing key concepts such as bounded rationality in *Administrative Behavior: A Study of Decision-making Processes in Administrative Organizations* (New York: Macmillan Free Press, 1965). Wilensky focused on the issue of problem formulation, pointing out that managers must be skilled at asking the right questions and gathering the right information in

order to promote learning; see *Organizational Intelligence: Knowledge and Policy in Government and Industry* (New York: Basic Books, 1967). C. Argyris and D. A. Schön looked at how organizational learning systems promote or impede efforts to identify and solve problems and developed the distinction between single-loop and double-loop learning: *Organizational Learning: A Theory of Action Perspective* (Reading, MA: Addison-Wesley, 1987). B. L. T. Hedberg developed a model of organizational learning based on the key processes of searching and perceiving, acting and reacting, designing and choosing, and linked organizational learning to situational variables such as stability, availability, and cost of information, and filters such as worldviews. He also highlighted the importance of unlearning—the ability of organizations to shed outmoded ways of formulating and solving problems. See his "How Organizations Learn and Unlearn," in *Handbook of Organizational Design*, ed. P. C. Nystrom and W. H. Starbuck (New York: Oxford University Press, 1981): 1–27. R. Daft and K. Weick extended these ideas to argue that organizations are interpretation systems and focused attention on cycles of scanning, interpretation, and learning in "Toward a Model of Organizations as Interpretation Systems," *Academy of Management Review* 9, no. 2 (1984): 284–295.

4. For an overview, see R. J. Robinson, "Errors in Social Judgment: Implications for Negotiation and Conflict Resolution, Parts 1 and 2," Cases 897-103 and 897-104 (Boston: Harvard Business School, 1997).

5. "The Battle for Brent Spar," BBC.

6. B. D. Berkowitz and A. D. Goodman, *Strategic Intelligence for American National Security* (Princeton,NJ: Princeton University Press, 1989), 27–28

7. "But always will our whole Nation remember the character of the onslaught against us," F. D. Roosevelt, "Address to Congress Requesting a Declaration of War with Japan," *The American Presidency Project*, 8 December 1941, <http://www.presidency.ucsb.edu/site/docs/pppus.php?admin=032&year=1941&id=138> (accessed 12 March 2004).

8. R. Wohlstetter, *Pearl Harbor: Warning and Decision.* (Stanford, CA: Stanford University Press, 1962), 397.

9. Berkowitz and Goodman, *Strategic Intelligence for American National Security*, 28.

10. Wohlstetter, *Pearl Harbor: Warning and Decision*, 369–370.

11. R. Lawrence and J. Lorsch. *Organization and Environment: Managing Differentiation and Integration.* (Homewood, IL: R. D. Irwin, 1969).

12. Wohlstetter, *Pearl Harbor: Warning and Decision*, 1.

13. Ibid., 382.

14. Ibid., 180.

15. Ibid., 186.

16. Luce and Raiffa attribute the formulation of the prisoner's dilemma game to A. W. Tucker. See R. D. Luce and H. Raiffa, *Games and Decisions* (New York: Dover, 1957), 94. The literature on one-shot and repeated prisoner's dilemma games is vast.

17. See R. Axelrod, *The Evolution of Cooperation* (New York: Basic Books, 1984).

18. "The Battle for Brent Spar."

19. J. Pratt and R. Zeckhauser, eds., *Principals and Agents: The Structure of Business* (Boston: Harvard Business School Press, 1985).

20. "Finance and Economics Section," *The Economist*, 23 November 2002.

21. In their behavioral theory of the firm, Cyert and March developed the important concept of organizational learning; see *A Behavioral Model of the Firm*, 116. J. P. Walsh and G. R. Ungson developed a model of organizational memory consisting of three processes: acquisition, retention, and retrieval; see "Organizational Memory," *Academy of Management Review* 16, no. 1 (1991): 57–91. Recent useful works in this tradition include P. M. Senge, *The Fifth Discipline: The Art and Practice of the Learning Organization* (New York: Doubleday, 1990); D. Garvin, "Building a Learning Organization," *Harvard Business Review* (July–August 1993): 78–91; and G. P. Huber, "Organizational Learning: A Guide for Executives in Technology-critical Organizations," *International Journal of Technology Management* 11, no. 7/8 (1996): 821–832.

22. M. Polanyi developed the distinction between tacit and explicit knowledge and the notion of interpretative frameworks for making sense of experience, in *Personal Knowledge: Toward a Post-critical Philosophy* (Chicago: University of Chicago Press, 1958).

23. This story about Somalia is drawn from S. Rosegrant (with Michael Watkins), "A 'Seamless' Transition: United States and United Nations Operations in Somalia—1992–1993 (A) and (B)," Cases 1324.0 and 1325.0 (Boston: Harvard University Kennedy School of Government, 1996).

24. The operation that followed UNITAF was actually named UNOSOM II, as there had been an earlier and smaller UNOSOM I operation in Somalia before UNITAF.

25. Rosegrant and Watkins, "A Seamless Transition," 6.

26. "UN Security Council Resolution 837," United Nations Web site, 6 June 1993, <http://www.un.org/Docs/scres/1993/scres93.htm> (accessed 11 March 2004).

27. M. Bowden, *Blackhawk Down: A Story of Modern War* (New York: Atlantic Monthly Press, 1999).

28. Rosegrant and Watkins, "A Seamless Transition," 4.

Chapter 6

1. K. Pender, "Investor Advocates Leery of Appointees to Accounting Oversight Panel," *San Francisco Chronicle*, 29 October 2002.

2. Ibid.

3. "Judge Webster, Miscast," *New York Times*, 26 October 2002.

4. Pender, "Investor Advocates Leery of Appointees to Accounting Oversight Panel."

5. S. Labaton, "S.E.C. Orders Investigation into Webster Appointment," *New York Times*, 31 October 2002.

6. Ibid.

7. J. Pasternak, "FAA, Airlines Stalled Major Security Plans," *Los Angeles Times*, 6 October 2001.

8. Ibid.

9. G. M. Gaul, J. V. Grimaldi, and J. Warrick, "How Terror Could Break Through; At the Airports: Risks to Security Detected, Debated for Many Years," *Washington Post*, 16 September 2001.

10. Pasternak, "FAA, Airlines Stalled Major Security Plans."

11. The Cato Institute's conservative estimate ($87 billion in fiscal 2001) considers only government programs that provide direct subsidies to individual industries. Ralph Nader's Center for the Study of Responsive Law includes federal tax breaks that funnel money to specific industries, for a total of $167 billion. See D. Akst, "On the Contrary: Brother, Can You Spare a Dime?" *New York Times*, 2 December 2001; S. Moore and D. Stansel, *How Corporate Welfare Won: Clinton and Congress Retreat from Cutting Business Subsidies*, Cato Institute Policy Analysis No. 254, 15 May 1996, <http://www.cato.org/research/fiscal.html> (accessed 10 March 2004).

12. M. Green, *Selling Out: How Big Corporate Money Buys Elections, Rams Through Legislation, and Betrays Our Democracy* (New York: Regan Books, 2002), 172–173.

13. Ibid.

14. H. Varian, *Intermediate Microeconomics: A Modern Approach,* 2nd ed. (New York: Norton, 1987); A. de Moor and P. Calamai, "Subsidizing Unsustainable Development: Undermining the Earth with Public Funds," Earth Council, January 1997, <http://www.ecouncil.ac.cr/econ/sud/subsidizing_unsd.pdf > (accessed 10 March 2004).

15. Mineral Policy Center, "What Is the 1872 Mining Law?" 1999, <http://www.earthworksaction.org/ewa/1872.cfm> (accessed 10 March 2004).

16. Friends of the Earth, Taxpayers for Common Sense, and the U.S Public Interest Research Group, "Granddaddy of All Subsidies," *Green Scissors*

2002: Cutting Wasteful and Environmentally Harmful Spending (Washington, DC: Friends of the Earth, Taxpayers for Common Sense, and the U.S. Public Interest Research Group, 2002).

17. Ibid.

18. Friends of the Earth, Taxpayers for Common Sense, and the U.S Public Interest Research Group, "Granddaddy of All Subsidies," *Green Scissors '97: Cutting Wasteful and Environmentally Harmful Spending* (Washington, DC: Friends of the Earth, Taxpayers for Common Sense, and the U.S. Public Interest Research Group, 1997).

19. The Center for Responsive Politics, "Lobbyist Spending: Mining: 2000 Data" (2003), <www.opensecrets.org> (accessed 10 March 2004).

20. Green, *Selling Out*, 162–165.

21. Ibid., 163.

22. Ibid., 165.

23. J. Mayer, "The Accountants' War," *New Yorker,* 22 April 2002.

24. H. Smith, "Bigger than Enron: Congress and the Accounting Wars," *PBS Frontline* Web site, 2002, <http://www.pbs.org/wgbh/pages/frontline/shows/regulation/congress/> (accessed 10 March 2004).

25. Ibid.

26. Ibid.

27. Mayer, "The Accountants' War," 66.

28. H. Smith, "Beyond Enron: Capitol Investments," *PBS Frontline* Web site, 2002, <http://www.pbs.org/wgbh/pages/frontline/shows/regulation/congress/money.html> (accessed 10 March 2004).

29. Ibid.

30. J. Brainard, "Another Record Year for Academic Pork," *Chronicle of Higher Education,* 27 September 2002, 20.

31. Ibid.

32. Ibid.

33. Ibid.

34. Ibid.

35. K. Zernike, "Pull in Congress Tied to Grants for Research," *New York Times,* 6 August 2001.

36. Green, *Selling Out*, 55.

37. Ibid., 52.

38. J. Eilperin, "After McCain-Feingold, a Bigger Role for PACs; Groups May Be 'Soft Money' Conduits," *Washington Post,* 1 June 2002.

39. J. E. Cantor, *Soft and Hard Money in Contemporary Elections: What Federal Law Does and Does Not Regulate* (Washington, DC: Congressional Research Service Report, Library of Congress, 1997).

40. Green, *Selling Out,* 55.

41. Ibid., 57.

42. E. Drew, *The Corruption of American Politics: What Went Wrong and Why* (Secaucus, NJ: Birch Lane Press, 1999), 51–52.

43. Green, *Selling Out,* 58.

44. Ibid., 62.

45. This paragraph adapted from Green, *Selling Out,* 65–67.

46. Drew, *The Corruption of American Politics,* 54.

47. Common Cause, "National Parties Raise Record $457 Million in Soft Money," 15 December 2000, <http://www.commoncause.org> (accessed 10 March 2004).

48. Common Cause, "Editorial Memorandum: McCain-Feingold Legislation Offers Bipartisan Opportunity for Comprehensive Campaign Finance Reform in 1997," February 1997, <http://www.commoncause.org> (accessed 10 March 2004).

49. D. Van Natta Jr., "Executives Press for Political Finance Change," *New York Times,* 31 August 1999.

50. Ibid.

51. Ibid.

52. Green, *Selling Out,* 74.

53. A filibuster used to mean endless speechifying on the Senate floor to blockade a vote on a bill that would otherwise pass. In recent years, the mere threat of a filibuster provokes a vote of "cloture" to override it. Cloture is a vote to limit debate on a bill; for a cloture vote to be successful, sixty senators must vote to end the filibuster.

54. Eilperin, "After McCain-Feingold, a Bigger Role for PACs."

55. Ibid.

56. Green, *Selling Out,* 81.

57. W. M. Welch and J. Drinkard, "Supporters Turn to Defending, Extending Victory," *USA Today,* 21 March 2002.

58. Presidential candidates that abide by state spending limits receive a quarter of the amount of hard money they raise in federal matching funds. McCain-Feingold raises the limit on individual hard-money contributions from $1,000 to $2,000 yet does not change the percentage of matching funds given. Thus, instead of receiving 25 percent of their total amount raised in matching funds (25 percent of each $1,000 donation), candidates will receive just 12.5 percent from the government (25 percent of $2,000). It is expected that the smaller pool of matching funds will be less attractive and that more candidates will opt out of public financing in order to disregard state spending limits. See "Life after McCain-Feingold," *Pittsburgh Post-Gazette,* 19 April 2002.

59. Eilperin, "After McCain-Feingold, a Bigger Role for PACs."

60. Ibid.

61. M. McGrory, "McCain-Feingold Follies," *Washington Post,* 28 March 2002.

62. S. Taylor Jr., "Three Judges, Four Opinions, 1,638 pages, and One Good Idea," *The Atlantic Online,* 13 May 2003, <http://www.theatlantic.com/politics/nj/taylor2003-05-13.htm> (accessed 10 March 2004).

63. L. Greenhouse, "Justices, in a 5-to-4 Decision, Back Campaign Finance Law that Curbs Contributions," *New York Times,* 11 December 2003.

64. J. Abramson, "A Law Survives. Now, Let's Subvert It," *New York Times,* 14 December 2003.

65. "Federal Election Wrecking Crew," *New York Times,* 15 June 2002.

66. Ibid.

67. R. A. Oppel Jr., "Soft Money Ban Goes into Effect, but the Effect Is Uncertain," *New York Times,* 23 June 2002.

68. "Election Law Coup d'Etat," *New York Times,* 24 June 2002.

69. "Rescuing Campaign Reform," *New York Times,* 27 June 2002.

70. Campaign for Tobacco-Free Kids, Common Cause, American Heart Association, and American Lung Association, *Buying Influence, Selling Death,* 14 March 2001, <http://www.commoncause.org/publications/march01/tobacco/> (accessed 10 March 2004).

71. Ibid.

72. Ibid.

73. Georgia Department of Agriculture, "$340 Million Assistance Announced for Tobacco Farmers," *Farmers & Consumers Market Bulletin,* 2 August 2000, 1.

74. Action on Smoking and Health, "US to Give $53 Million to Tobacco Growers," 17 March 2003, <http://no-smoking.org/march03/03-20-03-3.html> (accessed 10 March 2004).

75. Public Citizen, "Tobacco PAC Contributions and 1998 Tobacco Votes," 22 June 1998, <http://www.citizen.org> (accessed 10 March 2004).

76. Public Citizen, "Soft Money Hurts Consumers and Taxpayers," 19 January 2001, <http://www.citizen.org/congress/reform/soft$hurts.html> (accessed 10 March 2004.

77. Green, *Selling Out,* 178.

78. Center for Responsive Politics, "Top Tobacco Money Receipts," 1999, <http://www.opensecrets.org> (accessed 10 March 2004).

79. Green, *Selling Out,* 177.

80. Campaign for Tobacco-Free Kids, et al., *Buying Influence, Selling Death.*

81. B. Herbert, "Whose Hands Are Dirty?" *New York Times*, 25 November 2002.

82. "Republicans Won't Own Up to Protecting Drug Giant," *Brown Daily Herald* (Providence, RI), 18 December 2002.

83. J. Zeleny, "Lobbyists for GOP to Hear Speech in Advance," *Chicago Tribune*, 28 January 2002.

84. Huffington, "Finding the Answer to Washington's Hottest Whodunit," 6 December 2002, <http://www.tompaine.com/feature2.cfm/ID/6844> (accessed 10 March 2004).

85. A. L. McGill, "Context Effects in Judgments of Causation," *Journal of Personality and Social Psychology* 57 (1989): 189–200.

86. R. E. Nisbett and L. Ross, *Human Inference: Strategies and Shortcomings of Social Judgment* (Englewood Cliffs, NJ: Prentice-Hall, 1980).

87. R. Lacayo and A. Ripley, "Persons of the Year: Sherron Watkins of Enron, Coleen Rowley of the FBI, Cynthia Cooper of WorldCom," *Time*, 30 December 2002, 30.

88. Green, *Selling Out*.

89. Ibid.

90. K. Q. Seelye, "Bradley Proposes Revamping Federal Campaign Finance System, *New York Times*, 23 July 1999.

91. M. H. Bazerman, *Judgment in Managerial Decision Making* (New York: John Wiley and Sons, 1998).

92. D. S. Broder, "Toothless Watchdog," *Washington Post*, 29 May 2002.

93. Green, *Selling Out*, 283–284.

94. Welch and Drinkard, "Supporters Turn to Defending, Extending Victory."

95. Green, *Selling Out*, 285.

Chapter 7

1. All quotes from Johnelle Bryant are taken from her interview with Brian Ross, "Face to Face with Atta," 6 June 2002, <http://abcnews.go.com/sections/wnt/DailyNews/WNT_ross-bryant_transcript1.html> (accessed 10 March 2004).

2. The term "intelligence community" (IC) refers to a group of fourteen government agencies and organizations that, either in whole or in part, conduct the intelligence activities of the U. S. government: the Central Intelligence Agency (CIA), the Department of the Treasury, the Department of Energy, the Department of State, the Defense Intelligence Agency (DIA), the Federal Bureau of Investigation (FBI), the National Imagery and Mapping Agency (NIMA), the National Reconnaissance Office (NRO), the National Security Agency (NSA), U.S. Air Force Intelligence, U.S. Army Intelligence, U.S. Coast Guard Intelligence, U.S. Navy Intelligence, and U.S. Marine Corps Intelligence. Various

state and local agencies also play key roles in protecting the United States from attack by terrorists. As established in the National Security Act of 1947 and the Central Intelligence Agency Act of 1949, overall responsibility for integrating the analysis and presentation of intelligence to senior elected officials is vested with the Director of Central Intelligence (DCI), although in practice the National Security Council (NSC) staff and the Defense Intelligence Agency (DIA) exert significant influence.

Between late March and September 2001, the IC detected numerous indicators of an impending terrorist attack, some of which pointed specifically to the United States as a possible target. E. Hill, "Joint Inquiry Staff Statement, Part I," 18 September 2002, <http://intelligence.senate.gov/0209hrg/020918/hill.pdf> (accessed 10 March 2004), 20.

3. "Despite these indicators of a possible terrorist attack inside the United States, during the course of interviews, the Joint Inquiry Staff was told that it was the general view of the U.S. Intelligence Community in the spring and summer of 2001 that an attack on U.S. interests was more likely to occur overseas. . . . One FBI official we deposed said that, based on the intelligence he was seeing, he thought there was a high probability—'98 percent'—that the attack would occur overseas." E. Hill, "Joint Inquiry Staff Statement, Part I," 22.

4. "In August 1996, after his move back to Afghanistan, Usama bin Ladin issued a public fatwa, or religious decree, authorizing attacks by his followers against Western military targets on the Arabian Peninsula. In February 1998, Usama bin Ladin and four other extremists publicly issued another public fatwa expanding the 1996 fatwa to include U.S. military and civilian targets anywhere in the world. In the May 1998 press conference, bin Ladin publicly discussed 'bringing the war home to America.'" E. Hill, "Joint Inquiry Staff Statement, Part I," 12–13. "While one could not . . . give too much credence to some individual reports, the totality of the information in this body of reporting clearly reiterated a consistent and critically important theme: Usama bin Ladin's intent to launch terrorist attacks inside United States." E. Hill, "Joint Inquiry Staff Statement, Part I," 14.

5. "These intelligence reports [concerning threats of domestic attacks] should be understood in their proper context. First, they generally did not contain specific information as to where, when, and how a terrorist attack might occur and, generally, are not corroborated by further information. Second, these reports represented a small percentage of the threat information that the Intelligence Community obtained during this period, most of which pointed to the possibility of attacks against U.S. interests overseas." E. Hill, "Joint Inquiry Staff Statement, Part I," 14.

6. "Turbulence," *The Economist*, 12 May 2001.

7. Associated Press Wire, 3 July 2001.

8. "The failure of the Intelligence Community (IC) to provide adequate forewarning was affected by resource constraints and a series of questionable management decisions related to funding priorities. Prophetically, IC leadership concluded at a high level offsite on September 11, 1998 that 'failure to improve operations management, resource allocation, and other key issues within the [Intelligence Community], including making substantial and sweeping changes in the way the nation collects, analyzes, and produces intelligence, will likely result in a catastrophic systemic intelligence failure.'" *Subcommittee on Terrorism and Homeland Security, House Permanent Select Committee on Intelligence,* "Counterterrorism Intelligence Capabilities and Performance Prior to 9-11," 17 July 2002, <http://www.fas.org/irp/congress/2002_rpt/hpsci_ths0702.html> (accessed 10 March 2004), i.

9. E. Hill, "Joint Inquiry Staff Statement," 17 October 2002, <http://www.fas.org/irp/congress/2002_hr/101702hill.pdf> (accessed 10 March 2004).

10. "Following the August 1998 bombings of two U.S. embassies in East Africa, Intelligence Community leadership recognized how dangerous bin Ladin's network was. In December 1998, DCI [Director of Central Intelligence] George Tenet provided written guidance to his deputies at the CIA declaring, in effect, 'war' with bin Ladin. . . . Despite the DCI's declaration of war in 1998, there was no massive shift in budget or reassignment of personnel to counterterrorism until after September 11, 2001." E. Hill, "Joint Inquiry Staff Statement, Part I," 9–10.

11. The House Permanent Select Committee on Intelligence and the Senate Select Committee on Intelligence, "Report of The Joint Inquiry into the Terrorist Attacks of September 11, 2001," December 2002, <http://a257.g.akamaitech.net/7/257/2422/24jul20031400/www.gpoaccess.gov/serialset/creports/pdf/fullreport_errata.pdf> (accessed 10 March 2004), 17.

12. Ibid., 347.

13. E. Hill, "Joint Inquiry Staff Statement, Part I," 10.

14. The other two events were the detention of Zacarias Moussaoui, the so-called twentieth hijacker by agents in the FBI's Minneapolis office, and the Intelligence Community's realization that two individuals with ties to Osama bin Laden's network were possibly in the United States.

15. E. Hill, "Joint Inquiry Staff Statement, Part I," 10.

16. E. Hill, "Joint Inquiry Staff Statement," 17 October 2002, <http://www.fas.org/irp/congress/2002_hr/101702hill.pdf> (accessed 10 March 2004), 5.

17. Ibid., 6.

18. Ibid., 2.

19. Ibid., 13.

20. Ibid., 8.

21. M. Watkins and C. Reavis, "Robert Shapiro and Monsanto," Case 9-801-482 (Boston: Harvard Business School, 2001), 10.

22. Ibid.

23. Ibid., 11.

24. Ibid., 12.

25. Ibid., 11.

26. Ibid., 1.

27. "The Nunn-Lugar Cooperative Threat Reduction Program," 22 March 1999, <http://www.nti.org/db/nisprofs/ukraine/forasst/ctr/overview.htm> (accessed 10 March 2004).

28. R. G. Lugar, "Nunn-Lugar Cooperative Threat Reduction Program," 2003, <http://www.lugar.senate.gov/nunn_lugar_program.html> (accessed 10 March 2004).

29. Ibid.

30. The authors would like to thank Michael Roberto for suggesting this example.

31. "A Glance at Our Past," 2004, <http://www.edwardjones.com/cgi/getHTML.cgi?page=/USA/aboutEJ/glance.html> (accessed 10 March 2004).

32. D. Landis, "By Keeping it Simple, Edward Jones Enhances Its Image While Rivals Are Bloodied by Scandal," *Kiplinger's Finance*, May 2003; "High Quality, Long-term Investing," 2004, <http://www.edwardjones.com/cgi/getHTML.cgi?page=/USA/aboutEJ/high_quality.html> (accessed 10 March 2004).

33. R. Simons, "How New Top Managers Use Control Systems as Levers of Strategic Renewal," *Strategic Management Journal* 15, no. 3 (1994): 169–189; R. L. Simons, "Control in an Age of Empowerment," *Harvard Business Review* (March–April 1995): 80–88.

34. R. S. Kaplan and D. P. Norton. "Balanced Scorecard: Measures that Drive Performance," *Harvard Business Review* (January–February 1992): 71–79. For approaches to implementation, see R. S. Kaplan and D. P. Norton, *The Strategy-Focused Organization: How Balanced Scorecard Companies Thrive in the New Business Environment* (Boston: Harvard Business School Press, 2000).

35. E. Vitt, M. Luckevich, and S. Misner, *Business Intelligence* (Seattle, WA: Microsoft Press, 2002), chapter 9. To support business intelligence-gathering efforts, some companies use "action-learning groups"—teams of future leaders that meet to share data and analyze a key business challenge. See Y. Boshyk, ed., *Business-Driven Action Learning: Global Best Practices* (New York: Palgrave Macmillan, 2000).

36. For a discussion of boundary-spanning roles, see J. Thompson, *Organizations in Action* (New York: McGraw-Hill, 1967). See also the work of Thomas Allen on "gatekeepers" in T. J. Allen, "Communication Networks in R&D Labs," *R&D Management* 1 (1971): 14–21.

37. Hank McKinnell, the CEO of Pfizer, is a good example of a leader who routinely calls on a group of external advisers to help him avoid predictable surprises. One of McKinnell's most valuable "leadership counselors" is Dan Ciampa, former CEO of Rath and Strong. By serving as both a sounding board and an adviser on key issues and decisions, Ciampa is reportedly instrumental in helping McKinnell avoid undesirable outcomes. See "CEO Coaches," *BusinessWeek*, 11 November 2002.

38. K. van der Heijden, *Scenarios: The Art of Strategic Conversation* (New York: John Wiley & Sons, 1996), 5.

39. I. Mitroff, *Managing Crises Before They Happen* (New York: Amacom, 2001), 42.

Chapter 8

1. M. Watkins, C. Knoop, and C. Reavis, "Coca-Cola Company (A): The Rise and Fall of M. Douglas Ivester," Case 800-355 (Boston: Harvard Business School, 2000).

2. C. Mitchell, "Challenges Await Coca-Cola's New Leader," *Atlanta Journal-Constitution*, 27 October 1997.

3. P. Sellars, "Where Coke Goes From Here," *Fortune*, 13 October 1997.

4. "Clumsy Handling of Many Problems Cost Ivester Coca-Cola Board's Favor," *Wall Street Journal*, 17 December 1999.

5. Navratilova's advice provides a counterpart to Hesiod's observation that, "It is best to do things systematically, since we are only human, and disorder is our worst enemy." J. B. Simpson, ed. *Simpson's Contemporary Quotations* (Boston: Houghton Mifflin, 1988).

6. U.S. Department of Defense, "Donald H. Rumsfeld, Secretary of Defense," March 2003, <http://www.defenselink.mil/bios/secdef_bio.html> (accessed 11 March 2004).

7. D. Rieff, "Blueprint for a Mess," *New York Times*, 2 November 2003.

8. Friedenspolitischer Ratschlag, "Duty to the Future: Free Iraqis Plan for a New Iraq," March 2003, <http://www.uni-kassel.de/fb10/frieden/regionen/Irak/future.html> (accessed 11 March 2004).

9. J. Brinkley and E. Schmitt, "Prewar Planning: Iraqi Leaders Say U.S. Was Warned of Disorder After Hussein, but Little Was Done," *New York Times*, 30 November 2003.

10. Ibid.

11. Rieff, "Blueprint for a Mess."

12. N. Scheiber, "Noam Scheiber's Daily Journal of Politics," 12 September 2003, *The New Republic Online*, <http://www.tnr.com/etc.mhtml?pid=703> (accessed 11 March 2004).

13. Rieff, "Blueprint for a Mess."

14. "Garner Admits Mistakes Early in Baghdad: Former Chief of Iraq's Interim Administration Says U.S.-Led Coalition Made Mistakes in Baghdad," Associated Press, 26 November 2003, reprinted on ABCNews.com, <http://www.abcnews.go.com/wire/World/ap20031126_272.html> (accessed 11 March 2004).

15. "[A]t least at senior levels, the Intelligence Community understood that bin Ladin posed a serious threat to the domestic United States. . . . What is less clear is the extent to which other parts of the government, as well as the American people, understood and fully appreciated the gravity and immediacy of the threat." E. Hill, "Joint Inquiry Staff Statement, Part I," 18 September 2002, <http://intelligence.senate.gov/0209hrg/020918/hill.pdf> (accessed 10 March 2004), 17–18.

16. Hill, "Joint Inquiry Staff Statement, Part I," 15–16.

17. Ibid., 15–16.

18. "[T]his may have been driven in part by resource issues in the area of intelligence analysis. Prior to September 11, 2001, the CTC [the CIA Counterterrorist Center] had forty analysts to analyze terrorism issues worldwide, with only one of the five branches focused on terrorist tactics. As a result, prior to September 11, 2001, the only terrorist tactic on which the CTC performed strategic analysis was the possible use of chemical, biological, radiological and nuclear weapons (CBRN) because there was more obvious potential for mass casualties." Hill, "Joint Inquiry Staff Statement, Part I," 28.

19. Ibid., 27.

20. "The FAA worked with the Intelligence Community on this analysis and actually drafted the section of the NIE [National Intelligence Estimate] addressing the threat to civil aviation. That section contained the following language:

> Our review of the evidence . . . suggests the conspirators were guided in their selection of the method and venue of attack by carefully studying security procedures in place in the region. If terrorists operating in this country [the United States] are similarly methodical, they will identify serious vulnerabilities in the security system for domestic flights.

The 1997 update to the 1995 NIE on terrorism included the following language: 'Civil aviation remains a particularly attractive target in light of the fear and publicity the downing of an airliner would evoke and the revelations last summer of the U.S. air transport sectors' vulnerabilities.'"

21. Ibid., 29.

22. "The common view held at the FBI prior to September 11 was that bin Ladin needed pilots to operate aircraft purchased in the United States to move men and material...however, the FBI had also received reporting that was not entirely consistent with this view of Usama bin Ladin's pilots. Two of the pilots

had been through al-Qa'ida training camps in Afghanistan where they were trained to conduct terrorist operations. One of them was trained in surveillance and intelligence, and apparently had been selected for the course due to his aviation skills." E. Hill, "Joint Inquiry Staff Statement," 17 October 2002, <http://www.fas.org/irp/congress/2002_hr/101702hill.pdf> (accessed 10 March 2004), 14.

23. Ibid., 2.

24. Ibid., 5.

25. Reuters, "Chronology: Key Events Since Aug 14 NE/Canada Blackout," *Forbes.com,* 3 September 2003, <http://www.forbes.com/business/energy/newswire/2003/09/03/rtr1071719.html> (accessed 11 March 2004).

26. North American Electricity Reliability Council, "Transmission Expansion: Issues and Recommendations," 20 February 2002, <ftp://www.nerc.com/pub/sys/all_updl/docs/archives/TransmExpansion_BOTapprvd_022002.pdf 1.> (accessed 11 March 2004).

27. R. Smith and J. Hallinan, "Splintered Midwest Grid Helped Outage to Spread," *Wall Street Journal,* 19 August 2003.

28. Ibid.

29. North American Electricity Reliability Council, "Transmission Expansion: Issues and Recommendations."

30. Smith and Hallinan, "Splintered Midwest Grid Helped Outage to Spread."

31. Ibid.

32. "Blackout Blues in Midwest," *CBS News.com,* 15 August 2003, <http://www.cbsnews.com/stories/2003/08/14/national/printable568353.shtml> (accessed 11 March 2004).

33. J. Fuerbringer, "Big Board's Hard Work Smooths Recovery From Blackout," *New York Times,* 15 August 2003.

34. J. Drucker, "Lights Out in the Northeast," *Wall Street Journal,* 18 August 2003.

35. J. Barron and K. Semple, "Some Parts of Country May Remain Without Power Through Weekend," *New York Times,* 15 August 2003.

36. E. Koblentz, "Tech Services Survive Blackout," *eWeek,* 15 August 2003, <http://www.eweek.com/article2/0,4149,1499756,00.asp> (accessed 11 March 2004).

37. M. Weissenstein, "Blackout Triggers Post-911 Security Plan," Associated Press, 15 August 2003.

38. N. Carr, "Millions in Ontario Hope for Steady Electricity, but Prepare for More Outages," Canadian Press, 15 August 2003.

39. D. Garvin and M. Roberto, "What You Don't Know about Making Decisions," *Harvard Business Review* (September 2001): 110.

40. A series of experimental studies suggest that formal, structured decision-making procedures are superior to less structured techniques in certain

situations. Schweiger and his colleagues demonstrated that both Dialectical Inquiry and Devil's Advocacy encouraged higher levels of critical evaluation, generated more alternatives, and led to higher-quality decisions than the less structured Consensus Method. Priem and his colleagues demonstrated that these structured methods promoted higher levels of team-member satisfaction and commitment, because individuals felt that they had a fair and legitimate opportunity to express their views and disagree openly with one another. This research does not suggest that structured techniques are uniformly superior to a consensus approach; conflicting findings have led scholars to suggest that the effectiveness of each type of process depends on the nature of the task. See D. M. Schweiger and C. Leana, "Participation in Decision-making," in *Generalizing from Laboratory to Field Settings,* ed. E. Locke (Lexington, MA: Lexington Books, 1986), 147–166; R. L. Priem, D. A. Harrison, and N. K. Muir, "Structured Conflict and Consensus Outcomes in Group Decision Making," *Journal of Management* 21, no. 4 (1995), 691–710.

41. This example is cited in Garvin and Roberto, "What You Don't Know about Making Decisions."

42. A. Fusenko and T.J. Naftali, *One Hell of a Gamble: Khrushchev, Castro, and Kennedy, 1958–1964* (New York: W.W. Norton & Co., Inc., 1998).

43. J. S. Hammond, R. L. Keeney, and H. Raiffa, *Smart Choices: A Practical Guide to Making Better Life Decisions* (New York: Broadway Books, 2002), 4. They further note that an effective decision-making process fulfills six criteria: (1) it focuses on what's important; (2) it is logical; (3) it acknowledges both subjective and objective factors and blends analytical with intuitive thinking; (4) it requires only as much information and analysis as is necessary to resolve a particular dilemma; (5) it encourages and guides the gathering of relevant information and informed opinion; and (6) it is straightforward, reliable, easy to use, and flexible.

44. Hammond, Keeney, and Raiffa call this "PrOACT," for problem, objectives, alternatives, consequences, and trade-offs. See chapter 1 of *Smart Choices.*

45. The expected value is the sum of the products of the probabilities and costs, in this case 0.3 x $6,000 + 0. 5 x $2,000 + 0.2 x 0 = $2,800.

46. R. Thorpe and G. Homan, *Strategic Reward Systems* (London: FT Prentice Hall, 1999), 12.

Chapter 9

1. This example is drawn from C. Devereaux, "TRIPS, Activists, and Developing Countries" (Boston: Kennedy School of Government, 2003).

2. "Thabo Mbeki," interview by G. Ifill, *"The News Hour" Online,* 23 May 2000, <http://www.pbs.org/newshour/bb/africa/jan-june00/mbeki_5-23.html> (accessed 11 March 2004).

3. B. Gellman, "Gore in Conflict of Health and Profit: Gore at Center of Trade Policy Reversal on AIDS Drugs to South Africa," *Washington Post*, 21 May 2000.

4. L. Chaudry, "U.S. to South Africa: Just Say No," *Wired*, 25 April 2000.

5. "The Protection of Intellectual Property and Health Policy," Press Release, Office of the United States Trade Representative, 1 December 1999, <http://www.ustr.gov/releases/1999/12/99-97.html> (accessed 11 March 2004).

6. Médecins Sans Frontières, "The MSF Role in Emergency Medical Aid," 13 December 2000, <http://www.msf.org/about/index.cfm> (accessed 11 March 2004).

7. See, for example, H. Stevenson, J. Cruikshank, and M. C. Moldoveanu, *Do Lunch or Be Lunch: The Power of Predictability in Creating Your Future* (Boston: Harvard Business School Press, 1998).

8. D. Yoffie and M. Kwak, *Judo Strategy: Turning Your Competitors' Strength to Your Advantage* (Boston: Harvard Business School Press, 2001).

9. M. Watkins, *Breakthrough Business Negotiation: A Toolbox for Managers* (San Francisco: Jossey-Bass, 2002), chapter 6.

10. This is the case, for example, when organizational change involves the introduction of complex new technologies and when skills that were previously highly valued become obsolete.

11. Southwest Research and Information Center, "Electric Deregulation Fact Sheet," February 2003, <http://www.sric.org/workbook/features/V24_3/69.html> (accessed 12 March 2004).

12. R. Smith and J. Hallinan, "Splintered Midwest Grid Helped Outage to Spread Oversight in Region Shared by 23 Utilities; FirstEnergy May Have Been the Trigger," *Wall Street Journal*, 19 August 2003.

13. Ibid.

14. U.S.-Canada Power System Outage Task Force, "Interim Report: Causes of the August 14th Blackout in the United States and Canada," November 2003.

15. R. Smith, S. Murray, and J. Fialka, "How Unlikely Coalition Scuttled Plan to Remake Electrical Grid," *Wall Street Journal*, 4 November 2003.

16. Ibid.

17. Ibid.

18. "Senate Gives Up on '03 Energy Bill," Associated Press, *MSNBC Online*, 24 November 2003, <http://www.msnbc.com/news/993612.asp?cp1=1> (accessed 11 March 2004).

19. D. J. Wakin, "Mbeki's AZT Claims Set off Debate," Associated Press, *AEGiS*, 2 November 1999, <http://www.aegis.com/news/ap/1999/AP991101.html> (accessed 11 March 2004).

20. T. Karon, "You Cannot Attribute Immune Deficiency Exclusively to a Virus," *Time*, 11 September 2000.

21. "Mandela Breaks with Mbeki on HIV-AIDS," *Nambian Africa News*, 29 September 2000, <http://www.namibian.com.na/2000/September/africa/00A6E609C5.html> (accessed 11 March 2004).

22. "Mandela Denies Rift with Mbeki on AIDS Policy," Reuters, 19 February 2002, <http://www.hivnetnordic.org/news/worldnews2002/news_february2002.html> (accessed 11 March 2004).

23. "Mbeki Vows to Step up AIDS fight," *CNN.com*, 8 February 2002, <http://edition.cnn.com/2002/WORLD/africa/02/08/mbeki.aids/> (accessed 11 March 2004).

24. "Call for 'Dishonest' Mbeki to Apologise for AIDS Gaffe," *Sunday Observer* (UK), 28 September 2003.

25. L. Moncur, "The Quotations Page," 1994–2004, <http://www.quotationspage.com/> (accessed 11 March 2004).

26. K. Lewin, *Field Theory in Social Science* (New York: Harper, 1951).

27. L. Ross and R. E. Nisbett, *The Person and the Situation: Perspectives on Social Psychology* (New York: McGraw-Hill, 1991), 10.

28. C. Tilly, *European Revolutions, 1492–1992* (Oxford: Blackwell, 1993), 13.

29. R. Andrews, M. Biggs, and M. Seidel, eds., *The Columbia World of Quotations* (New York: Columbia University Press, 1996). Kennedy was one of the first women to attend Columbia Law School, after winning a lawsuit that had prevented her admission.

30. M. Mitchell, *Propaganda, Polls, and Public Opinion: Are the People Manipulated?* (Englewood Cliffs, NJ: Prentice-Hill, 1970), 111.

31. J. Barnes, ed., *The Complete Works of Aristotle,* vol. 2 (Princeton, NJ: Princeton University Press, 1984), 175.

32. Many people tend to be *loss-averse*—that is, more sensitive to potential losses than to equivalent potential gains. Similarly widespread is the tendency to be *risk-averse*—to prefer guaranteed gains to risky choices, even if the latter are likely to yield much larger gains.

33. See chapter 11 of H. Raiffa, *The Art and Science of Negotiation* (Cambridge, MA: Harvard University Press, 1982).

34. See "Influencing Behavior," chapter 2 of P. Zimbardo and M. Leippe, *The Psychology of Attitude Change and Social Influence* (New York: McGraw-Hill, 1991).

35. See "Authority: Directed Deference," chapter 6 in R. B. Cialdini, *Influence: The Psychology of Persuasion* (New York: Quill, 1993). This book is an excellent introduction to the psychology of interpersonal persuasion, exploring key processes such as consistency and commitment. D. Lax and J. Sebenius term these "patterns of deference"; see "Thinking Coalitionally," in *Negotiation Analysis,* ed. P. Young (Ann Arbor, MI: University of Michigan Press, 1991), 64–85.

36. D. Krackhardt and J. R. Hanson, "Informal Networks: The Company Behind the Chart," *Harvard Business Review* (July–August 1993): 104–111.

37. In their studies of the 1940 presidential election, Lazarfeld and his associates made the early observation that people were influenced both directly by information that they were exposed to and by people who either passed along the information or to whom they went for clues about "right thinking." The result was a "multi-step flow" model of opinion formation. See P. Lazarfeld, L. Bereson, and H. Gaudet, *The People's Choice: How the Voter Makes Up His Mind in a Presidential Campaign* (New York: Duell, Sloan, & Pearce, 1948). See also chapter 8 of M. A. Milburn, *Persuasion and Politics: The Social Psychology of Public Opinion* (Pacific Grove, CA: Brooks/Cole, 1991).

38. See "Commitment and Consistency," chapter 3 of Cialdini, *Influence: The Psychology of Persuasion*. This approach to persuasion presumes that people can be led from point A to point B in a succession of small, irreversible steps when doing so in a single leap would be impossible.

39. T. Kayser, *Building Team Power: How to Unleash the Collaborative Genius of Work Teams* (Carlsbad, CA: Irwin, 1994), 208–209.

40. For a discussion of productive ways to structure individual and group problem-solving, see R. L. Ackoff, *The Art of Problem-solving* (New York: John Wiley & Sons, 1978).

41. I. Mitroff, C. M. Pearson (Contributor), and L. K. Harrington, *The Essential Guide to Managing Corporate Crises: A Step-By-Step Handbook for Surviving Major Catastrophes* (Oxford: Oxford University Press, Book and Disk edition, August 1996), 6.

Chapter 10

1. A. Nicholson, "Fishermen May Learn to Love Faceless Eurocrats," *Daily Telegraph* (London), 31 December 2002.

2. Ibid.

3. C. Clover, "Europe's Fishing Fleet Plunders the Seas of Africa," *Daily Telegraph* (London), 15 March 2003.

4. C. Mortished, "Africa Caught in Net of Fisheries Crisis," *The Times* (London), 12 March 2003.

5. This section on Senegal adapted from Clover, "Europe's Fishing Fleet Plunders the Seas of Africa."

6. Mortished, "Africa Caught in Net of Fisheries Crisis."

7. Nicholson, "Fishermen May Learn to Love Faceless Eurocrats."

8. Mortished, "Africa Caught in Net of Fisheries Crisis."

9. *Webster's New Collegiate Dictionary* (Springfield, MA: G&C Merriam Company, 1977).

10. Akst, "On the Contrary: Brother, Can You Spare a Dime?" *New York Times,* 2 December 2001; S. Moore and D. Stansel, *How Corporate Welfare Won: Clinton and Congress Retreat from Cutting Business Subsidies,* Cato Institute Policy Analysis No. 254, 15 May 1996, <http://www.cato.org/research/fiscal.html> (accessed 13 March 2004).

11. L. Wayne, "A Guardian of Jobs or a 'Reverse Robin Hood'?" *New York Times,* 2 September 2002.

12. "Harvesting Poverty; The Long Reach of King Cotton," *New York Times,* 5 August 2003.

13. "Harvesting Poverty; The Rigged Trade Game," *New York Times,* 5 August 2003; E. Becker, "Republicans Back Down on Raising Farm Aid," *New York Times,* 13 February 2003.

14. R. Lazio, "Editorial: Some Trade Barriers Won't Fall, *New York Times,* 9 August 2003.

15. "Harvesting Poverty; The Rigged Trade Game," *New York Times,* 5 August 2003.

16. T. Rosenberg, "Globalization," *New York Times Magazine,* 18 August 2002.

17. Ibid.

18. Ibid.

19. N. D. Kristof, "Editorial: What Did You Do During the African Holocaust?" *New York Times,* 27 May 2003.

20. "Harvesting Poverty; The Long Reach of King Cotton"; Kristof, "Editorial: What Did You Do During the African Holocaust?"

21. A. T. Toure and B. Compaore, "Your Farm Subsidies Are Strangling Us," *New York Times,* 11 July 2003.

22. Ibid.

23. "Harvesting Poverty; The Long Reach of King Cotton."

24. T. Fuller, "European Union Votes 14–1 to Reform Agricultural Policy," *New York Times,* 26 June 2003.

25. D. Leonhardt, "Globalization Hits a Political Speed Bump," *New York Times,* 1 June 2003.

26. "Harvesting Poverty; The Rigged Trade Game."

27. Leonhardt, "Globalization Hits a Political Speed Bump."

28. "Harvesting Poverty; The Rigged Trade Game."

29. E. Becker, "Republicans Back Down on Raising Farm Aid."

30. "European Welfare Farmers," *New York Times,* 14 July 2003.

31. P. Meller and D. Barboza, "Deal Reached on Subsidies for Farmers," *New York Times,* 14 August 2003.

32. Ibid.

33. Toure and Compaore, "Your Farm Subsidies Are Strangling Us."

34. This section is adapted from M. Bazerman, J. Baron, and K. Shonk, *"You Can't Enlarge the Pie": Six Barriers to Effective Government* (New York: Basic Books, 2001).

35. S. H. Schneider, ed., *Encyclopedia of Climate and Weather* (Oxford: Oxford University Press, 1996).

36. J. M. Wallace and P. V. Hobbs, *Atmospheric Science: An Introductory Survey* (San Diego: Academic Press, 1977).

37. Bazerman, Baron, and Shonk, *"You Can't Enlarge the Pie."*

38. W. D. Nordhaus, "Discounting and Public Policies That Affect the Distant Future," in P.R. Portney and J.P. Weyant, eds., *Discounting and Intergenerational Equity* (Washington, D.C.: Resources for the Future, 1999), 145–162.

39. Bazerman, Baron, and Shonk, *"You Can't Enlarge the Pie."*

40. The medical component of this section was inspired and improved by discussions with Professor Richard Bohmer, Harvard Business School.

41. D. M. Cutler, J. M. Poterba, L. M. Scheiner, L. H. Summers, and G. A. Akerlof, *Brookings Papers on Economic Activity* 1990, no. 1 (1990): 1–73; "The Council of Economic Advisors on the Challenge of an Aging Population," *Population Development Review* 23, no. 2 (June 1997): 443–451.

42. Cutler et. al., *Brookings Papers on Economic Activity.*

43. D. P. Rice, "Papers and Proceedings of the Hundred and First Annual Meeting of the American Economic Association," *American Economic Review* 79, no. 2 (1989): 343–348.

44. "The Council of Economic Advisors on the Challenge of an Aging Population."

45. Ibid., 17.

46. Ibid., 44.

47. The White House Office of Management and Budget, *Mid-Session Review* (Washington, DC: GPO, July 2003).

48. E. L. Andrews, "Budget Office Says 10 Years of Deficits Could Total $5 Trillion," *New York Times,* 26 August 2003.

49. R. S. McIntyre, "Is the Bush Economic 'Stimulus' Plan Effective, Fair, and Fiscally Responsible?" U. S. Senate, *Democratic Policy Committee Hearing,* 21 January 2003, <http://democrats.senate.gov/dpc/hearings/hearing1/mcintyre.pdf> (accessed 14 March 2004).

50. Citizens for Tax Justice, "Year-by-Year Analysis of the Bush Tax Cuts Shows Growing Tilt to the Very Rich."

51. "Economists' Statement Opposing the Bush Tax Cuts," advertisement, *New York Times,* 11 February 2003.

52. Ibid.

53. The White House Office of Management and Budget, *Mid-Session Review.*

54. W. Neikirk, "Bush Fails Consumer Credit Test, Critics Say," *Chicago Tribune,* 14 August 2003.

55. Ibid.

56. Ibid.

57. R. E. Moffit, P. Peterson, E. James, W. Prewo, D. Harris, and M. Rutkowski, "Perspectives on the European Pension Crisis: Some Lessons for America," *Heritage Foundation Lecture* (Washington, DC: The Heritage Foundation, 2002).

58. Ibid.

59. R. Bernstein, "An Aging Europe May Find Itself on the Sidelines," *New York Times,* 29 June 2003.

60. Moffit et al., "Perspectives on the European Pension Crisis."

61. Ibid.

62. W. G. Shipman, "Retirement Finance Reform Issues Facing the European Union," *Cato Project on Social Security Choice,* 2 January 2003, <http://www.socialsecurity.org/pubs/ssps/ssp-28es.html> (accessed 14 March 2004).

63. Bernstein, "An Aging Europe May Find Itself on the Sidelines."

64. Shipman, "Retirement Finance Reform Issues Facing the European Union."

65. Moffit et al., "Perspectives on the European Pension Crisis."

66. J. Niessen and Y. Schibel, "E.U. and U.S. Approaches to the Management of Immigration," Migration Policy Group paper, 2003, <www.migpolgroup.com> (accessed 12 March 2004).

67. Ibid.

68. Ibid.

69. F. Norris, "Will Congress Let Accounting Fiction Obscure Pension Reality?" *New York Times,* 18 July 2003.

70. The number of frequent-flyer miles had accumulated to 800 billion by 1990, according to *Barron's.* Twenty thousand miles are typically redeemable for a free flight within the continental United States. If we value a free flight anywhere in the United States at $300, the estimated cost to the airlines in 1990 stood at approximately at $12 billion. A. Zipser, "Sky's the Limit? Frequent-Flier Programs Are Ballooning out of Control," *Barron's* 70, no. 38 (17 September 1990), 16–17, 44.

71. "Free-for-All in the Skies," *Time,* 7 March 1988.

72. "Cutting Back on Flier's Freebies," *Fortune,* 6 June 1988, 149–152.

73. For comparison, the imputed average value for United Airlines is $68 per ticket and $118 for American Airlines.

Further Reading

Measurement system redesign

Kaplan, R. S., and D. P. Norton. *The Strategy-Focused Organization: How Balanced Scorecard Companies Thrive in the New Business Environment.* Boston: Harvard Business School Press, 2000.

Simons, R. "How New Top Managers Use Control Systems as Levers of Strategic Renewal." *Strategic Management Journal* 15, no. 3 (1994): 169–189.

Intelligence-gathering networks

Boshyk, Y., ed. *Business-Driven Action Learning: Global Best Practices.* New York: Palgrave Macmillan, 2000.

Vitt, E., M. Luckevich, and S. Misner. *Business Intelligence.* Seattle, WA: Microsoft Press, 2002.

Scenario planning

Lindgren, M., and H. Bandhold. *Scenario Planning: The Link Between Future and Strategy.* New York: Palgrave Macmillan, 2003.

Van der Heijden, K. *Scenarios: The Art of Strategic Conversation.* New York: John Wiley & Sons, 1996.

Disciplined learning processes

Argyris, C. *Knowledge for Action: A Guide to Overcoming Barriers to Organizational Change.* San Francisco: Jossey-Bass, 1993.

Mitroff, I. *Managing Crises Before They Happen.* New York: Amacom, 2001.

Structured dialogue

Garvin, D., and M. Roberto. "What You Don't Know About Making Decisions." *Harvard Business Review* (September 2001): 108–116.

Decision analysis

Bazerman, M. *Judgment in Managerial Decision Making*, 5th ed. New York: John Wiley & Sons, 2001.

Denardo, E. V. *The Science of Decision Making: A Problem-Based Approach Using Excel*. New York: John Wiley & Sons, 2001.

Hammond, J. S., R. L. Keeney, and H. Raiffa. *Smart Choices: A Practical Guide to Making Better Life Decisions*. New York: Broadway Books, 2002.

Incentive systems redesign

Thorpe, R., and G. Homan. *Strategic Reward Systems*. London: FT Prentice Hall, 1999.

Wilson, T. B., and R. M. Kanter. *Innovative Reward Systems for the Changing Workplace*, 2nd ed. New York: McGraw-Hill, 2002.

Persuasive communication

Cialdini, R. B. *Influence: The Psychology of Persuasion*. New York: Quill, 1993.

Zimbardo, P., and M. Leippe. *The Psychology of Attitude Change and Social Influence*, 3rd ed. Philadelphia: Temple Press, 1991.

Coalition building

Lax, D., and J. Sebenius. "Thinking Coalitionally." In *Negotiation Analysis*, ed. P. Young. Ann Arbor, MI: University of Michigan Press, 1991, 153–193.

Watkins, M. *Breakthrough Business Negotiation: A Toolbox for Managers*. San Francisco: Jossey-Bass, 2002.

Structured problem-solving

Kayser, T. *Building Team Power: How to Unleash the Collaborative Genius of Work Teams*. Carlsbad, CA: Irwin, 1994.

Kim, W. C., and R. Mauborgne. "Fair Process: Managing in the Knowledge Economy." *Harvard Business Review* (January/February, 1997): 65–75.

Crisis response organization

Fink, S. *Crisis Management: Planning for the Inevitable*. IUniverse.com, 2000.

Mitroff, I., C. Pearson, and L. K. Harrington. *The Essential Guide to Managing Corporate Crises: A Step-By-Step Handbook for Surviving Major Catastrophes*. Oxford: Oxford University Press, 1996.

Index

About the Authors

Max H. Bazerman is the Jesse Isidor Straus Professor of Business Administration at Harvard Business School. He is the author of *"You Can't Enlarge the Pie": The Psychology of Ineffective Government* (with Jonathan Baron and Katherine Shonk), *Smart Money Decisions, Judgment in Managerial Decision Making, Cognition and Rationality in Negotiation* (with Margaret Neale), and *Negotiating Rationally* (with Margaret Neale).

Michael D. Watkins is the founder of Genesis Advisers, a leadership strategy consulting firm (www.genesisadvisers.com). He is the author of *The First 90 Days: Critical Success Strategies for New Leaders at All Levels* and *Breakthrough Business Negotiation,* and coauthor of *Right from the Start* (with Dan Ciampa), *Winning the Influence Game* (with Mickey Edwards and Usha Thakrar) and *Breakthrough International Negotiation* (with Susan Rosegrant).